Life's a Scream

Also by Ingrid Pitt

Cuckoo Run
The Peróns
Eva's Spell
Katarina
The Bedside Companion for Vampire Lovers
The Bedside Companion for Ghost Hunters
Bertie the Bus

INGRID PITT

Life's a Scream

The autobiography of Ingrid Pitt

WILLIAM HEINEMANN : LONDON

The title was suggested to me by Barry Langford.

Published in the United Kingdom in 1999 by
William Heinemann

1 3 5 7 9 10 8 6 4 2

First published in the United Kingdom in 1999 by William Heinemann
Random House UK Ltd
20 Vauxhall Bridge Road, London SW1V 2SA

Random House Australia (Pty) Limited
20 Alfred Street, Milsons Point, Sydney
New South Wales 2061, Australia

Random House New Zealand Limited
18 Poland Road, Glenfield
Auckland 10, New Zealand

Random House South Africa (Pty) Limited
Endulini, 5a Jubilee Road, Parktown 2193, South Africa

Random House UK Limited Reg. No. 954009

A CIP catalogue record for this book is available from the British Library

Papers used by Random House UK Limited are natural, recyclable products made from wood grown in sustainable forests. The manufacturing processes conform to the environmental regulations of the country of origin

Typeset in Palatino by SX Composing DTP, Rayleigh, Essex
Printed and bound in the United Kingdom by
Biddles Ltd, Guildford and King's Lynn

ISBN 0 434 00762 5

for Steffanie and Tonio

Prologue

Las Vegas loomed out of the shimmering heat haze like a mirage. I tried not to do the touristy thing and lean forward to look out of the window but that sort of control is beyond me. As we circled to land I thought I could pick out the constantly flashing, glaring names hyping the star-studded hotels that have taken the place of whitening bones and tumbleweed in the cardboard-brown desert. The plane levelled up on finals and sank decorously to the painted black strip of tarmac edged by low-level buildings and washed-out palm trees. My excitement increased – this was it. Three days of the biggest press junket they'd ever seen in America. And I was part of it. I checked my make-up as well as I could in a pocket mirror and tried to think of scintillating titbits for the press. After all, this was the big one. When I left the States a few years earlier I had flogged my heap of automotive rust at the airport and taken the first available flight out with the proceeds. Now was the triumphant return. Ticker-tape, gold-chained mayors, counter-marching mayorettes and a gold key. Or is that only in New York?

The doors opened and the heat hitting me in the face took my breath away. I shuffled out with the throng and looked for what, in those days, was the epitome of a status symbol – a stretch limo, preferably black, a Lincoln Continental no less. Zilch! Deflated, I followed the crocodile across the griddle-hot concrete into the ice shower of the reception buildings. Things started to look up immediately. A smartly dressed woman, with a clipboard welded to the crook of her left arm, gave a nurtured welcome smile and invited me to follow her. I had a moment of panic. What about my luggage? All that trendy gear I had spent hours trying on and visualising in action? Before I could communicate my secret horror of losing everything, my guiding light hailed a distant crumpled linen suit and told the wearer to pick up my bags and take them to the hotel. It wasn't a scenario I was happy with but my misgivings were put on hold as I walked between rows of aggressive fruit machines, standing with arms at the salute like a well-trained band of military robots, into the sumptuous VIP lounge.

Another suit, this time immaculate in blue, slobbered over my hand at the door, told me archly that he was the vice-president of something or other and was on call to make my every wish come true. I gushed back and was disappointed that it wasn't the President of MGM himself, putting his body at my beck and call. I turned to meet the press. What's the collective noun for pressmen? A 'flash'? Maybe a 'clutter'? Whatever, there were more hot shots sucking pencils and burning flash bulbs than I had ever seen in my life. And they all called me 'Heidi' – the name of my character in the film I was there to promote, *Where Eagles Dare.* Rather sweet, really. And surprising. My role in the film was pretty good but it didn't deserve this sort of attention. I should have been worried. Where were Richard Burton and Clint Eastwood? Or even Mary Ure? Making other movies – that's where. Leaving me to do the ego-stroking job of promoting the film while they moved on to pastures new and pay-cheques big.

After half an hour of primping and posing the clipboard lady threw me a lifeline and suggested we move on to the hotel. I was torn between the thought that there might be someone who hadn't captured my image on his emulsion and the knowledge that in spite of the ice-blast air-conditioning, the wedge of bodies had produced a temperature that was melting my make-up. I followed her out to the car. At least I rated a Cadillac. The short drive through the tawdry streets was a little depressing. Las Vegas was built and designed by a gang of vampires. Everything looks glitzy and expensive at night. The senses are overwhelmed by the millions of watts pumped out through the sparkling light from every ledge, roof-top and revolving door. Reality kicks in as the sun, a mephistophelean red, edges up over the hills and desert scrub. I tried not to notice the light sockets and angle iron, the paper blowing in the wind which carried sand in from the desert and coated everything in a dull layer of khaki. This was my day. I didn't want to know about reality.

The booking in at Caesar Palace, again saluted by rows of attention-grabbing fruits, was satisfactory. Another 'vice' something or other went through the knuckle-grazing ritual and assured me that his *casa* was my *casa*. I dimpled prettily. By now I had got the picture. If there wasn't too much effort involved I would be in line for an underling in an expensive suit and all the pressmen I could eat. I was beginning to come down off the mountain. Then the door to my suite was thrown open and I was sparkling again. Wall-to-wall flowers and a note that suggested I wasn't going to be confined for ever to the realm of vice-presidents and under-managers. I waited until my escort left with renewed promises of eternal servitude, then leaped on to the flowers and shuffled through the wad of visiting cards: 'For Heidi – welcome to Las Vegas – Bo Poke – President/MGM.' 'Welcome to America, F. Melnicker, President of Finance/MGM.' 'Knock 'em dead, kid! Luv – Alistair' (MacLean). 'Sorry not to be there with you, darling, Good Luck, Richard & Elizabeth.' A sop, that one. Richard was much better off where he was making *Staircase* and knew it. I read the rest of the ritualised billets-doux and stored them carefully away in my little box purse that was all the rage in London but had also taken on a tackiness in my ostentatious surroundings. I considered a bath but rejected it in favour of crashing out on the luxurious charpoy, as big as a singles court, and buried myself under a heap of cushions and pillows.

Bad move!

My eyelids had hardly started to flutter when the telephone chirruped. Dazed after thirty hours with only a spine-snapping doze on the plane to fizz up the old batteries, it took me quite a while to realise that the one-armed bandit poised on the bedside table was doubling as a telephone. It was the lady with the clipboard whose name, if I remember rightly, was Soledad, and she had exciting news. *El Presidente,* Bo Poke, was already in the hotel and would like to meet me before the reception banquet – which, incidentally, was due to start in half an hour. I panicked. It would take me that much time to find a suitable frock. Never mind meeting the Poke bloke and doing all the things I should have done before diving into the pillows.

I made my entry into the Titanic-sized banqueting hall twenty minutes late and hating everybody. I was reminded not to get big ideas about my part in the PR operation by the fact that all of them were already seated at their tables and, if they weren't exactly at the cheese and coffee stage, they were prodding the bread rolls and had their napkins strategically placed to catch any dribbles.

Bo Poke did his bit. After all, he was strapped into the chair that could become a throne or electric according to the international performance of the film that I was fronting. He massaged my ego into some sort of shape and made a big fuss of seating me beside him. I had been curious to meet him. There were so many stories going around the industry that I didn't know what to expect. Someone pretty extraordinary, at least. You don't get head-hunted by a super-conglomerate like MGM unless you are something a bit special. Only three months earlier he had been little more than a glorified grocer – well, president of General Foods, actually – but what had that to do with film? I asked him. He laughed. He had been given a crash course. It was, *au fond*, all the same thing. You buy a commodity, price it attractively, get a few dumb broads to waggle their butts suggestively and you are in profit.

I looked at him and struggled with the concept that he saw me as a dumb broad wiggling my assets and went off him. It didn't bother him. He came out with 'present company excepted' but I read that as 'accepted' and withdrew my favours. As if he cared. Everyone was talking to everyone, tearing down reputations and questioning what everyone else was worth. I painted on a smile and went to sleep behind it. Which was fine – until Bo Poke jumped up and launched into a spiel which ended in a fanfare for Clint Eastwood. Nobody had bothered to tell me Clint was going to be there. It turned out that he had a couple of days off filming and had let MGM fly him in. I was glad of the distraction, I had the distinct impression that the head of finance was about to make a take-over bid for my prime assets. Clint and his wife Maggie were wonderful. He sailed charmingly down the line of executives, who stood to give him a welcoming ovation, until he reached me. I didn't know what to expect. Clint gave a big hello, gathered me in his arms and let the suits know that we were brothers under the skin. It got better after that. He sat on the other side of Poke and made a point of chatting to me across the President's soup plate.

I was beginning really to enjoy myself. Then Poke blasted out a corporate message about *Where Eagles Dare*, smarmed over Clint, threw me a titbit and thanked the Nazis for being the greatest source of entertainment since Nero burned down Rome.

As if on cue some joker smashed through the double doors of the banqueting hall in Adolf Hitler gear: stupid little black moustache, SS hat and Führer uniform. Just in case anyone missed the allusion, he kicked his heels together, shot up his arm in the Nazi salute and shouted, 'Heil Hitler!'

Everyone laughed.

I felt sick. I had to get out of there. I stalked from the room, leaving the laughter to fade in the distance, overwhelmed by the morass of memories of my nightmare childhood – a lifetime ago.

One

I had a strongly developed sense of the dramatic even before I was born. It has to be admitted that if you are trying to escape from your oppressors, having a baby in front of them is not a wise move.

My parents were on their way from Nazi Germany to England via Poland when I decided to arrive. Grimly my mother tried to hold me off but when the train pulled in to Częstochowa station I was on my way out. My father managed to find someone who contacted a doctor and my mother was made more or less comfortable in a little room at the rear of the station. It was only just in time. I had already made my way into the world virtually unaided when the midwife arrived. I have a picture of smiling faces hovering above me and in the distance through the driving snow the sound of a train whistle welcoming me into the world.

In haste and without much thought – and to my continuing distress – my mother called me Ingrid, which in Swedish means 'victorious on horseback'.

My father was a true-blue Prussian, a scientist and reluctant officer in the cavalry during the Great War. A man who knew how to live well. He was born in 1870 in Potsdam, although his family came from Torbetzkoy in the province of Kaluga, not far from Moscow, where they owned land until the Bolshevik revolution. The family was proud of its connection to the great Russian General Mikhail Larinovich Kutuzov, Prince of Smolensk, who stuck it to Napoleon pretty conclusively when he had designs on taking over Russia.

My father was my hero. He'd been educated at Heidelberg and later Oxford where he took up rowing. When competitors were rounded up to enter the first Olympic Games in 1896 in Athens he was there. He won a medal and was received by the King. He could have gone anywhere to live but turn-of-the-century England suited him. My father's immediate claim to fame was his invention of a special electrical battery which he patented in 1900. To prove that his battery was a viable product with a modern application, he took his battery-driven car on a London-to-Brighton run – and finished, which was enough to prove a point.

Always looking for greater challenges, he worked on developing a purely British aeroplane. He also started on the design of a British airship. Then Archduke Ferdinand was assassinated in Sarajevo and World War One became inevitable.

After twenty years in England my father considered himself British in everything but birth and wished to stay there. Kaiser Bill wanted him back, since my father was one of the top designers of lighter-than-air aircraft, and he therefore had the negative choice of staying in England in a detention camp or returning to Germany. He closed up his house in New Malden and served in the Prussian cavalry.

The war over, my father tried to return to England but his initial overtures to old British friends and business acquaintances met with a less than enthusiastic response. The horror and futility of the Great War had left a psychological scar on the nation's psyche which was not easily healed. He always said that the detention camp would have been the lesser of two evils – and he would have improved his cricket . . .

He was a renowned engineer and inventor, a man of passion and intellect, of courage and conscience.

It was a love of horses which brought my parents together. They'd met when he spotted her competing skilfully in a dressage event at a horse show in Treptow. She was thirty years younger than him and from a Lithuanian background, but their interest in horses bridged the gap. My father was never one to hang around and within the year they were married.

External events were not to allow them much time to enjoy their newly wedded happiness in Berlin. The Nazis were gaining influence and their rhetoric was directed with growing ferocity at the huge Jewish section of the community. My mother's Jewish blood put her in jeopardy. My father thought long and hard about the situation. He would probably have decided to sit it out and see what happened if he'd been able to continue to design non-military airships, but already the Nazi influence was beginning to show so he decided to leave his job. Despite the fact that he was over retirement age, he was ordered to stay on. It was time to leave.

Reacting quickly, he sold whatever he could and left the rest with his friend and partner, Abe Mandelstamm. It wasn't easy. The mounting number of attacks on Jews was turning the once elegant city into a hell-hole of racial discrimination and any Jew with a sense of history realised it was time to get out. This meant that the market was flooded with household goods and minor masterpieces. My family weren't too badly off. In the good old days my father had bought a number of shares in British engineering companies. When times were hard, after World War One, he had been tempted to sell them. Now he was glad that he hadn't. They would provide a nest-egg that would set him up in England.

My parents decided to take the route favoured by most *émigrés*, via Poland. There was just one small difficulty – me. I was due to be born at any minute. My father initially wanted to wait until after my birth but the authorities were getting heavy about his refusal to work on their war machines. He was picked up one night by men from the SSD, the State Security Service, and taken to Sachsenhausen – one of the first concentration camps – where he was told in unmistakable terms what would happen to him and his Jewish wife if he didn't co-operate. It was four days before they put him in a black SSD car and dropped him off at home. My father had learned his lesson. My appearance would have to be postponed until the family was safely out of the country.

That might have been the plan but no one had consulted me. The train was crossing the Polish border when I made my untimely arrival. Once I was safely delivered, my mother begged my father to get back on the train and continue the journey. She would follow in a couple of days when she had recuperated. He should have listened to her. My arrival without a ticket hadn't gone unnoticed and to ingratiate himself with an enquiring SSD man the station-master passed on the news. The SSD man checked with Berlin and my father was held for 'further questioning'. They decided to take him back to the capital. At this point everyone's attitude to us changed. Before, they had been almost happy that the small railway station of their medieval town had been turned into a makeshift maternity home. Once my father had been fingered everyone wanted my mother – and me – out.

My father had no intention of returning with the SSD man to Berlin if he could help it. When the train pulled in at Gdansk he took a chance and managed to slip away. He returned to us and decided that it would be wisest to lie low with members of my mother's family in Grodno.

I have vague memories of life in Grodno, of idyllic, exciting fields to play in. Of course, in the wider world the war was now raging and when the SSD got wind of my father's new address it did not take them long once more to 'invite' him to go to Gdansk with them to 'discuss' his contribution to the war effort. He tried to tell them that he had retired but they didn't want to know about that. Reluctantly he agreed to go with them.

I was always allowed to sleep with my parents to keep warm and feel safe. They thought if there was any danger they could just grab me and be off. Now I watched my mother stand at the window most of the night, wrapped in her coat, blowing warm breath on the glass to make the ice flowers melt and wipe it clear so she could see my father coming back. She waited and watched but for many nights the road was empty.

At last one night her vigil was rewarded. My father had been devious. He had agreed with everything the SSD had said. They wanted him to work on long-range rockets, V2s at Penemünde. He told them he had no problem with that. The fact that he would have to work with forced-labour battalions wasn't anything to get excited about either. They were so impressed that they made the error of letting him come home to pick up his family. He arrived in the middle of the night and, in spite of my grizzling, we were packed and on our way before the sun breached the eastern horizon.

My mother wanted to go to Vilna where her parents

lived but my father was being masterful so we headed towards Bialystok.

Whenever I think of Poland it's cold. Cold that cuts into your face like tiny razors and burns out your sinuses. There's a smell about extreme cold that in small doses can be exhilarating. Day after day, for weeks on end, it gives you an overdose that has a touch of death about it. If you're fuelled up with food and can occasionally find somewhere warm it can be endured. When you're near starvation it's not so easy to be sanguine.

But the cold was not our worst enemy. My family had no status, no money, no passports, no roots. If we stayed in one place for more than a couple of days our hosts became terrified and made it clear that they wanted us out of their house and miles away.

At last we found a safe haven with one of my mother's relatives, who fixed up a barn so that, if soldiers came, we wouldn't be in their home and they could pretend they didn't know anything about us. It wasn't at all bad. It was reasonably draught-proof and clean and, most important, we felt almost safe.

My parents would leave me in the barn for short spells while they helped around the farm. One morning I was on my own, asleep in the hay, when the door was thrust open and a woman ran in followed by a soldier. She seemed happy enough, giggling and playing some sort of game with the man. I was about to jump up and join in the fun when the mood changed. The woman's squeals of laughter became shrieks of fear. I knew about fear. You have to keep away from its source in case you were contaminated. I stayed where I was hidden but could see everything. After a lot of thrashing around and moaning in the straw the soldier stood up, pulled up his trousers, buttoned his coat and left. The woman lay on the straw, whimpering to herself. I rushed to the kitchen and told my parents what I had seen. They were terrified. The thought of a soldier so close at hand had them practically in hysterics. They kept asking me over and over what exactly his uniform was like. I didn't know. I couldn't possibly know if he was German, Polish or Russian. No one thought to go and see if the woman was all right. They were too busy packing their bags.

Determined finally to get to Bialystok, we left that night. But whatever decision my parents took they would never be able to outrun the Nazis. They wanted my father and they were going to have him. He had become an 'enemy of the Reich' for deserting his country in its hour of need.

We arrived in Bialystok in the early hours of the morning. By wonderful coincidence my maternal grand-parents had left Vilna a couple of months earlier and had come to Bialystok, where for some reason they felt safer, to stay with my grandmother's brother. My maternal grandparents seemed genuinely pleased to see us. Our obvious distress surmounted the hostility they had expressed when they'd found that their darling daughter, Katja, had married a man so much older than herself. We spent the summer and autumn with them and everyone began to relax. Having my father living with them helped to warm my grandparents' attitude towards him. It's one of the happiest times I can remember from my early childhood. There were children of my own age to play with and we spent hours catching crickets and making them jump, and digging up mounds in search of moles. In spite of long hours invested in the sport I don't think we ever actually unearthed one.

The fields were surrounded by ditches which were part of an old irrigation system. There were a few small dams at strategic places which could be released if too much water was backing up. It only happened a couple of times while we were there but it was something to remember. Once, the river dried out in places, leaving only small, deep pools. The fish knew about those pools and made for them when the water level started to sink. They should have been safe. But that's life. Just when you think you are home free something falls on you from a great height. When the water was low it was us kids that fell on the corralled fish. We harvested enough trout and crayfish to keep the table supplied for days.

German activity in the area had been pretty spasmodic so far. There had been a little detachment of troops bivouacking about two kilometres away in an old quarry but they were generally civil and the few times they had come to the house it had been merely to buy eggs. My father told everyone to treat them like guests in the hope that they might act the part and not embarrass their hosts. The ploy worked for a long time.

By this time we were surrounded by a lot of refugees. Nobody liked the danger they represented but to turn them away seemed so heartless that neither my father nor my grandfather nor uncle could bring himself to do it. Unfortunately the increased refugee activity had drawn the Nazis' attention and they were only too happy to vent their anger over the reverses at the front. These, combined with the *Luftwaffe*'s inability to clear the skies of British Spitfires and the demoralising raids on Berlin, had changed how the Nazis saw themselves. Before, they had been able to strut around making high-handed decisions under the illusion that they were masters of the universe. Slowly it now dawned on them that maybe the whole of Europe wasn't going to roll over and play dead. The assurance of their leaders that reverses in Russia, the annihilation of the *Luftwaffe* and America entering the war were just annoying blips in the master plan was beginning to sound a bit like drowning by numbers. The result was another push to round up anyone who could be called a threat to the 1000-year Reich.

The troops arrived in their usual impressive manner: a couple of motor-bike outriders to clear the road, a saloon car and three trucks to pick up anyone they came across. They had obviously had a busy day. The trucks were already bulging with depressed-looking citizens stoically enduring the teeth-chipping experience of riding in the back of the rudimentarily sprung lorry. The people were unloaded from the trucks and stood around in the freezing night, waiting for further developments.

A man in a long leather coat and a smart snap-brimmed trilby knocked on the front door and politely asked my father to accompany him. There was nothing my father could do but agree. He did get a bit of a concession. He was allowed to bring my mother and me along. My mother wanted time to pack but was told there was no problem, she would be back long before she knew what was happening. Nobody believed that but so far everything had been fairly restrained and no one wanted to push at the shaky envelope of safety.

Outside, the little group of refugees, who had been our house guests for weeks, were made to join the people who had arrived on the lorries and looked pretty discouraged. My grandparents, Albert and Melanie, were among them. My father asked the trilby if they could come with us and, unbelievably, he agreed. As we climbed on the back of the lorry and jolted off along the rutted cart track the soldiers started herding the new arrivals and the refugees into one of the barns. I still wonder what happened to them.

Two

My father held me under his coat to keep me warm and put his arm around my mother to steady her as the lorry sped through the night. My grandparents had great trouble sitting on the truck floor and my poor grandpa couldn't do a lot to ease Baba Melanie's discomfort.

It seemed inevitable that the truck should finish up at the railway depot. We were ordered to join hundreds of people sitting on the cobbled stones of the station.

I didn't really have any idea of what was going on. Why had I been snatched up and taken to this place where everyone seemed to be afraid, where the only sounds were frightened cries and harsh, terrifying shouts? I wanted my father to reassure me, to tell me that it would only last for a moment and then everyone would go away and we could return to our big, warm bed. I kept as close to him as I could but he had other problems: Grandpa Albert and Baba Melanie for a start. All their lives they had lived at peace with the world and they had no way of coping with these unfamiliar harsh circumstances. My father understood this and tried to make them as comfortable as possible, mentally as well as physically. Amid all the noise and confusion he battled to keep us together, to reassure us that everything would be all right.

We sat on the ground but my grandparents remained standing, their arms locked around each other. The guards were walking along the track-side, shouting at people to sit down and, when they didn't react smartly enough, giving them a whack with their guns. My father helped Baba Melanie sit down. It was difficult for her. She suffered from arthritis and it was agony having to lower herself on to the damp cobbles. We all crouched around her and when the guard had passed my father disappeared into the building behind us and emerged with a chair. He put it at the back of the track-side area where it was less conspicuous but still in touch with the mass of prisoners on the crowded platform and, with Grandpa Albert, gently lifted Melanie up and almost carried her to the chair. My mother gathered me close and watched the guards. They hadn't noticed our movements so we crawled back to where my grandmother was now sitting in the chair.

All around, everyone was talking in whispers. I still didn't understand what was going on but the atmosphere of fear was subsiding now. We were beginning to be philosophical about our position. The grown-ups reasoned that there was surely no mileage in doing anything nasty to us. It was obviously in everybody's best interest to buckle down and work in the resettlement camps and show that we could be depended upon to pull our weight.

A guard walked past and we all cowered down, trying to look as inconspicuous as possible – which wasn't easy with Grandma Melanie perched above us on the chair. He stopped and looked at her. My father's arm tightened around me. Melanie inclined her head and smiled at the guard as if greeting an acquaintance. The guard smiled back and moved on. We all relaxed.

I dropped off to sleep. I don't know how long I slept on my father's lap but I was awakened as he shifted his position to claim the attention of the guard who was walking along the line calling his name. Papa carefully transferred me to my mother, then got up and picked his way through the people lying on the ground. I wanted to cry out, to tell him to come back, not to leave me, but my mother put her hand over my mouth.

A man in a long leather coat came over to Papa, asked him a question and checked a detail in a sheaf of papers. My father shook his head and pointed to us. This did not suit his interrogator. He took my father by the arm, but Papa pulled away and again pointed towards us. The leather coat wanted my father to go with him but Papa was desperate. Rashly he grabbed the man's arm in an attempt to detain him and, although the guard tried to shrug him off, my father wouldn't let go. Without warning, the man took out his Luger and smashed it across my father's head. For what seemed an eternity Papa stood and stared at the man with the leather coat, then he crumpled at the knees, fell on his back on to the cobblestones and lay very still. I screamed and clung to my petrified mother who, wisely, didn't react. The man nodded to my mother as if they were acquaintances acknowledging a chance meeting and walked off.

Mascha dropped to her knees beside my father and cradled his head on her lap. She tried to see how bad the wound was and looked around desperately to find something to staunch the bleeding. I was shrieking my little lungs out. The blood covering my father's head was something I couldn't cope with. Mama opened my coat and tore my pinafore off me, folded it and pressed it to my father's head. Someone tried to comfort me but I wasn't having it. Without warning my father's eyes opened and he looked solemnly at me for a moment or two, then smiled reassuringly and opened his arms. I threw myself on him and sobbed hysterically.

It was almost light. A train arrived with a haunting blast of its whistle, then set about shunting the cattle trucks around until the guards were satisfied that they occupied the exact position designated for them. Then, with their dogs, they began to round us up and force us aboard the train.

The man in the leather coat was standing near our group. He obviously had a problem with my father. As Papa desperately tried to get to his feet, he roughly pushed him out of line and snapped questions at him. My mother tried to stay with him and my grandfather also attempted to help but the night on the cold ground had been too much for him. He could hardly move and Grandma Melanie was even worse. My mother, half carrying my father, tried to assist her parents but it was impossible. The guards were shouting and shoving everyone on to the train. Grandfather Albert told Matka to help my father to the train. They would follow. My mother hesitated but Grandmother gave her a reassuring smile and waved her away. I clung to my father's coat and went with them. When I looked back Baba Melanie was sitting like a queen on a throne and Albert was at her feet, his back resting against the chair leg, holding Baba's hand. They saw me looking and gave a wave and a reassuring smile. It was the last I ever saw of them.

We were pushed on to the train. My father's dazed state saved him. The man in the leather coat tired of not getting a coherent reply and pushed him roughly towards the door of the cattle truck. Mama elbowed the people getting on the train out of the way, held her position in the entrance by force and practically hauled my father aboard single-handed.

More and more people were hustled into the already packed cattle truck. A cacophony of shouts and shots fired outside cut into the screams and cries. Abruptly the doors slammed shut and bolts crashed home. It was pitch black inside. I couldn't see anything but I could hear the mass of people crammed around us pushing against each other, moaning and cursing. I started crying again. I was terrified.

The train began to move, very slowly at first, then gained traction and speeded up. But it was not long before it stopped again. We could just make out that it was snowing and we were standing in the middle of nowhere. A freezing draught blew through the slits in the wall and it was better not to look out. But the doors didn't open. With a lot of grumbling and shuffling everyone settled down again. The train stood and stood. Matka had managed to worm her way into a corner. She acted as a comfortable buffer against the cold wooden walls. Poor Mascha, her back must have been frozen. She held my father's head on her lap and cradled me in her arms.

It was daylight again when the doors crashed back and a metal container was heaved on board. Everybody instantly started shouting questions and making demands. They fell on deaf ears. The doors were slammed shut, bolts driven home and there was the shrill cry of a whistle which signalled that we were about to continue our journey.

The train finally came to a halt at a small provincial railway station called Stutthof Waldlager. The bolts were pushed back and the doors opened. It was night time but glaring lights blinded the semi-comatose prisoners on the train. Freezing wind drove snow into our faces as we tried to obey the shouted orders from the guards: *'Raus! Raus!'*

The guards gave their dogs a bit of slack to help the lazy 'Yids' to get a move on. Huge black shapes jostled and pushed at me. I was too terrified even to whimper. My hand was welded to my mother's but it didn't seem to help. I wanted to run away somewhere, anywhere. For a moment I was out of the crowding figures and in the glaring light – and that was even worse. The shouting and crying was horrendous. Everyone was running, stumbling. A number of times I would have fallen and been ground into mincemeat underfoot if it hadn't been for my mother's strong hand. I was crying now and, in my fear, trying to sit down. My mother knew something I didn't and wasn't allowing me to give way to my terror. And I wasn't her only concern. My father's head was bleeding again and in spite of his determination to keep on his feet it was touch and go whether he would make it to wherever we were headed. A couple of times we found ourselves on the outside of the bustling crowd. Even I knew it wasn't a good place to be. There were men in daunting black uniforms with sticks and dogs with sharp teeth.

My father, seventy-two years old and suffering from the blow to his head, sank to the floor. Torn between helping him and keeping me close, my mother was desperate. Her anxiety was transmitting itself to me through her fingers. I was screaming and trying to wrench my hand from the vice-like grip. Relief came just in time. The soldiers called a halt and everyone sank down where they stood on to the snow-packed ground.

Time was unimportant. Pain was what counted. Pain from sitting on the ice-cold ground, pain from bruises and cuts picked up along the way, pain from the separation from family and pain from hunger. I'd never been a particularly great eater but my small appetite hadn't been satisfied for many hours. I swayed in and out of consciousness, so cold that I couldn't even cry. A man in a Nazi uniform stopped in front of my parents and ordered them to follow him. My mother tried to pull me to my feet and I fought against the unrelenting pressure. I wanted to stay where I was, movement meant pain and I had had enough. My mother picked me up and we followed the man in uniform who seemed to know where he was going. He took us to a truck waiting by the side of the platform and my mother put me on board and then, with the help of the man, heaved my father in beside me. I was terrified that we would leave without Matka and tried to jump down. Papa attempted to stop me but he was too weak. A stinging slap to my bare, ice-cold leg brought me momentarily to my senses. My mother climbed in beside me and took me in her arms. Two guards followed us on and one of them banged on the cab with the flat of his hand.

The truck moved off immediately into the pitch-dark night. Naked to the elements, we sat shivering as the snow fell on us. Papa pulled me on to his lap and covered me totally with his coat. We bumped and thrashed along for some time, the engine straining and the tyres trying to keep traction until we got to an area with bright lights, a big iron gate and barbed-wire fences with watch towers at intervals. Soldiers with guns stood on the watch towers, pointing their weapons at us. The truck passed through the gate and stopped outside a brick building with lots of tall glass windows.

Cold, hungry and miserable, I started crying again. My father's wound frightened me. Who would take care of us if Papa couldn't? My father had always been so positive, sure in what he did and what he wanted. To see him sitting on the floor listless, not making his mark on the surroundings, was terrifying.

We went inside the building and were told to sit and wait in the corridor. Mama pulled me up on to her lap and, out of the snow, I began to feel comforted. We sat there for hours. Mascha made a little nest with her coat and I dropped off to sleep.

Heavy footsteps woke me up. The *Kommandant* of the camp, Max Pauly, wearing an impressive uniform and an overbearing manner, stopped in front of my father. He tried to get to his feet but the effort was too much. Matka was on her feet, speaking fast and persuasively. I couldn't follow what she was saying but I could tell it was important. But not as important as my hunger. I started whining again in the hope that the big man would be more sympathetic than my parents and give me some food. Nobody took any notice.

That night we were ordered to sleep in a hut, empty except for cubicles with rows of rough wooden bunks three high. Mascha put me on one and I thought it was the most luxurious place I had ever known. It was out of the icy wind and snow, and I had a thin mattress, a blanket and even a wonky pillow. I snuggled down and fell asleep at once.

At dawn, still hungry and miserable, I noticed a terrible stench, and the cots that had appeared so wonderful the night before were damp and unyielding. There was also a loudspeaker shouting a few inches from my ear – enough to make anyone cry. Mama tried to go in search of food but was stopped at the door by a couple of men in 'pyjamas'. Shortly after, I learned that they were prisoners. Everyone in pyjamas was a prisoner and those who weren't were to be feared and avoided.

I needed to go to the loo and left my poor mother in no doubt that if I didn't go immediately the result would be all her fault. One of the prisoners offered to take me. That first encounter with a camp latrine was memorable. It was open on three sides with a long seat with round holes roughly cut at equal distance along the whole length. The stink was eye-watering but the companionable seating appealed to me. And it's surprising how easy it is to get used to vomit-inducing odours.

Back at the hut, Mascha was trying to light the pot-belly stove but without dry tinder her efforts were getting her nowhere. Later in the day we were taken back to the warm offices with the big windows. My mother sat on a bench, very upright, very tense. I was bored and tried to persuade her to play with me but she wasn't in the mood. She sat staring at the door through which my father had vanished as if our lives depended on it. And they probably did. What seemed like hours later my father suddenly appeared. He seemed better now – more confident. He grabbed me by the hand and hustled us both outside as if he was afraid that his good fortune might leak away if he hung around too long. We went back to the hut. It was still empty. My father settled down on one of the bunks and pulled me in beside him. I felt warm and protected. My mama had gone off somewhere. I was just explaining my hunger to him when she returned. She had some bread and a tin pot containing a dark liquid. I hated both but Matka's patience was wearing thin after listening to my non-stop whining and she gave me a take-it-or-starve alternative and I took the former.

I was lying in the crook of my father's arm on the bunk, almost asleep, when the door opened and a man entered. My father gently extricated himself and stood up. My mama was crying and seemed to be on the point of collapse. I was embarrassed. Until recently I had never seen my mother cry – now she never seemed to stop. My father cuddled her and then came back to me and gave me a quick kiss. I was amazed. He also seemed close to tears.

He turned away abruptly and followed the man out of the hut. Matka picked me up and held me so that I could see out of the window. A car stood a little way up the path between rows of huts. It was big and shiny and black. My father turned and waved, then climbed into the back. As the car sped off I could see my papa's white face staring back at us through the little window. Mama was crying openly now, not making any attempt to hide her sorrow. She didn't seem to know what to do. It was the only time I can remember her appearing hopeless. I didn't really know what was going on but I joined in her tears anyway.

A man in a uniform came into the hut and spoke to my mother. I was fascinated by his black shiny boots and the way he kept swatting them with his riding crop. The man saw my interest and flicked me gently on the arm. I didn't like that and glared at him. He patted me on the cheek with the floppy end of the whip. Angry, I grabbed at it. He teasingly flicked it away, then pushed it back again. Again I tried to grab it but he was too quick. He laughed, nodded to my mother and left. She picked me up and wept into my hair. I didn't know what it was all about and struggled to get down. She held on tightly. So far, my whining and sniffling had been about normal for a healthy five-year-old. My mother's tears and seeing my father being forced to leave us opened the dam, and I sank to the ground, shrieking and crying. Perhaps our situation had finally sunk in: Welcome to Stutthof concentration camp, my home for the next three years.

Three

We were taken to Block 5. There were two doors in the hut. Just inside the main door was a little cubicle that was inhabited by an ogre in human form: the *Kapo* – overseer. She looked and sounded just like everyone else but was to be avoided. She handed us our camp uniform, wooden clogs, leggings and striped shift.

Behind the huts there was a double line of latrines. The huts were locked at night and admission to the latrines outside the normal hours was by direct permission of the ogre only. Not to be allowed to go to the latrine, with diarrhoea rampant in the camp, was torture. If anyone messed herself or her bunk, she would be badly beaten, which could result in death. The washing facilities were spartan and I tried to avoid them at all cost. To wash with cold water in the wind and draft was hell. But the latrines were a lot worse. This dark, stinking corrugated hut built on pressed earth concentrated an odour which, mixed with the stink from the smoking chimney, could be smelled all over the camp. Nowhere was free of it, especially on the days when the latrines were cleaned out. That was the day to have a streaming cold. The method for cleaning them was quite interesting. There were no cubicles and the seats were just a row of holes in a wooden plank, cut so close together that you actually touched the next bottom when you sat down. To clean the latrines the plank was taken off to reveal an awesome pit below, filled with bubbling excrement. The recommended method of emptying it out was to drop a bucket in and then carry it to the pits near the barbed-wire fence which had already been dug by a more fortunate group of prisoners. But it didn't work – a fact that everyone recognised as soon as they got on the job. The only way, and the cleanest, was to jump in the pit, scoop out a bucketful and hand it to someone else to dispose of.

My mother was detailed to work in the camp laundry. In the morning, which was 4 a.m., the alarm bell went and everybody rushed to get ready for roll-call. On the first day I woke up in our bunk squashed in beside my mother and another woman. It was still pitch dark and the noise of over a hundred or so women banging around was terrifying. I tried to cuddle up to my mother but she had already got the idea that lying around in the bunk might not be the healthiest way to spend the morning. The door at the end of the hut crashed open and I could hear a dog snapping and snarling. It was so horrifying I don't think I even cried.

My mother gripped my jaw, put her mouth close to my ear and told me to stay in the bunk, to keep out of the way, not to be seen. That got the tear ducts going. I demanded she take me with her. For once she wasn't going to be seduced by tears. I tried to cling to her back but she broke my grip and was gone. I lay there sobbing to myself.

A new sound distracted me from my tears: a rustling and high-pitched squealing. The big room was lighter now and hanging over the side of the bunk I could see dark shapes scampering across the floor. Rats. That did it. No more tears. I pulled the blanket over my head and just quaked – with an occasional convulsive kick when I thought my area was being invaded.

The day passed slowly. Occasionally I heard a sound outside and hoped it was my mother coming back. Once someone entered the hut and walked through it. I knew it wasn't my mother and lay as still as a straw doll under my protective blanket. As the day dragged on I became a little more adventurous. I came out of my nest and wiped the glass window-pane above my bunk with my sleeve. Outside was a barbed-wire enclosure which was empty. I guessed they would bring cattle and horses there in the spring. I would love that.

As the days passed I began to develop a routine. Matka had been told that children in the camp were groomed to be given to childless Germans. She was terrified that she would lose me. When prisoners brought new straw I hid under one of the bunks in the far corner and watched their legs go to and fro until they left. My mother had drilled it into me: no one must be aware of me. When I asked her why not, she told me that if I were found they would send me away and I would never see her again. I asked if I would be with my father. She just took me in her skinny arms and rocked me backwards and forwards. I didn't ask her about going away or my father after that. I was too frightened of her reaction.

Somehow I got through the days, sitting on the bunk and awaiting my mother's return. How long this went on I have no idea. Probably not as endlessly as it seemed. It was long enough for me to shrug off my original fears and become almost daring. Even the rats no longer bothered me. They represented life, of a sort, and, if the opportunity had arisen, I would have had a bedful of rats as playmates.

Then everything changed. One morning the doors to our block were thrown open, uniformed guards charged in and screamed at everybody to get up and get out. This morning there was no comforting chatter as the women prepared for the day, no reassuring hug from my mother. There was barely time for her to hide me. Everything was confusion, dogs, shouts, cries, stomping feet. It was so frightening that I forgot I was supposed to stay quiet and added to the cacophony with wild yells and entreaties of my own. I still might have been overlooked – there was so much general noise – if it hadn't been for the dogs. Drawn by my high-pitched screaming, they tugged at their chains until their handlers pulled aside the blanket that my mother had draped across me. Terrified by the dogs, I screamed for Matka, who came running into the hut, weeping and begging them not to hurt me. I hung on to Mascha's legs with all my strength but they pulled me off her, marched her off with her work detail, and one of the guards, who seemed to find the situation amusing, bore me off, still shouting and crying.

Where I finished up was a surprise. All the time I had been hiding in the barrack hut I had not seen anyone near my age. Now I was carried through a little gate and into a hut: the *Kinderschuppen* – children's shed. A tall woman in a white coat was sitting at a desk. The guard put me on my feet, said something to her and left. She asked me my name but I wasn't in a talkative mood. She shrugged, went to the door and called to someone. A woman with a hump appeared in the doorway. I was terrified. I had been brought up on Babi Yaga fairy tales and standing in the doorway with the sun low behind her she reminded me of a witch. She came forward and bent to pick me up. I tried to seek protection from the woman in white but she just pushed me into the arms of the witch. It took me a long time to calm down but when I did I reassessed my opinion of my new 'keeper'. She was gentle and kind. She asked me if I wanted to pick a place to sleep where I'd feel at home. I went straight to the back where the little window was in the old block and found there was one there, too. And it had a better view of the field where they would be putting cattle and horses soon, when the spring came, when the sun would shine and the grass would look green, not grey and cold like now.

I soon decided that Fräulein Gloge was nice, not like the other *Kapos*. She didn't shout and at times she even smiled. In truth, she was more of a nanny than a *Kapo*. I soon forgot her hump. When I kept crying for my mother and peeing in the bunk, she whispered that my mother was all right, she was in the laundry, nice and warm . . . She would soon come and see me. As I began to calm down I was amazed to find that the little area set aside from the main camp was full of children. They all appeared to be more or less my age. I was given a smock and a bunk, with a proper mattress and two blankets. But the best thing was the toilets, which were four low buckets that we could use day and night and that hardly smelled at all and were emptied regularly by prisoners from the main camp.

We were sleeping three to a bunk, head to toe, a great luxury compared with the other hut where there was even less room. And I had my little window. It almost felt like home. To indoctrinate and prepare us for our future glory deep in the bosom of a truly teutonic family we were given German lessons. Although we were from many different countries and spoke different languages, we were forced to talk to each other in German. Sometimes Fräulein Gloge took us off to play in the wired enclosure, which was magical because there was no restriction on noise making or running around. There was even a see-saw of sorts and Fräulein Gloge would sit on a wooden plank left over from building the watch towers and occasionally smile if you did something she liked. I must admit I loved her a little. I used to show off like mad whenever I thought she was watching.

Fräulein Gloge came to my bunk one morning and told me I could expect a visitor. My mother, along with several others, was being allowed to come. I had the unworthy thought that Matka might spoil it and take me away with her. It was pouring with rain when she arrived so we sat on my bunk and she hugged me until I wished she'd stop. Later the Fräulein brought a piece of bread. It was a real treat. I can still remember the taste. After we had eaten we were all told to go out for a 'routine inspection'.

Outside, the mud was up to our ankles, sucking at the clogs we had to wear. I noticed that my mother was shaking all over and knew it was a bad sign. A couple of men in uniforms with another in a long leather coat arrived. My mother became even more agitated and I could hear her keening to herself, which scared me. The three men walked along the line. Occasionally they stopped and the man with the leather coat looked at one of the children while a guard made notes in a book. They came to me. I was curious. The one with the long leather coat smiled at me. He looked quite nice. I couldn't see what all the fuss was about. He turned my head from side to side and looked at my knees. He was particularly taken with my head. It was a lot better now but the lice in the main camp had done a good job on it and my endless scratching when my mother wasn't there to stop me had produced some really impressive scabs. Evidently the leather-coated one wasn't a scab fan and gave a negative shake of his head. The trio got to the end of the line, said something to the woman in the white coat, and left. She walked over and with the help of Fräulein Gloge separated the selected children from their mothers, who howled and screamed and tried to hang on to them by force.

My mother stopped shaking. She hurriedly bent down, held me for an instant so tight it took my breath away and whispered 'Lucky day . . . !' and hurried off to her work.

The selected children were bundled aboard a truck which left at once. These chosen ones were going to German families who wanted children and couldn't have any of their own. It's a sobering thought that with my almost white-blonde hair I would have been carted off to be brought up as a staunch supporter of the Third Reich if it hadn't been for a particularly virulent attack of scabies.

Later they took dark-haired children too. Like my best friend Rachel who was the most beautiful girl I'd ever seen. I envied her dark curly hair and black eyes, and the way she could dance. She told me she was a gypsy. We'd entertain the guards sometimes, she would dance and I would sing. We had rehearsed a routine with Fräulein Gloge. What a riot it must have been. I didn't really know any songs and just made them up. We'd laugh a lot and the guards would give us an apple or chocolate.

We were playing something like 'Round the Mulberry Bush' outside the *Kinderschuppen*. We were seven that day, sometimes we'd be more. If we were less we wouldn't play *'Ringel Ringel Reihe, wir sind der Kinder Dreie* – one has gone to breathe the gas – *jetzt sind wir nur noch zweie!'*

Two guards Rachel and I had been singing for came along and watched us playing for a while. One was quite good-looking, tall and neat. He smiled. The other one was fat and ugly, pink like a pig. He kept whispering in his companion's ear. He had to stand on his toes to reach it. Suddenly the tall one grabbed Rachel, held her tight by her shoulder and smiled at her. He said something I couldn't hear and opened his trousers. He slammed Rachel against the wall of the *Kinderschuppen*, which vibrated. All the kids disappeared in a flash. Me too. I crawled under the hut and listened to the thuds her body made against the *Kinderschuppen* as the SS man pushed into her body again and again. His hat fell down, rolled under the hut and stopped in front of me. The silver death's-head insignia grinned at me. I crept further to the back of the hut, into the darkness. Rachel dropped to the ground. Eager hands grabbed her and pulled her up again. The other guard had a go. The same thudding noises . . . He let Rachel drop to the floor. A face appeared under the floorboards of the *Kinderschuppen*. A hand reached for the hat. The shiny boots walked away, crunching on the gravel.

Rachel's body lay on the ground. Slowly I crept closer. I pulled her under the hut. It was hard – she was four years older than me. Blood ran down her legs. For a moment she opened her eyes and looked at me, then she stopped breathing. I held her, but the rats came back and I crawled away.

Four

We had a great trade going with new arrivals. It was easier for the children to organise this than the grown-up prisoners. We could rush around without being accosted, hide behind the huts and slip into them unnoticed when everyone was away on work detail. Some of the older children, about eight or nine years old, had organised us into gangs. One particular boy, probably the oldest in the *Kinderschuppen*, had even got some sort of black market going. He was a regular little Fagin. Before long, we were all part of his empire. His main line of business was spoons. At that time, the top currency was the simple tablespoon. It was what kept you alive. Without it you were reduced to lapping up what little food was available like a dog. With it you were in at the cooking pot, shoulder to shoulder with the best of them. Unfortunately, spoons were a fast disappearing commodity. When the camp had first opened everybody had been issued with pyjamas, wooden clogs, a threadbare blanket, a canteen and a spoon. By the time I got there you grabbed what you could and hung on to it for grim life. In the children's compound there were spoons which were handed out each mealtime. Our budding Fagin made us filch them. If we didn't perform he would beat us up. I became one of his ace suppliers.

Before long, the spoons' disappearance was noted and typically the *Lager* – camp – officials over-reacted. There we were, twenty or so little ones, asleep in our bunks, when the door crashed open and two dog handlers burst in, barely able to control the huge Alsatians, shouting at us to get out while they searched the hut. Standing outside in our draughty shifts, we clung to each other, petrified. We had been there long enough to know that we could be in deep trouble very soon. The guards crashed about inside and then stormed out, triumphantly bearing a cardboard box full of spoons. They called the 'Fagin' boy out from the cold and wet line-up and took him away. We never saw him again.

They also took one of the boys whom I didn't like, a bossy eight-year-old. I didn't mind that he'd gone. Life went on as usual after that. I discovered years later that the children the Germans had no use for were sent to Mauthausen and Ravensbrück and were gassed. Why they didn't just kill everyone at Stutthof no one knows. But who knows why the Nazis did anything . . .

It's surprising how easy it is to fall into a routine. At least when you are very young and have no recollectable experience to compare with your present life. The nightmare of mass murder is all around you every moment of every day and even at night, too. Gone were the times of waking up in the morning, all three of us together, warm and safe, holding a mug of tea or cocoa, nattering about moles and ditches and butterflies. All I knew now was that it was bad to cry, you were always cold, food was something you bolted down as quickly and as often as possible and you kept out of the way of the men and women in hats with silver badges on the front.

Long lines of people arrived every day, but the number of prisoners in the camp never rose. Some kids joined the *Kinderschuppen* and lots of people queued up outside a small brick building which was the gas chamber. The chimney smoked all the time. I had got used to the constant stench, the shouting, the snarling dogs which never barked, the armies of scurrying filthy rats which spread disease and the constant hunger. The vicious beatings and ghostlike prisoners, running around, pushing carts with clothes or cases piled high. When something fell off, guards would be on hand at once and beat the prisoner trying to pick up the fallen bits and pieces and avoid the club blows at the same time.

Instead of cows and horses, uniformed prisoners of war began to appear in the barbed-wire enclosure behind the *Kinderschuppen*. At first there were only a few dozen or so. Gradually more were driven in and before long the enclosure was full to bursting point. Fräulein Gloge told us not to be seen speaking to them. They were Russian POWs and were being held there until they could be taken to a more permanent camp. I watched them from my little window over my bunk. They milled around, trying to keep warm in the open, without any cover, not even a blanket, and with very little food. As winter drew in many were carried away dead.

I thought I knew about the Russians. I kept waiting for them to rise up and shout 'Hurrah!' like my papa had told me the great General Kutuzov's army had done, crushing the wicked Napoleon. I fervently believed my Russians would rush the fence, trample it down and liberate the camp. But they never did.

We were taught German by a professional teacher who was hellbent on teaching me to write with my right hand. I didn't take to it and he made me lay my hands on the desk in front of me so that he could hit them with a thin yellow stick. It hurt like hell. When he did it his face turned red; so did my hands. I still kept on writing with the left. God only knows why I didn't even try to do what he wanted.

One day, in the middle of the German lesson, a couple of soldiers stormed in, grabbed our teacher by the neck and dragged him outside. He pleaded with them, appealed to us kids to do something and hung on to the door frame screaming. One of the guards smashed his rifle butt on to our teacher's fingers and he let go quickly enough. We were all in our usual state of terror. Adults were always warning us to keep our heads down when violence was being meted out. The wrong look, the wrong word could soon put you on the receiving end. Nevertheless we crept to the window and watched as our poor teacher, still begging for mercy, was made to stand at the centre of our play area. Without any preamble they shot him in the head and left the compound.

Terrified, Fräulein Gloge urged us to return to our seats but we waited to see a couple of prisoners come into the yard and take the body away before doing as she asked. It was the last day of school for a long time. The teacher was never replaced. Fräulein Gloge tried to fill the role but she was too soft-hearted. There was one unexpected outcome from the brutal scene – I never wrote with my left hand again.

Another selection parade was held and the more acceptable children were loaded on to lorries. I had again failed the audition. As I watched them disappear I felt rejected and a little envious.

The half-dozen rejects were playing quietly in the compound when the gate opened and four or five soldiers barged in with rifles and dogs. The woman in the white coat watched, expressionless as usual, as, stunned by fear into silence, we were rounded up. Instead of being marched up the road to the brick-built compound with the gas chamber and the black smoking chimney that we had learned to fear, we were led in the opposite direction into the main compound. Outside the building with the tall windows we were brought to a halt and one of the men went inside. It was starting to rain. We huddled together on the packed earth and watched it become a mire of mud. The man returned and we were marched off again, this time towards the huts. Again we were herded together and made to wait . . . and wait . . . and wait. Too wet and confused even to cry, we tried to guess what the next move would be. Around us, activity in the camp was picking up. Marching groups of women shuffled past us. Some looked at us curiously, others were too exhausted to care. Then I saw my mama in another group. They were heading in our direction. I had never been so pleased to see her. The group consisted of mothers of some of the children. There was a lot of crying. The soldiers left us for a while to enjoy our reunion, then got bored and drove us away. I soon found out that a new regime was in place. The size of the Russian compound was being extended, taking in part of the children's area. In future, the youngsters would spend the day in the *Kinderschuppen* with the white-coated *Kapo* and the nights in the main camp with their mothers.

Being back with Matka was wonderful. She spoiled me rotten. The conditions in the hut were awful compared with what I was used to but being reunited made it worthwhile.

My mother had made a new friend, a young Lithuanian woman called Annie Jadkowska. Annie and she shared a bunk, and worked together in the laundry. Sometimes Annie was forced to work in the brothel. That impressed me, although I had only the vaguest idea of what it meant.

Sex wasn't a prime subject of conversation in the barracks. Food and death were.

I loved Annie. She was big and warm, and had a way of giggling that was infectious. She would clutch me in her arms and hug me and hug me, and not let me go. I have a passion for big breasts because of Annie. Hers were big and soft and warm, whereas my mother was just skin and bones, and it hurt when she cuddled me. Annie would tell me about her little boy in Vilna and how she would soon see him again. In the meanwhile I would have to fill her 'empty arms' . . .

Annie had worked in Berlin for some time as a spy for the Russians. She used me to take notes and throw them towards the Russian compound as I passed on the way to the *Kinderschuppen*. I never saw anyone pick them up and nobody ever tried to get a note back to her but I guess the sense of doing something helped her to get through each dreadful day. The trouble with Annie was that she never learned to keep quiet. How she ever managed to be a spy I'll never know. Obviously she wasn't a good one or she wouldn't have been in the camp in the first place. The Nazis let her shoot her mouth off for a long time without doing anything about it – probably because they appreciated her activities in the brothel – but one day, inevitably, they decided they'd had enough. It was the middle of the night when the guards crashed into the hut. They came straight to our bunk and ordered Annie to get down. There was no place to hide. When I saw them coming I crept under my blanket and shut my eyes tight. I didn't want to see them march Annie away. She didn't say anything. She knew it was the end, that she was done for. Everyone in the hut knew.

The next morning all the prisoners were lined up to watch the hanging. Even the children were forced to look on. I couldn't breathe. I tried to keep from weeping. They brought her out and marched her to the gallows. A square frame of timber with five ropes tied off and boxes strategically placed beneath the nooses. Annie could hardly walk. She looked terrible. Her pyjama frock was torn, there was blood all over her face and they must have broken one of her arms, for it dangled at the side of her body at an awkward angle. She crouched forward and walked with enormous effort. The prioners had to lift her on to the box under the scaffold. They put the noose around her neck and kicked away the box. Her body shook and went limp. I wanted to scream and shout but not a sound came out.

Annie's body hung there for days as a warning. Eventually prisoners wheeled her away to where the smoke climbed into the sky.

A few days later they came and took my mother while I was in the *Kinderschuppen*. The security officer, SS Captain Hoppe, had found out she was a friend of Annie and assumed she was tarred with the same revolutionary brush. After all, she was Jewish and had a Lithuanian background. When I arrived back at Block 5 that evening the other women looked after me. They tried to make light of the fact that my mother had been taken to the dreaded punishment block but I was an old lag by now and knew the score. What would become of me if Mama didn't come back? Without her I would die.

I spent the night in the bunk of two other women. By the morning I was like a furnace. Too weak to get up, I didn't join the other children when they were taken off to the *Kinderschuppen*. I lay in the bunk all day, drifting in and out of consciousness. I woke up once to find that I had been sick and messed myself. I was worried about what my mother would say – but not for long. When the women at last arrived back from work I was unconscious – and I had a swelling on my neck the size of a carpenter's fist. I'd had problems with my glands for a long time but I guess the added torture of having to watch the hanging of my dear Annie and losing my mother had brought on a crisis. I couldn't eat or talk. But most awful of all, I couldn't breathe. And my condition was getting worse. It was a miracle that neither Mama nor I had fallen really sick before. The marshes bordering the camp bred sickness and the vermin scurrying around the huts spread it to the prisoners.

Suddenly Matka was back. I didn't question the fact that she was there. It was natural. She was always there when I was really in trouble. She made a fuss of me and never let on about the pain she had suffered, although it was clear that she had been badly beaten. I was sure that everything would be all right now. The next thing I knew I was stretched out on a table with my mother standing over me holding my head while prisoners held me down and a man, who I later learned was called Steiner, looked at my neck. I tried to twist my head round to see what he was going to do but my mother's grip and the vice-like hold of the prisoners kept me in place. Out of the corner of my eye I could see a candle burning. The blade of a knife passed through the flame. I felt a sharp cut. My body convulsed as pain seemed to explode in my head. I passed out and dreamed of ferns and trees. When I woke up I could feel the man's hands on my throat. Now the suffering was different. The wild searing pain was gone, leaving just an ache that wasn't being helped by the man's determination to get any residual puss out of the wound. I tried to struggle but there were too many hands holding me down.

They couldn't sew up the wound. Catgut was not an easy commodity to find in the camp. Steiner poured some burning liquid over the hole in my neck and wrapped me up with a bandage. The prisoners carried me to my mother's bunk and I fell asleep in her arms.

As a result of her connection to Annie, my mother lost her job in the laundry and was put on a torturous work detail, unloading rocks from lorries on the main road outside the camp and cutting them up into smaller pieces. The camp was being extended again and building materials were needed. The place was constantly growing and evolving. Even the *Kinderschuppen* had undergone a radical change. The *Kapo* in the white coat had been joined by a couple of other women. These were prisoners. But often the prisoners were worse than the Nazis, wanting to ingratiate themselves with the camp hierarchy in return for life-supporting extra rations. The *Kapo* in the white coat seemed indifferent to our fate, which was fine with me, but the new women were determined to turn us into perfect little German schoolchildren. I, for one, didn't like that and it was back to the old routine of dumb insolence followed by a slap, crying and more dumb insolence. I tried to tell my mother what a trial my life had become but she was so exhausted from a sixteen-hour day humping rocks that I didn't get a lot of sympathy for my whining.

My mother's new job was horrendous and the women dropped like flies. She knew she wouldn't last the week. Part of the agony was wearing wooden clogs. They made the feet bleed, which then became infected and if you couldn't march properly in your work detail you'd get picked out for the gas chamber. I recognised that Matka was in a bad state and wondered what would happen to us.

The *Kapo* of my mother's work detail, Peter Steiner, was the 'surgeon' who had saved my life. Before the camps he'd been a shoemaker and now earned a little preferment by making boots for the Nazi officers and guards. He expiated his guilt by helping out some of the less fortunate prisoners and soon he began to take an interest in my mother and her scrawny, sickly kid. Mama always told me after the war that without me she would have given up straight away. She wouldn't have endured the hell it took to survive. Protecting me gave her superhuman strength and a purpose to live. Steiner found such a purpose by helping us. He organised food for us and alcohol to disinfect my poorly healing wound. Somehow he got a new bandage and some antiseptic cream and, after repeating the treatment with the alcohol – which was terribly painful – the incision started to close up and heal.

Steiner was a whittler. With the same knife he used to operate on me, he carved little ornaments. He knew that if it was found on him he would be a candidate for the 'road to heaven', as the Nazis called the gas chamber, but the knife was his symbol of resistance. He carved Mama a small wooden Star of David. She kept it hidden under her straw mattress, then gave it to me to keep safe. I lost it and my mother was heart-broken. Years later, in Buenos Aires, I found a carved wooden Star of David, an exact replica, at an antiques market. When I gave it to my mother, to my surprise, she thanked me matter-of-factly and took it to her room. I didn't see it again until after her death. She kept it in a little box with my father's medals. I still have it, and wear it and pretend it's Steiner's star.

One day Steiner brought me a little Cossack doll, no bigger than a child's hand. I took it with me everywhere.

My mother never found out how Steiner managed to get her transferred to the kitchens. It saved our lives. She cooked exclusively for the Nazis, having learned from my father what kind of food Germans like and how to prepare it. She had to make out a shopping list once a week. She soon became quite a dab hand at sorting away little titbits and bringing them back to the hut. It was dangerous and if she had been caught there would have been no reprieve. But she didn't seem to care. I think at this point she was seriously doubting that we would survive the camp. There were too many knives pointing our way.

Every two weeks children were selected and left the camp by the wagonloads. Transports arrived each day, the children would be taken to other huts as well as the *Kinderschuppen*, but they weren't there for more than two weeks. Then there would be the routine selection and lorries would come and spirit them away. By now, none of my former class-mates was left. I was the runt whom nobody wanted. I should have been happy with that but I was older now, and felt rejected and despised. I never realised how much of my good fortune was due to my mother's survival antennae. She had become friendly with the illiterate Lithuanian guards. In return for information about selections, she would write gooey, emotional letters to the guards' loved ones or read their letters from home to them. The Lithuanians were considered the most brutal and dangerous, but their need to be loved provided my mother and me with some degree of security.

When it was time for a selection my mother would hide me in the latrines. Not too many people came there during the day and the guards wouldn't go near them. Once the lorries had left, she would collect me, scrub me down with ice-cold water and hurriedly take me back to the hut. The next day the *Kinderschuppen* would have a completely new host of faces, tearful and ready to do anything I told them to do.

Five

Our precarious routine was finally broken by events on the front: the Russian army at last crossed into Poland and approached Stutthof. Suddenly the glorious Nazi war machine was on the back foot fighting to get away. Frightened that the POWs might rise up and join the approaching Russians, the SS men moved in and overnight machine-gunned the lot. The sudden, overt blood bath threw the *Lager Häftlinge* – camp prisoners – into a frenzy. Everyone rushed around trying to rationalise their position, to convince themselves that the Nazis wouldn't hurt them. The rising hysteria was cut short by reality. The unmentionable was happening. The SS were closing down the camps – and getting rid of all the incriminating evidence. That didn't just mean the files they had efficiently kept on 'the final solution for deportees' but also the prisoners themselves. Now the Nazis weren't using euphemisms. Hut after hut was cleared and taken to the gas chamber. As prisoners could no longer believe they would be spared, an unnatural silence descended on the camp. People held on to each other, cuddling, or else hid away, either facing despair or trying to meet the inevitable with dignity.

I was in the *Kinderschuppen* when Peter Steiner arrived unexpectedly. He grabbed me and took me to my mother's hut, where he lifted me into her bunk. 'Stay there!' he said. 'Don't move.' He had received information that the *Kinderschuppen* was to be liquidated and all the children taken to the gas chamber, and had risked his life crossing the compound in glaring daylight to fetch me. In silence, the women came back from their work details and went to their bunks. When she reached ours, Mama was bewildered to see me huddling there. She took me in her arms and was very still. She fumbled under her thread-bare blanket and put bits of bread in my mouth as she held me and rocked me back and forth.

The emptying of huts progressed through the long afternoon, coming nearer and nearer to the one we were in. The waiting was horrendous. At last the dreaded squad ran up to our door.

It was almost a relief when a sergeant came in and ordered us out. 'Block 5! *Antreten*!' he yelled.

Everybody shuffled out without protest. We all knew what was happening but obeyed the shouted orders as if refusal might bring some punishment. What punishment could be greater than the fate we knew awaited us? I knew things were bad but I don't think I really comprehended that we were going to die now. The thought of death is a very abstract concept to an eight-year-old.

Shivering in the falling dusk, we waited for the command to move off to the small brick house, the gas chamber. Everyone was silent, contemplating what they believed awaited them. Half a dozen more guards appeared and talked to the ones already in place. No one knew what was said. Then, with the usual shouting and screaming, dogs straining at the leashes, panting and slavering, the order came: '*Marsch, vorwärts!*' The guards stirred us into movement.

But instead of marching left – to the Death House – the column followed the guards to the main gate of the *Lager.* My mother squeezed my hand so tight it hurt. We weren't going to die. A whisper went through the colum, that the gas chamber had broken down.

In a dream the raggedy column of fifty or so women *Häftlinge* shuffled through the open *Lager* gate and followed the guards along the road. The euphoria at not being marched off to the gas chamber was replaced by more rational thought. No one knew what would happen but believed we had to be killed. The Nazis would not let us survive to tell our story.

Whispers went through the column:

'They'll kill us in the forest.'

'We're being spared for the labour battalions.'

'We're going to be shot dead as soon as we get into the woods.'

Matka kept pushing me out of sight when guards approached. It was strangely comforting hearing the guards shouting at us, *'Schneller machen, schneller ihr verdammten Juden Schweine . . . !'* We didn't care where we were going as long as we were leaving Stutthof concentration camp.

Walking along the dark road in our clogs was agony. We were freezing and hungry. Some of the women collapsed and the guards shot them where they lay. After a few hours we came to a barn. We were marched inside and the doors were locked. Again hysterical suppositions filled the air:

'Nazi guards don't want to be seen with concentration camp prisoners. It's too risky. They have to get rid of us.'

'They're going to set fire to the barn and run off.'

But the guards were just tired. They didn't set the barn on fire. They sat down and ate. We didn't get anything but no one cared. We smelled the Nazis' food and were glad and surprised to be alive to sense it.

The cold was less severe in the barn. We climbed into the hay and covered ourselves up. Its fresh smell reminded me of Bialystok. We must have fallen asleep because shots being fired outside woke us up. What was happening? We couldn't see anything. One of the taller women put me on her shoulders and I was able to look out of a slit high up in the barn. Outside, flashes of light were followed by a bang. The guards were being attacked by partisans! Something hit the side of the barn a few inches above my head and a splinter just missed my right eye. I overbalanced and was caught by my mother who wasn't happy about me being the look-out.

Meanwhile some of the women were trying with their bare hands to prise away the wooden planks at the back of the building so we could escape while the SS guards were busy fighting. But the planks wouldn't give without proper tools.

The partisans killed one or two of the guards but then the SS men got the upper hand and the partisans left us to perish.

It was not long before we were once again shuffling along the road like freezing, starving skeletons. The guards, too, were sombre and had stopped shouting.

Suddenly there was a noise in the sky. Looking up we saw aeroplanes, their machine-guns at the ready. We threw ourselves into the ditches at the side of the road, quivering as the planes swooped down and raked us with their guns. Why were they doing this? we wondered. Couldn't they see we were just a pitiful bunch of skeletons, crawling along the road hoping to live another hour?

When we looked up we saw that the planes had killed some of the guards but more of the prisoners. Matka ripped strips off a dead woman's shift to wrap around our feet, then, prodded by the guards, we marched on again. We hadn't gone far when the planes came back. Mascha dived into a ditch, pulling me with her. Gently, she rolled herself on top of me. Once more I heard the guards ordering everyone to march on but my mother stayed motionless on top of me. I feared she was dead. One of the men came to the edge of the ditch and shoved a boot into her still body. Convinced that she'd been hit by the aeroplane fire, he didn't waste his bullets.

For a long time Matka and I lay in the ditch. Eventually, my mother lifted her head slightly to survey the area. Gingerly, she raised herself up a bit more to make sure the column had gone and we were safe, then she sat up, dragged me out of the ditch and we slowly walked towards the forest.

When we got into the trees, we sat on a fallen trunk and rested. My mother suddenly pulled me on to her lap and hugged me, and fiercely kissed my face over and over. Then she wept. All the pent-up tears poured out of her big, hollow eyes. 'This is our lucky day, baby . . .' she whispered and rocked me back and forth, trying to stop crying. She knew that every day in the last three years had been our lucky day.

We were still a long way from being safe. Partisans – made up of Polish freedom fighters, foreign workers, political refugees, deserters and even bandits, but very few Jews – were all over the forests of Poland. They killed prisoners from the camps.

When Matka had stopped crying, she took my hand and we started off once more. We had to find somewhere to sleep before nightfall. We went deeper into the dark forest. I was mesmerised by the mass of trees. I couldn't remember ever seeing such big beautiful specimens. But it was hard going, I kept losing my clogs and hardly had the strength to climb over the roots, and through the brambles and underbrush. I was starving and the cold wind whipped viciously through my flimsy shift. At frequent intervals we had to rest. We had no idea where we were going.

Suddenly Matka stopped and listened. We heard twigs breaking. Mama fell to the ground and pulled me down under her but it was too late. We had been spotted. An older man and a boy, a few years older than I and with a gun that was nearly as big as he was, stood right in front of us. The man spoke in Polish and my mother begged him not to hurt us. He wanted to know where we came from. She tried lying but it was no use. The boy said, 'They're from the camp, Grandad.' It was obvious from the tone of his voice that he didn't think much of us. 'Let's go,' he urged.

'Please,' my mother begged, 'let us go with you. We won't be any trouble.'

The old man asked if we were from Sztutowie. Mama hesitated. She decided it was useless to deny it. Anyone could tell from our appearance. She slowly nodded her head. The old man looked at her for a moment, then at me. I tried a smile but it only stretched the snot cascading out of my flame-red nose. 'We'll see what the others think,' he said and, trailed closely by his grandson, he plunged off into the trees leaving us to follow as best we could. Now that we had a goal we reached into our small reservoir of strength and kept our saviours in sight.

The partisan camp looked like a palace to me. In reality it was a jumble of make-shift tents and lean-tos grouped around a small decaying Babi Yaga cottage. Old tarpaulins, sacks and rotting pieces of cloth were draped over the shelters in an effort to conserve as much heat as possible. The people in the camp weren't much to look at either. What rags they hadn't draped over their accommodation, they were wearing. But they were dressed in proper clothes, no pyjamas. And there were no *Kapos*, no guards and slavering dogs, no shouting, no stinking stench, no smoking chimney.

The old man talked to two others. They looked at us without a lot of enthusiasm. The boy showed how he felt by walking straight into the cottage without a backward glance. Nobody else seemed interested.

The old man signalled to us and we followed him into the cottage. Inside, we found a small furnitureless room with about a dozen or so men sitting on the floor. They barely looked at us. We went through to a makeshift kitchen. From a heavy bucket sitting on a cut-down oil drum that had been pressed into service as a stove came a delicious smell. A man, evidently the cook, scowled at us and didn't seem inclined to feed us, but the old man insisted. With bad grace the cook sloshed some soup into a couple of earthenware bowls and practically threw them on the greasy table in front of us. I wanted to snatch up the steaming broth but I wasn't convinced that it was really for me. I watched Matka reach for her bowl and was about to ask for a spoon, when she scowled at me and put the rim to her mouth. I followed her example. The rich soup tasted even better than it smelled.

After much discussion it was finally decided that we could stay. Eagerly my mother thanked them. Finding somewhere to sleep, however, wasn't easy. A spot in the cottage was prized above everything and all places were taken and jealously guarded. The alternative was one of the lean-tos. With her usual brio my mama found us a nice dry spot under a bush by a massive oak tree. A woman in a battered Russian uniform, with some skins and a blanket, came up to Mama and squatted down beside us. She told us her name was Tchechia and she had escaped into the forest two years before when the Nazis had come to her village to round everybody up. She was the first woman we had seen in the camp. She was beautiful, with dark curly hair and laughing eyes, and asked my mother a lot of questions about what was happening outside the forest, but, other than the fact that the Russians were getting close, we had nothing to add to what she already knew. She was obviously disappointed in us. She shoved the skins and blanket towards Mascha and left.

As I lay down to sleep, listening to the night sounds of the forest, I thought I was in heaven. The luxury of a little nest far away from the constant fear and threat of death in the camp and a full belly couldn't be compared with anything I had known before.

Then I spoiled it and threw up all over our blanket.

Six

I woke up with a hacking cough, a nose which felt as if it was on fire and hands and feet swollen to twice their size by chilblains. Although I protested that I liked sleeping beneath the trees, Mascha faced the fact that somehow she had to work up a shelter for us by nightfall. I was no help. I was mesmerised by the boy with the gun and his surly attitude. His name was Yuri and he didn't think much of girls, especially this skinny one with a snotty nose and a funny accent. I didn't care. I thought he was wonderful. Yuri got tired of me following him around and kicked me on the leg. I didn't flinch. He could do no wrong and I wasn't going to be put out by a little thing like physical violence. But I did have enough savvy to realise that our relationship wouldn't get better unless he wanted a friend.

As I mooned around, my mother was getting organised. She had insinuated herself into a space between one of the less substantial lean-tos and the chimney. The chimney radiated some warmth but unfortunately it also gave out great billows of suffocating smoke, which was why the spot had remained unoccupied.

Our next-door neighbour was the woman we had

talked to the night before, Tchechia. Apart from Mascha, she was the only female in the camp with a child. She took a shine to my mother, probably because she was beset with the same problems. Tchechia's daughter, Mila, was five months old, a black-eyed little cherub with a mass of black curls. I thought she was wonderful until I found that my freedom was restricted by having to care for her. With ill grace and poorly concealed resentment I humped the poor infant around.

Tchechia was in a privileged position as she was Kuragin's woman. There was little organisation in the camp, not even a designated site for latrines, but everyone deferred to Kuragin, a big, boisterous Russian. We were told that he was a Russian fighter pilot who had been shot down and captured by the Germans. They'd tortured him but he'd escaped and now was just waiting for his chance to get back at the enemy. It was a comforting story.

Mama was transformed by life in the partisan camp. Tchechia gave her some nice raggedy clothes and Russian boots, and she looked like the other women, big and as tough as a man. Her hardy Stutthof shell crumbled and she became soft and gentle, and cuddled me all the time.

My mother also worked to transform the camp. Within days she had taken over the kitchen. The food improved and our stock went up. Next she had the 'stove' moved to a rough shelter at the side of the cottage. That freed up the room in the cottage where the cooking had been done and we moved in. She also tried to get Kuragin to sort out some kind of schedule that would give the men something to do instead of lying around playing cards. He tried but without much enthusiasm. The only positive thing to come out of it was that an area was designated for latrines, pits dug and a tree trunk slung across them to sit on – luxury!

*

Burdened by my little charge, Milusia, I was even less cut out to be Bonnie to Yuri's Clyde. At least I thought that was how it was going to be – except that behind all the macho blustering Yuri was as soft-hearted as the next partisan.

I was sitting on a log amid the birch trees and conifers, looking after the baby, when Yuri turned up and sat at the other end of the tree trunk. We glowered at each other and I made a fuss of little Mila to show I had something important to do. He got up and leaned against a tree, rolling a fag. He lit it and sat back down – a little closer. After a few minutes he asked about the baby and that broke the ice. He told me he was going to look at the traps he had set the night before and asked me if I wanted to come along. When I hesitated he offered to carry the baby. I made sure Mascha was looking the other way, then happily deserted my post.

The traps turned out to be a disappointment, containing nothing for the pot, but Yuri didn't seem particularly worried. He had another surprise for me. Half an hour from the camp was a ruined castle that had been the family home of the people who owned the land on which the cottage was built. The place had briefly been the barracks for a small garrison of Germans but they'd blown it up when they'd left. Most of the furniture had been taken back to the camp but there was still enough there to make it interesting. My prize find was a box on wheels with a pulling handle, which had probably been used for transporting logs in the old days. It was a most cumbersome contraption but I loved it and bullied Yuri into helping me take it back to the camp. It became a sort of perambulator and shopping trolley. It was daft but it was mine.

The cart came into its own shortly afterwards. One of the men found a dead horse and asked if he could borrow it to bring back the meat. As I wasn't keen to let my prize possession out of my sight, they took me along. The horse had been dead for some time and I found the smell frightening, reminiscent of Stutthof. I watched as the men hacked the swollen carcass to pieces and loaded it on to my cart. In spite of the smell the meat must have been okay as everyone ate great chunks of it and I can't remember anyone being particularly ill.

Yuri told me that our camp was just one of many that had sprung up in the last year or two. There was much talk about what the partisans would do to spike the Nazi war machine and help the Russians when they arrived, but little was done to implement the ideas. In reality, there was not much they could do for they had few rifles and even less ammunition. The shotguns were needed for hunting and the ammunition for those was so precious that hunting parties sometimes came back empty-handed because they were afraid to shoot unless they had a rabbit practically squinting down the barrel. If we were amazingly lucky the huntsmen might come across a German supply wagon or a train shunted into a siding. On occasions, when the food situation got really wretched, some of the men would raid a farmhouse, but this was attempted only in desperate circumstances as the reward was rarely worth the enormous risk.

When I wasn't minding Milusia or running after Yuri, I was drawn inexorably to the oldest member of the camp, blind Boris. Borja was large and jolly, and had a halo of white hair and a beard that made him a dead ringer for Father Christmas. Boris had been in Treblinka. With his disability he would have been exterminated straight away but the Germans are very sentimental about Christmas and so his likeness to Santa Claus probably saved him. Whatever the reason, they decked him out in robes, put him in charge of the latrines and gave him the title of

'*Scheissmeister*'. When the revolt had come in Treblinka, Borja hadn't let his blindness hold him back. While everyone else was ducking and diving or fighting, he just walked straight ahead and out of the camp. Yuri told me that Boris had carried a baby out with him but hadn't been able to look after it so he gave it to someone to care for. When the war was over, he said, he was going to find the baby.

Boris used to sit with me under the leafy canopy, holding Milusia, and tell me wonderful fairy stories about witches and demons, goblins and gnomes, in the dark Russian forests far, far away.

Almost daily, now, there were rumours that we were about to be liberated by the advancing Russian army. Planes flew constantly over the forest and everyone claimed to be able to spot which nation they belonged to. They came and went above the trees so quickly, however, that it was impossible to get a good look. Someone would say, 'That's a Messerschmitt!' Someone else would argue that it was a Yak. I always shouted 'Spitfire!' because it was the only name I could remember from the days with my father.

We had been in the partisan camp some time now. Winter was giving way to spring and the sun warmed the earth. Buds appeared overnight and grass pushed up out of the ground. Leaves thrust from stark branches, covering the camp in a light-green blanket.

We decided that it was my mother's birthday as she had been born on the first day of spring. Tchechia announced that she was going to take us to a special place, deep inside the forest and, carrying Mila, led Mama and me to a small clearing. At the centre was a fire pit. She lit a fire, which was strictly forbidden in case Germans were in the area, and told us to fan the smoke away gently. As we sat by the burning twigs, Tchechia pulled our Stutthof shifts from her bag. She ripped the hated striped cloth into small rags and solemnly laid them into the flames. Tears streamed down Mama's face, but still she tried to smile at Tchechia. Each year on my mother's birthday I remember that day when we burned the past.

Because of the better weather, I was able to leave little Milusia behind in a hammock in the open most of the time, and Yuri and I became inseparable. The old ruined castle was our domain. Yuri used to pretend we owned it and were husband and wife. He was just moving into puberty and we indulged in a few innocent 'show me yours and I'll show you mine' games.

One day Yuri and I, with the reluctant help of a few of the men, were ripping up floor planks in the castle to help build up the roofs of the lean-tos. We had filled my little cart and were about to go back when an aeroplane roared overhead, so low everyone ducked, then we heard the sound of it crashing into the trees. We didn't hang around. Yuri was first at the wreck. When I arrived the three men were standing a safe distance from the plane looking warily at the smoking, hissing carcass. I suppose they expected it to burst into flame at any moment. I had no such hang-up and ran straight for it. I knew it was an English plane because I remembered my father teaching me the RAF insignia: blue and white circles and a red dot.

I heard Yuri shout but I had seen something that the others hadn't. The pilot was half in, half out of the cockpit and looked in a bad way. Cautiously the men approached the plane. It had settled down now and no longer appeared to be in danger of exploding. Yuri climbed up on to the wing and looked into the cockpit. He shouted for the men to help him get the pilot out of the plane. The pilot was unconscious and blood was leaking from a head wound. One of the men said he thought he had a broken leg. They didn't seem too concerned about it. Instead, they were interested in seeing what they could scavenge from the plane.

The pilot groaned and woke up. Surprised, I screamed, and the three searching the plane ran back to see what was going on. I suggested that I fetch my cart but the offer was turned down and the men carried the pilot back to the camp. He was unconscious again by the time we arrived.

My mother, the only partisan who could speak English, discovered that the pilot's name was Mike and that he came from Yorkshire. His injuries were painful but not life threatening and soon he was hobbling about. He suggested that the men fetch from his plane the radio and a little medical kit that had been overlooked. Back in the camp, they fiddled with the wireless for days. I'm not sure what was wrong with it but at last they got something very special. In that little huddle of makeshift hovels in the middle of a Polish forest, backed by a symphony of whistles and crackles of static, the sounds of Big Ben rang out. It was followed by Winston Churchill. Nobody but my mother understood a word, but for once, for a few seconds, everybody felt that something magnificent had been achieved. The station drifted off and the radio shut down – permanently. People have said that the whole incident happened in my mind, that it was impossible to get a radio from an aircraft tuned in to London from Poland. And Churchill *and* Big Ben. All I know is that it happened. And Churchill said that the Hun was beaten, or words to that effect.

The mood in the camp was very different now. With Mike hobbling around in his uniform and the assurance that in a very short time we would all be free to go home, there was an effort to do something. Volunteers for scavenging parties were easy to find and even dared to go as far as the nearest town. They came back with stories about the Nazis that made us feel our efforts in the forest hadn't been in vain and, equally sustaining, brought back salt, which improved our stews no end.

Mike was more anxious than anybody to get away. He didn't relish missing the victory parade. Contact with the town established, his departure became possible and some time later a pony and trap came and took him away. We all stood by the side of the little track where he was picked up and waved a misty-eyed farewell. Once he was out of sight I burst into tears and Yuri moved his heart and actually put his arm around my shoulder.

We were convinced that the Russians were coming. We could hear the far-away rumble of the artillery but it never seemed to get any closer. Every day somebody went down to the road to see what was happening. And each day came back and said the troops would be there on the next. It went on for so long that spirits began to droop. Then the artillery went silent and no one volunteered to go down to the road, so Yuri was sent. Forbidden from accompanying him, I nursed Mila, keeping an eye on the path. Sure enough, Yuri came into the camp at a run, too excited to tell what was happening. Kuragin grabbed him and made him slow down. The Russian front was on its way! Yuri had seen them in the distance and they were definitely heading in our direction. Everybody seemed to be relieved by the news but I was elated. For so long I had heard everyone talk about this idyllic life which would start when the Nazis were overpowered and the Allies came. Now it was happening and the adults merely seemed bemused. Not so Yuri and I.

We rushed off through the trees to the other side of the forest, where our column had been attacked and where my mother and I had lain, pretending to be dead. When the Russians finally appeared it was a wonderful sight to behold. At the front were the tanks, at least fifty of them, then came the artillery, armoured cars, marching troopers, more tanks, horses, hundreds of horses pulling cannons and wagons, more cars, more artillery – everything an army has to have passed us by. Overhead, Russian Migs and Yaks roared. The noise was deafening and exhilarating.

Yuri and I marched along with the soldiers for a little way, but by now it was night and he thought we'd better get back to camp. I couldn't bear to leave the Russian army, and broke down and cried my eyes out. Yuri was quite patient about it and waited for me to stop. He rolled himself a fag and looked up at the stars twinkling through the trees. I guessed he was bored and embarrassed, so I pulled myself together and we ran back to camp as fast as we could.

Many of the people in the forest were phlegmatic in the face of our excitement. They were sick of fighting, sick of the war and wanted to go home. After a few days we couldn't hear the front any more, the planes stopped coming over and the artillery had fallen quiet. Everyone hoped that the war was over but no one knew anything for sure.

Meanwhile, my mother had contracted typhus. Soon she was so ill that I believed she would die. She told me to stay away from her, so she didn't infect me, and to keep the baby away. She thought she was done for. After all she had endured, this was going to be the end. I kept telling her that I could foretell the future and we had a lot to do yet. And what about my papa? We had to find him. He was waiting for us. She tried to smile but it was a hollow attempt.

Everyone debated what to do with Mascha. Kuragin and Boris decided they should take her to the nearest village the next day, but they didn't know whether there was even a doctor there. It was a big risk. Yuri said they hated Jews in that village. They had denounced all their Jews to the Nazis and the SS had then murdered them. I stared at him, stunned, and my breath stopped flowing and my whole body shook in terror. Kuragin took me in his strong arms, rocked me to and fro, and slowly I felt better. He assured me that no one would suspect Mama of being a Jew. She looked like a Polak. Just as I did.

We were laughing about this when the Red Cross arrived at the camp. They were systematically combing the forests looking for bands of partisans who, like us, didn't know about the end of the war. The news was almost a shock. The war really was over! Suddenly we were all very quiet. The nightmare we had suffered, each in his own way, had been horrendous. To know it was done with released the tears and the pain that everyone had kept locked away.

My mother had a hard time grasping the news. Kuragin told her over and over. He held her head in his hands and said it again. She smiled and said he mustn't hold her, he'd get infected. 'We're safe here,' she said.

'No,' Kuragin insisted. 'The war is over. Finished. We all go home! You go to hospital and get well!' Mama started to cry then and Kuragin cuddled her for a while before leaving her to it.

Now that I'd had my cry I was bored with Mama having a go and I shouted at her that it was over, and there was no need to cry. She stretched out her skeleton-like arms and pressed my hand. I threw caution to the wind and clutched her thin body close to me. We banged heads. It made us laugh. We couldn't stop laughing. We laughed hysterically until we cried and had no more energy.

The Red Cross took us to Kraków hospital. My mother pumped herself up as much as she was able to make the journey. She couldn't believe that we had survived the impossible. We'd had a lot of luck. If the Nazis hadn't wanted my father at any price we would probably have been killed with the other refugees in Bialystok. And if it hadn't been for Steiner, we wouldn't have survived Stutthof.

Now Mama could allow herself hope to get well, to find my father, hope for a future she had stopped believing in.

Our lives in the forest were over. We said goodbye to the partisans. I loved them all, especially Yuri and Boris and Kuragin, Tchechia and little Milusia. I love the Russian custom of everyone sitting down for a moment to reflect on the journey ahead before parting. We did that, then embraced each other, but of course there were no addresses to exchange and so we all lost each other for ever.

My greatest loss was Yuri. We sat together holding hands. Yuri had his very own way of holding my hand, with so much love. He was strong and kind and understanding. I looked into his green eyes and suspected they were wet. He looked around at everyone, leaned forward quickly and kissed me. I put my arms around his neck and held him tightly to me.

Matka and I were lifted up on to the back of a big truck. As it pulled away, I turned round one last time and yelled at Yuri, 'Goodbye, husband!' He laughed and nodded but was having trouble talking. I watched him until we were out of sight. There is a picture in my mind as clear as on the day it was formed: Yuri standing there in clothes too big for him, the rifle he loved to carry even though he had long ago run out of bullets in his arms. Just before we turned a bend and lost sight of each other for good he raised his gun above his head and waved me goodbye. I cried for hours.

Forests for me will always mean Yuri and the partisans. Surely it was the best part of my childhood. The only time I remember without pain.

Seven

Leaving the forest saved my mother's life. Mine as well, as it turned out. I had a bad case of tuberculosis and needed treatment at once.

The hospital was a frightening place for me. I remember glaring white walls, people in white coats with needles and a large cold machine which burred when I was forced to press my chest against it. I thought the machine would kill me and screamed for my mother.

Having survived the X-ray machine, I was put in a big white bed. Matka was in a different ward from me and I kept asking if I could be with her but it wasn't allowed. I wanted to get upset but I recognised that the Red Cross nurses and doctors were being very kind to me. They brought me paper and picture books, including one called *Gebrüder Grimms Märchen*. I so wanted to read it, but my education had been patchy and I found it too hard.

It took seven months to get us back on our feet. Once we were strong enough to leave our beds we were given clothes, shoes, blankets and a small parcel of food, mainly lard biscuits made from grits and oats, and told to move on. There were queues of refugees in need of our beds.

We were taken from the hospital to a huge, partly

demolished factory, which had been turned into a large dormitory. Braziers burned day and night but in spite of them it was still freezing cold.

The factory was a depressing place. Endless lines of displaced persons queued for days on end to be interviewed by soldiers, only to be told that the army could do nothing for them. We were advised that if we could get to the next Red Cross station we might find help there. So began a long trek between displaced-persons camps.

I admire my mother enormously. In the camp she had been a survivor. She had kept her head down, sheltered me and had done whatever it had taken to live from day to day, from moment to moment. In the forest she had worked all hours of the day to bring some sort of order to the chaos and make sure that we were still around when deliverance came. These were enforced reactions to circumstances. Our odyssey around the displaced-persons camps was a display of sheer guts and determination. She could have given up at any time. Thousands did. We passed them everywhere, sitting in bombed-out houses, staring ahead, all the fight knocked out of them by the lack of food and the gnawing conviction that 'home' no longer existed for them. Matka would have none of that. She was determined to find my father. Unfortunately, she had no clear idea how this could be accomplished. Where would he be? Would he come looking for us? Would we pass each other in the night and be separated for ever? I wasn't much help although I was nine years old now. Life in the camp and my brush with TB had left me as thin as a rake and with about as much energy as a drink of water.

The only transport that could be relied on at that stage of the aftermath of war was Shank's Pony. From somewhere, however, my mother dug out a battered old cart. The wheels were at crazy angles and it always seemed on the brink of disintegrating but it helped. I was able to rest on it every so often while my poor mama ploughed on to the next camp, pulling me along.

The Red Cross camps were the desert oases which made it possible to carry on. There you could rest for a couple of days, eat hot food, catch up on your medication and, most important, spend hours scanning the boards around the camp which carried thousands of names and messages. The only names we were interested in were my father's and my grandparents' but they were never there.

With winter came the snow and I fell ill again. I spent most of the time on the little handcart, wrapped in whatever rags my mother could find. We lived like bag ladies. Anything which might be useful was loaded on to the cart or put into the bundle wrapped in a blanket that my mother carried over her shoulder. How she survived, day after day in freezing temperatures with minimum nourishment, I'll never know.

Just when it looked as if, in spite of all her efforts, we were going to be defeated by cold and hunger, we met Pani Philipska. Pani Philipska was an anachronism in that shattered world. Everyone around her looked on the verge of death and she was life. She was little and plump, warm and jolly. She was an oasis of elegance in the displaced-persons camp, with her outrageously blonde hair piled on top of her head, and her chic and expensive clothes. She had come to the camp to try to find her brother who had disappeared at the beginning of the war, when he had had the luck to be away when the Gestapo had come for his family. Pani Philipska had been living with her husband but had been widowed just before the end of the war.

My mother was spellbound and a bit in awe of Pani Philipska. We thought it best not to ask where the clothes and hair dye came from, especially as she soon took a bit of a shine to Mascha and, when she saw the state I was in, wanted to help. Out of the blue she asked my mother to come home with her for Christmas. Matka didn't hesitate. She could see that if I didn't get some real food, warmth and rest, I would not last much longer.

Pani Philipska's large, elegant apartment building, just outside Lodz, had been practically untouched by the war. I was so ill now that I wasn't able to appreciate it fully. But I did appreciate the big dry bed with a cloth-wrapped hot brick in it. Pani Philipska arranged for a doctor to come and see me. When Mama told him about the camp and TB he didn't give me much chance of survival. At this time TB was a big killer – and the recommended treatment was a long stay on a Swiss mountain top with a fortifying diet.

Christmas came and went, and I just lay in the warm bed, drifting in and out of consciousness. Most of the time Mascha sat beside me but sometimes Pani Philipska would come to give her a break. Pani Philipska gave me a big baby doll with a china head and a long flowing frock. It was the most beautiful thing I had ever seen. I pulled it into bed, lay down and looked at the puffy pink cheeks and huge staring blue eyes. Pani Philipska laughed and swept me up into her big soft arms. I loved the mist of exotic perfume that surrounded her and couldn't get enough of it. When she left the room I took out Sonja, the little Cossack doll that Steiner had given me, and laid her beside the baby doll. For looks there was no contest. The baby doll was so real you half expected it to cry at any moment. Sonja was crude and showed the marks of our adventures, and sweat from my hand where I had clutched her for months. I left Baby Doll on the pillow and hid Sonja down between my legs in the warmth.

Pani Philipska insisted that Matka ate heartily and rested as much as she could. Nevertheless, my mother worried that Pani Philipska would expect us to leave once the Christmas period was over. She went to the displaced-persons camp and tried in vain to get us a place there. When she returned and confessed where she had been Pani Philipska was offended. Did my mama think so little of her that she could imagine that she would throw us out? Especially with me knocking at death's door?

The food and warmth were having a beneficial effect on me. The doctor even seemed to think I might make it. My recovery was a source of joy to Mama and Pani Philipska. Slowly I began to gain some strength. Pani Philipska by this time had almost forgotten that we weren't actually part of the family, so took it quite badly when, in the spring, Mama announced that we must be off. I wasn't too happy about her decision either. I wanted to stay in the big warm apartment with lots of food and dry clothes. Patiently Mascha explained that my father was waiting for us. She said we would leave in two days. Pani Philipska gave us some money to buy food for the journey and Mascha and I walked into the village to get provisions.

The trees were just bursting into bud and the sun was warm and friendly. It was so revitalising I almost forgave Matka for wanting to give up our safe haven and go back to the miseries of the open road. In the middle of the village, which was quiet and orderly and a million miles from the devastation I had been used to, was a baker's shop. The smell wafting from it was mouth-watering. I stared through the window, mesmerised by the cakes and bread on offer, and was soon whining to my mother, begging her to buy me a cake. She was made of sterner stuff. Although she had devoted her life to me, to my survival, she had a code of discipline and refused to pander to me. She went to buy the basic necessities, leaving me to slaver over the pastries.

A girl about half my age came out of the shop, saw the Baby Doll I held in my arms and tried to grab it. I pulled it fiercely away. The girl promptly burst into tears. Instantly her mother was there, wanting to know what had happened. I was ready to run but I had been so taken with the cakes I hadn't noticed which way Matka had gone. Before I could make a decision the baker's wife asked me if I wanted to sell my beautiful doll. Indignantly I said, 'No!' The woman had obviously seen me lusting after the pastries. She went into the shop, looked at me through the glass and pointed at a big gooey cake. It was so gorgeous that I hadn't even considered it. I nodded. It was a deal. Frightened of what Mama would say when she discovered what I had done I stood and woofed the whole cake down on the spot.

I don't think my mother noticed what I had done with the doll. If she did, she kept quiet about it. She decided that as it was such a lovely day she would give me a chance to try out my legs, for it was a long time since I had walked anywhere. We set off towards the displaced-persons camp, which was a couple of miles outside the village, with the intention of looking through the cards for one last time to see if by some miracle my father's name had appeared among them. Soon I began not to feel very well. I wanted to go back to Pani Philipska's apartment and lie on my bed but Mascha ploughed on, ignoring my entreaties. Without warning I was sick. The rich cake was too much for my stomach and it had rejected it. When my mother saw what I had brought up she wasn't amused. She didn't question me, just grabbed my arm and dragged me at a fast pace up the road.

By the time we got to the DP camp I had recovered enough to force down the slice of black bread we were handed on arrival. Mama then checked in with the Red Cross officer and, full of optimism, told him that we were setting off and that anyone who might want her could find her at our old house in Berlin.

As we were leaving the Red Cross tent, Mother drew up short, a look of surprise on her face. Following her gaze I saw, leaning against a tree with a cigarette in his mouth, a man I faintly recognised.

'Peter?' Mother said hesitantly.

The penny still didn't drop. To my mother the events of Stutthof and the kindness of Peter Steiner were just a moment away. To me they had already taken on a touch of grey unreality.

Peter hugged Mama and picked me up, joked that I had put on a lot of weight, swung me around and set me on my feet again. I looked at him suspiciously. I knew I had seen him before but I had trouble knowing where.

He seemed to read my thoughts. 'How's Sonja?' he asked.

Finally identifying him and remembering all his kindnesses, I was full of remorse. I pulled Sonja out of my pocket and showed her to him in an effort to overcome my embarrassment at not recognising the man who had constantly saved us. I was dismayed by my seeming ingratitude and it exacerbated the guilty feelings which had weighed me down since I'd been sick. Inside I knew I was a horrid child. I'd so easily been persuaded to give up my beautiful Baby Doll. And for a piece of cake! What if I'd had a mother like me? I'd be dead now. Peter didn't know about my misdeeds. He put his arm around my mother's waist, took my hand, found a sheltered spot and sat us all down. The adults had a lot of catching up to do and I needed to sleep.

Bringing Peter Steiner back to Pani Philipska's house turned out to be an excellent idea. She liked him straight away. He looked like hell but he had twinkling eyes and a great sense of humour, which won her over. He started flirting with her at once.

When he had cleaned himself up and shaved, she asked him where he was staying. 'In a castle with fountains and paintings inside,' he replied. Pani Philipska told him to stay the night with us. I went with him to the 'castle' to fetch his belongings and when we got back from the hovel he had been sleeping in, we told of the vast riches and treasures he had left behind.

Instead of leaving as planned, Matka and I stayed on in the flat. With Steiner there it felt as if we were a real family. He brought laughter and noise into our home. We would listen to him hammering away on Pani Philipska's grand piano, trying not to let him see us cringe when he hit a wrong note.

To my disappointment Peter's arrival didn't change my mother's mind about continuing the search for my father. After a couple of weeks she again announced that we had to leave. I was devastated when I found out that Peter wasn't coming with us. I had already accepted him as a factor in my new life. But he was also a factor in Pani Philipska's life and we found out later that they married.

For one year we walked in the snow and cold, schlepping mounds of accumulated rags and scraps of deteriorating food from displaced-persons camp to Red Cross station to government office. Occasionally we'd get a lift on an army truck or a farm cart, or the Red Cross would give us a train ticket if a stretch of line had been opened and the rolling stock had been repaired. Mostly, we walked.

I had shoes now, given to me at the hospital by the Red Cross, and a coat. It was a massive ex-army coat that reached to the floor and swept the snow as we walked along the roads. At the displaced-persons camps Matka would read endless lists of names nailed to wooden boards. My papa was never there. On one occasion she found the names of her parents, killed at Treblinka. It set us back. She was so upset that she couldn't go on. She thought of the time at Bialystok railway station seeing her little mum sitting on a chair like a queen, holding Albert's hand, while people pushed all around them to get on the train which they thought meant safety. If only they had known what fate awaited them. I hoped that they had managed to stay together . . .

My mother's need to find my father still obsessed her and eventually gave her the strength to continue. It was now nearly two years since the official ending of hostilities, yet life was still very hard. Even in peacetime much hatred remained and, as refugees and former camp prisoners, we felt it. There weren't a lot of Pani Philipskas about. Most people saw us coming and shut their doors. Children would throw stones at us and call us names. I became accustomed to it.

Occasionally we found a farmer or a cottager who gave us shelter for a couple of days. The farms were warm and comfy, full of food and milk. Even though it meant leaving the warm hay or the occasional feather bed, I loved getting up at dawn and helping to milk the cows. But with nothing to offer the farmers in return for their hospitality we always felt uncomfortable and would push on as quickly as possible.

At one smallholding the farmer offered to keep me while my mother went on alone to locate my father. She could come back for me when she had settled down. Matka wouldn't consider it. She hadn't gone through living hell to leave me behind now. But sometimes I had the tiniest, smallest thought that it might have been a good idea to stay at Pani Philipska's . . . Then I felt very ashamed of myself. There was no life without Mascha. She had the answer to everything.

On the border with Germany was a large DP camp. I

wasn't keen on entering that country. It seemed to me that all my life I had been running away from the Germans, that every conversation about them had emphasised how terrible they were. So what were we doing putting ourselves at their mercy?

The camp was run by Americans and they seemed keen to help us. Mascha went wearily through all the formalities and was told to return the next day. They gave us some coupons for food and an address where we could stay the night. This turned out to be an old brewery that had been gutted and fitted out with beds in little cubicles. The smell of beer was overpowering but we had smelled far worse and enjoyed a good night's sleep.

The next day, with still no word about my father, Matka decided we should continue on our way to Berlin. The Red Cross woman was aghast at our precipitous departure. She had expected my mother to accept that there was nothing she could do but sit around and wait until someone arrived with news of my father. She didn't know my mother. Finally, Mama was persuaded that it would be better for me if we rested a few days, so we waited two more nights before taking a train, courtesy of the Red Cross, over the border.

Walking was now easier. The snow had melted, and the sun warmed our bodies and put new strength in our hearts. In the evenings Matka would call at farms and houses, and ask for shelter from the cold night air. Mostly she was treated to abuse and told to clear off. Once dogs were set upon her and we were vilified as 'stinking Yids'. Didn't anyone know about the camps? Didn't they care?

At last we neared Berlin. I was ill again and needed all my concentration just to keep going. My mother would urge me on – 'Not much further now, baby. We're nearly there' – trying to encourage us both to keep putting one foot in front of the other.

One night we were walking along a dark winding road and it occurred to me that my mother was smaller than me, that her head was nearly level with the earth. She was weighed down with the rucksack and bags, and they dragged her to the ground. 'Let's stop and rest, Mama,' I said. 'I can't go on.'

She stopped, tried a smile and said, 'Really, it really is just around the corner . . . if the bombs didn't get it . . .'

And for once it *was* just around the corner.

Past a towering burned-out ruin rising up into the dark sky, a driveway lined with beautiful mature trees led to a funny-looking little house with a pointed roof. Matka dropped our bags and leaned on me to catch her breath. Silently, she dragged herself up the few steps to the front door and rang the bell. 'If there's no one there I'll break the back door down, I don't care,' she muttered.

But the door opened and a little man with a long beard, holding a pipe in his mouth, stood there. My mother told him who we were and he opened the door wide to welcome us into our home.

Eight

The post-war government had assigned our house to the Totenhoefer family. They warmly put aside the worries that must have surfaced with our arrival and took great care of us. I was immediately given a cup of hot chocolate, which I thought was the most amazing drink I had ever had, my grubby clothes were removed and I was plonked into a hot bath and after that into a massive feather bed. Mama also had a bath and then crawled into bed with me. I fell asleep thinking of all the wonderful things that would happen now that we were 'home'.

All the way from Poland Matka had told me that Papa would be waiting for us at home. In her mind I think she had nurtured an image of my father opening the front door, sweeping us into his arms and heralding an end to our troubles. But Papa wasn't here. Mascha sat around for days, overwhelmed by exhaustion and disappointment.

The Totenhoefers were wonderful. Here they were, probably about to be dispossessed, but they showed understanding above and beyond the call of self-interest. Mrs Totenhoefer watched my mother for days, not wanting to intrude. Then she asked to have a heart to heart with her. Whatever she said worked. Once more my mother started bustling around, taking an interest in things and making plans.

Matka was at first reluctant to go to Papa's relatives. The rift between my father and his family, which started when, widowed, he married his second wife, my Jewish mother, widened considerably when my father made known his views about the Nazis. He had even disowned one of his sons by his previous marriage on learning that he had joined the SS and he never forgave him. When she finally plucked up the courage to visit her brother-in-law's house, her reception was anything but cordial. They told her they had not heard from my father and implied they hoped they never would. They were living on a very short fuse, worried about what was going to happen to them for they had been influential Party members. Every day the Allied forces' Nazi hunters were widening their net, taking into consideration new categories of guilt. Each knock on the door worked like a laxative: they couldn't waste valuable worrying time with my mother. Mascha cursed herself. She should have known she would get no help from that quarter.

We realised we would have to find Papa through a different route. Every day Matka left me with the Totenhoefers and set out on the rounds of friends and Red Cross offices in search of information on my father's whereabouts. She still had the utmost faith that he was out there, waiting for her to find him. Each evening she'd return exhausted and dispirited but the next day she'd pump herself up and set off again. Eventually some government department in Schoeneberg said that they had a record of my father leaving Terezina concentration camp but since then he had disappeared. They promised to look into where he might have gone. Twice a day my mother would go to the office, stand in line, only to be told there was no news.

One morning Mama woke up, shook me awake and kept repeating the word 'Haneli'. I didn't understand until she explained that Haneli was the Polish wife of my father's best friend, Utz Droemer. Utz and my father had been at Heidelberg University together and Utz had helped my father get to England following a fencing duel where Papa thought he had accidentally killed a fellow student. They'd later been in the cavalry together on the Somme. Matka was furious with herself for not thinking of Haneli earlier.

The Totenhoefers found a map and looked up where the Droemers had lived before the war. They decided that old Herr Boettcher, who had opened the door to us and who was Frau Totenhoefer's father, should go to a friend's house and ask for the loan of his car. This was something that needed major discussion. Cars were still a luxury that very few could afford. Boettcher was willing to presume on this friendship to help us out, despite the fact that finding my father could make his family homeless.

Early the next day Herr Boettcher came home with the car. Mama was so happy she kissed him on both cheeks. I got dressed quickly, excited at the prospect of an adventure. I had never been in a car before – trucks I was familiar with and even an occasional jeep – but never an honest-to-goodness car.

The journey to Steinstuecken took hours. I wasn't used to travelling in a closed car with springs and several times we had to stop so that I could be sick. Herr Boettcher took it all philosophically. Matka was getting a little impatient by the fourth stop. The roads were in a terrible state but everywhere gangs of people were beavering away trying to clear the rubble. There were many road blocks and we had to cross from the West to the East sector and back to the American sector where Steinstuecken was a US enclave inside the Russian zone. Most of the time we were waved through the checkpoints quickly but once or twice we were hauled out of the car and subjected to interrogation. Years of experience had taught Mascha how to deal with petty officials and we were never in danger of a serious delay. A more difficult problem turned out to be the signposting, which was practically non-existent, and most of the time we had to rely on finding someone who could give coherent directions. Finally Herr Boettcher pulled into a checkpoint and had a long conversation with a bored sergeant who really did know the district. He drew a map and before long we turned into the road where Haneli and Utz had lived.

Matka had told me all about Haneli's lovely house and what great fun she was. As Herr Boettcher brought the car to a halt and surveyed what was left of the road ahead I heard my mother sob. The entire area had been bombed and, two years after the war, little had been done to reclaim it. It looked as if nobody could possibly live amid the jumble of bricks and timber.

After a few minutes' silence Mama told me to stay where I was and opened the car door. She had come too far and waited too long just to give up and leave. She reasoned that if my father had decided to go to Haneli he would have assumed we would follow. If, subsequently, he had moved on he would have left a note to let us know.

Herr Boettcher got out of the car and looked around. He called Matka's attention to a building on the far side of the road. The top had caved in but the bottom seemed reasonably intact. And, more important, a pathway had been cleared through the rubble to the side of the building. Matka was off like a shot. I didn't know what to do. I stuck by Herr Boettcher and watched anxiously as Mama disappeared. Herr Boettcher surveyed the area and, satisfied that there was no one around who might pinch our wheels, took my hand and we too followed the path.

Matka was standing by a little fence looking down into what had been the entrance to the building's cellar. Boettcher leaned as far over as he could, then decided to investigate. Cautiously he negotiated the stairs, looked up at us and banged on one of the planks covering the door. A pause. Then a woman's voice called out cautiously, 'Who is it?'

My mother didn't hang around. She rushed past me and skidded down the steps. I wasn't going to be left alone in the gloom of the late afternoon and followed. It was damp and smelly, and I was sure there were rats among the debris.

'Haneli?' my mother called out. 'It's me, Katja!' She pulled futilely at the planks across the door. A sound behind her made her turn towards a shutter on a casement window, which was slowly being opened. Matka pulled at it eagerly to reveal the worried face of a woman.

'Katja?' she said.

Mama leaned over the sill, clasped the woman in her arms and burst into tears. Behind Haneli a shadowy figure struck a match and lit a candle. He slowly came forward.

'Katja?' he asked, hope in his voice. He came to the window, his arms outstretched. Mama was already in them as I stood stunned, amazed that this skeleton of a man could be my gloriously handsome father.

Nine

My papa lived only another five years. As if she'd known that time was short, my mother had powered through Poland and Germany to find the man who was her whole life. When I saw him for that first time after the war in Haneli's little cellar I somehow knew, because of my mother's desperation perhaps, that every day would be a gift.

My father was now seventy-seven years old and had spent the last five years in conditions that had killed many thousands of younger men. After the war he had headed for home in the hope of finding my mother and me but had collapsed, and, when he'd come to, could no longer remember his address. The only address in his head was that of Utz Droemer. The Red Cross didn't have either the time or the facilities to go looking for his real home so they'd contacted Haneli, who'd been glad to look after him. In spite of the hell he had lived through in Terezina and in spite of his age, under her care he'd gradually grown stronger.

We all crowded into the dismal cellar and after the initial shock of his debilitated appearance I threw myself into my father's arms and sobbed. When I looked at him again he was the old, smiling, handsome Papa that my mother had promised me and that I had held close to my heart. Five years is a long time to a ten-year-old, but as I stood there in that little cellar, with everyone around me in tears, it really didn't seem as if we had been apart at all.

At the house the Totenhoefers continued to look after us. Matka and Papa decided they should stay on and my father divided up the house so that the Totenhoefers had the rooms upstairs and we the two downstairs. The bathroom was shared. This meant that my father had to climb upstairs to wash. He said it would help build up his muscles but it was torture to see him pull himself up the stairs, step by agonising step, refusing to be helped. In the end, Matka couldn't stand the pain of watching him. She found a huge pannier-like pot which she filled with water and heated in the fireplace, then filled an enamel bath in front of the fire. Every time she washed him I saw tears in her eyes. He was so thin and weak, and it took a long time before he got a bit of flesh on his bones. How I hate the Nazis still for what they did to my father.

With Papa home, for the first time I saw my mother relax. It was as if, now that they were together again, she could go back to being the wife she had enjoyed being before the war, as if she believed that our trials and tribulations had ended with the reunion with my father.

Matka never worried about herself. She maintained that she had the appetite of a bird; my father would joke that it was a vulture. My mother would cut our rations into three equal parts. I saw her once eat her whole day's ration at one go. She said it saved time and she might as well feel full for a little while as be perpetually hungry.

I refused to be separated from my father. I don't think my mother minded, although sometimes I wondered if she wasn't just a little bit jealous. After all, we had been through so much together and now I was deserting her. But I think she was pleased that I got on so well with my dad. She loved him so much.

Herr Boettcher was a gardener by profession. He was about my father's age and they got on famously. Most of the time they reminisced about life before the war, sometimes they talked about the Great War, although they had been in different battle zones. When spring came at last, Herr Boettcher and my father decided that they had had enough of sitting around. Herr Boettcher commented that the earth in the garden was very good and it was a shame nothing was growing there, so they began to make plans for cultivating it. I found it very exciting. My mama wasn't so enthusiastic. She was afraid that it would be too much for my father in his frail state of health. She needn't have worried. Now that he had made a positive decision and had a goal in sight he was a changed man.

The first thing Herr Boettcher wanted to do was cut down several trees to let in some sunlight. They would also provide wood for the fire. Since my time in the forest I'd had a thing about trees and I hated this plan. In old Borja's stories the trees had personalities and could be hurt. I tried to explain that to Herr Boettcher but he just said you had to get your priorities right. If you needed food, sacrifices had to be made. He and my father almost became sacrifices themselves. Maybe in his younger life Herr Boettcher had had a way with felling trees but time and ageing sinews turned our tree-felling into a farce.

Herr Boettcher asked his grand-daughter Henny to climb up and attach a rope to the top of the first tree so that it would fall away from the house. He then cut a big chunk out of the trunk and everyone pulled – and pulled, and pulled. The tree, a beautiful old English oak, hardly moved. Just when we thought we were getting somewhere the rope broke. We all staggered backwards. Herr Boettcher was at the end of the rope and he tripped and fell into a muddy fishpond that hadn't been cleaned out in years. My father fell on top of him. After the initial shock, and finding that neither of them was hurt, we all fell about laughing.

Later we felled the tree and one other. My father pretended not to care although I knew how much the trees meant to him. He'd chosen to build the house on this spot because of those big oaks. They reminded him of England. But Papa said he could at last sit in the sun and warm his heart.

Once the land had been cleared, or nearly cleared – we never did manage to get rid of the massive roots of the trees – we were press-ganged into helping prepare the ground for planting. I loved it, although I got in the way more than I actually worked. Matka came up with a solution that kept me from under everyone's feet and made me feel happy and productive. She dug over a little patch of earth at the side of the house and gave me some seeds to sow. It was amazing how quickly they sprouted and before long I had rows of lettuces, radishes and carrots. They were the pride of my life and I spent hours touching them, making sure they had enough water and getting quite vicious with any snails or other pests that tried to harm them.

When we weren't gardening I would sit on my father's lap or cuddle up beside him on the bench on the covered balcony at the front of the house. We'd chatter about everything from Spitfires and cricket, to wildlife and the stars in the sky. He would enthral me with stories about England, and amaze me with his knowledge and love of animals, especially elephants. Thirty or more years later when I worked in a circus and they asked me if I'd lie under an elephant and let him walk over me, I had no qualms about it. I remembered my father had told me that elephants would never step on anything soft.

My father's knowledge of the stars was fantastic. He loved the idea of space travel. It was a shame he didn't live just a few more years to see Yuri Gagarin take off into space.

I guess at this time my father and I were a bit of a drag on my poor mama. It was summer and the air was warm so most of the time we just sat about in our pyjamas. Matka wasn't too keen on that. She had always been very disciplined, even the camp hadn't managed to knock that out of her, but in the end she had to acknowledge defeat and let us slum around as we liked. While we lazed, happy in each other's company, she spent most of her time in government offices trying to get financial aid or some assistance to repair the house. I felt a bit guilty about not going with her when, until recently, we'd been together all the time – but not guilty enough to want to leave my papa now that I had him back. It seemed that now he was with me I didn't need Mascha any more. Much later she told me that she was glad I stayed with my father. She didn't want him sitting by himself, dwelling on the past. Anyway, she was much faster on her own.

I have never in my entire life known anyone as strong and determined as my mother. And she had more love in her heart than anyone. I always wanted to be like her but I will never be that strong.

Mama's relentless efforts were rewarded at last. Our little family was granted a reparation payment by the German government and was able to make repairs to the house. Her ultimate achievement was getting central heating installed, which made my father very happy.

I'd finally been forced to go to school. The other kids hated me. I hated them back. The big boys took me round the back of the bicycle shed and beat the shit out of me every day after school. Suddenly I had become a victim again, a non-person, *ein Untermensch*. They joked about my father as well. When they passed my house on their way to school they mocked him for sitting on the balcony all day in his old dressing-gown and to my fury called him grandad.

Years of being told to keep a low profile had taught me to bide my time. I decided they could say what they liked – for the moment. My chance to get my own back came soon enough. Once, on being pulled behind the shed, I let myself go limp and when Heinz, the leader, thought I was ready for the hit, I jumped on him and bit into his cheek, hard. Heinz never touched me again. Years later I ran into him in the interval of a play at the Schiller Theatre and with great satisfaction I saw that he still bore my tooth-marks on his cheek.

Matka went to the school after a complaint was made against me for biting this supreme *Herrenvölkler*. The headmaster demanded that I apologise to Heinz or be removed from the school. My mother said that in no circumstances would I apologise and yes, I would leave the school at once. No one mentioned the fact that I had been beaten up day after day.

Now I had sorted out my problem and defended my father's honour I quite fancied the idea of staying at the school, but Mascha said it was a matter of pride and that people like that had nothing to teach her daughter. I had twice as far to go to the new school and the problems were just the same. But I was going to win respect. I was never going to be a victim again.

Ten

Although the war was long over, its shadow still fell on our lives. Control of Berlin at this time was divided between Eastern and Western forces. When the Russians decided they weren't going to allow Allied supply convoys to pass through their territory, a new war, the Cold War, was teed up.

Food trucks queued at Helmstedt, the border between East and West Berlin, and weren't allowed into the city. Without food, coal or clothes, Berliners, still in poor health after the war, began to drop like flies. The Allied forces, determined not to give in to bullyboy tactics, decided to airlift supplies into their sector. When they offered to take children out to West Germany on the same planes, Matka was at the front of the queue. I didn't want to leave my parents, especially my father with whom every day was to be cherished. I wasn't that hungry. But my mama wouldn't listen. She would brook no arguments. I tried all kinds of blackmail in an attempt to persuade her to let me stay but to no avail. She knew I had a lot of catching up to do, my health was poor and I was still undernourished. My heart was too small for my long scrawny body, my TB had not cleared up properly and I was underweight. I was going and that was it.

I was flown out of Berlin in a Dakota. It was exciting to make my first flight but I hated leaving. I was homesick from start to finish. The parting from my parents was terrible. My father got his suit out and with my mum took me to Tempelhof airfield. I couldn't bear to go. To distract me my father talked about the plane, the flight, how great flying was and how one day he wanted me to be a pilot. He got me all excited about the Dakota I was going to fly in and of course brought up the great Spitfires again. Talking about flying made the trip look exciting but I assured him that I could be very happy just hearing him talk about it. I didn't have to leave to know how good flying was. I could fly later. Papa told me to write to him and tell him every detail of the flight, and to say hello to the pilot if the chance presented itself.

I walked in the little gaggle of evacuees, determined not to cry. I couldn't believe that after all we had been through my mama was willing to let me go off by myself. I kept looking back. There they stood, my frail father and my brave mother. Why didn't they run after me, sweep me up in their arms and tell me it was all a mistake? The door of the plane swung shut and they were lost to sight. I wondered if I would ever see them again.

I was surprised to find the seats lined along the wall of the plane. In the middle were stacks of empty sacks. The planes were configured for bringing in food and coal – taking kids out was a bonus. We were strapped in along the benches and soon the plane was heading along the runway and we had lift-off. I was in tears – and not only because I had just left the two people I loved most in the whole world – I'm always in tears at take-off.

Flying was just as my papa had told me it would be and I loved it. I spent the entire flight wrenching my neck round, trying to see out of the window behind me. I saw ugly Berlin disappear below, I saw us climb into the clouds, then break through them and into the sun. 'Yes!' I shouted in my head. 'I love this. Flying is the greatest invention of all time.' Then I had to go and get airsick. The first time and the last. It didn't lessen the glory of the flight for me, though, just made me mad that my stupid body wouldn't behave and was threatening to spoil my enjoyment of those initial magic moments up in the sky. Gliding over the sea of pink cotton wool, seeing the clear blue sky and the sun so near and so large, I thought that perhaps this was what dying was like. To be flying like that seemed like eternal life.

The landing was both exhilarating and sad. It was sad to end the dream but it was as exciting as the take-off. I could feel the flaps come down, the roar as the throttle opened and closed, the thrill of seeing the earth loom larger as the plane lost altitude and that orgasmic moment when the wheels slap down on the tarmac and the plane is captured by the runway. Before climbing out I went to the cockpit and spoke to the pilot. I told him how much I admired him and said that I would learn to fly even if it took years and years. He smiled and patted my cheek, and complimented me on my English. That made me really proud – all the time my father had spent talking to me in English was suddenly worthwhile.

A bus took us to the railway station. Everywhere the houses were little more than tall piles of rubble. Along the sides of the roads men and women worked, scraping bricks and piling them up into stacks.

I didn't want to get on the train. I still dislike them: they bring back bad memories. It's a bit better now because trains have fundamentally changed: they look and sound different. But then it was not long after the war and they were still pretty much the same as they had always been. I infuriated everybody by throwing a tantrum. Eventually they pushed me on board and I found myself not in a cattle truck but a passenger car, with upholstered seats and window curtains. I was so overcome I threw up all over the plush red carpet. The other kids yelled and called me '*Sau*' and '*Schwein*', which I had heard plenty of times before, but I was so frightened and lonely it all seemed very unfair. I wanted others to understand what I felt, to share my pain, so with a scream I leaped upon the nearest kid, scratching, biting and kicking. I was so far gone that even the man in charge of us had difficulty controlling me. Then, all of a sudden, my rage evaporated. All I wanted to do was be alone so that I could savour my sorrows.

When we reached the 'orphanage' it was dark. My anger at being parted from my parents rose up again. I shouted that I didn't want to be in any orphanage. I still had my parents! I still had a home! No one took any notice. They had dealt with it all before. A *Kapo*-type shouted out a string of instructions. We were lined up and an older girl marched us up the stairs to our dormitories, where I crept into a freezing bed covered with only one thin blanket.

I was calmer now and a little ashamed of my outbursts. I gave myself a good talking to and was determined not to let anyone know how unhappy and scared I was. I tried to take a leaf out of my mother's book and bear my new tribulations with stoicism. But I was not as strong as my mother. I was cold and lonely – and very, very stubborn. I got up and put all my clothes back on. That felt warmer. When the *Kapo* woman saw what I was doing she stormed towards me, shouting that I must put my pyjamas back on immediately. It was the regulations. She was not going to let her authority be undermined by an evacuee. For a moment I stood defiantly in front of her but then it was all too much. I put on my PJs and shivered through the rest of the night.

The next day I wrote a letter to my parents demanding to be brought home as soon as possible. This place was another *Lager*! It was not long before I was called in to see the headmistress. She asked me if I really wanted to worry my poor parents. I burst into tears and screamed at her at the top of my voice that I wasn't prepared to have people shout at me like an *Untermensch* ever again. I was cold and I wanted to go home. I was shaking and couldn't breathe. My TB had got better at the Kraków hospital but whenever I became upset the breathless attacks would return with a vengeance. Frightened by my attack, the headmistress made some concessions. For the time being I would be allowed an extra blanket, and she would talk to the doctor when he came to check on my state of health. She could see how thin I was and even mentioned the possibility of arranging extra rations.

The added blanket had hardly any effect so one day I decided to wear my coat to bed. We'd been to football practice. In reality the boys played football and the daft girls walked around the pitch watching. It was freezing and utterly boring. When we got back to the orphanage I refused dinner and went to bed. The *Kapo* woman stormed up to the dormitory. Defiantly I stared at her and dared her to hit me. I even thought of hitting her. I wanted to be 'punished' by being sent home. Unfortunately we both thought better of physical violence, she contented herself with calling me names and I was forced to come down to dinner, where I was at least allowed to sit next to the big vats which pumped out heat.

When I went back to my bed there was a lump in it. Slightly apprehensive, I slowly rolled back the blanket. Before me lay a big piece of sausage. I ate some at once and wondered who had given it to me. The next day on

Left: With my father in Bialystok, 1942. You can just make out the duelling scars on my father's cheek. These were considered the mark of a man at the turn of the century when he was at Heidelburg university.
Right: The house at Bialystok, where the Nazis finally caught up with us.

Middle: The headquarters of Stutthof Concentration Camp. This is where my father was questioned on arrival at the camp.
Below: Stutthof Concentration Camp. The *Kinderschuppen* was just behind the right-hand hut.

The house in Berlin where we lived after the war.

My parents, reunited after the war.

IP, Haneli, Mama and Papa.

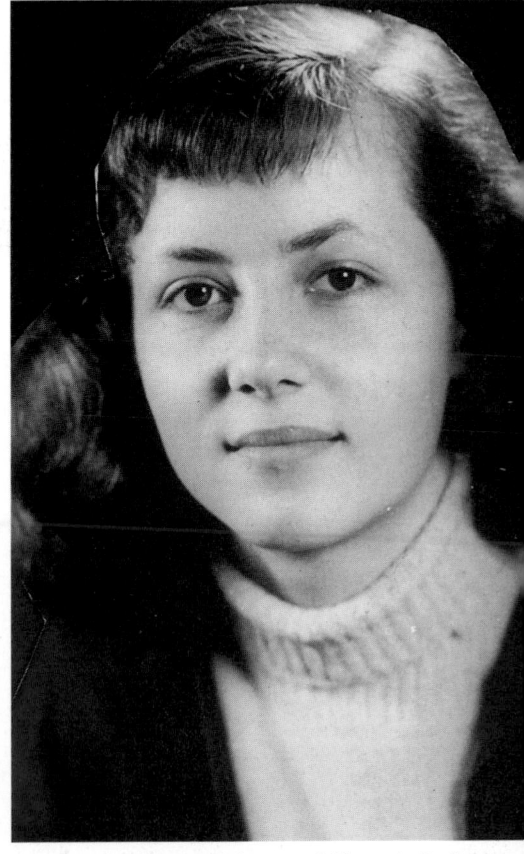

IP around the age of fifteen, in Berlin.

Major Pitt.

Steffi with her father.

Living on the reservation, with Johnny and Woman.

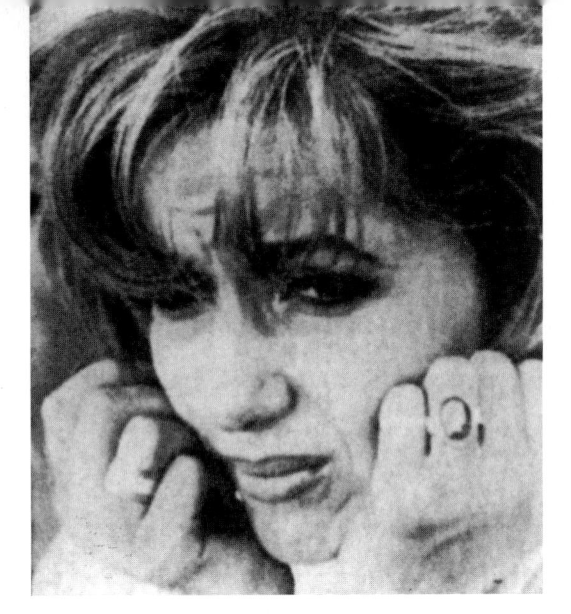

The newspaper photo of me crying at a bullfight which launched my film career in Spain.

Steffi helping out on location.

Steffi and I in a Spanish milk advert which appeared on billboards all over the country.

With Maximo, who taught me Spanish, on set of *Los Duendes de Andalucia*.

With Willy Wilder in the Philippines, shooting *The Omegans*.

With John Mills in *Dundee & the Culhane*.

The photo that got me the part in *Where Eagles Dare*. I went to see Brian Hutton in his Hollywood office. As I had laryngitis I just smiled, pointed to my throat, laid this photograph on his desk and wrote 'HEIDI' all over the picture. He got the drift – and I got the job.

With Alistair MacLean, author of *Where Eagles Dare*. Alistair inspired me to turn to writing after location shooting had finished and I was at a bit of a loose end.

With Richard Burton.

Clint Eastwood taking me for a spin on his bike during a quiet moment in the filming of *Where Eagles Dare*.

With Brian Hutton, director of *Where Eagles Dare*.

At the Vegas launch of *Where Eagles Dare*. Clint sailed charmingly down the line of executives who stood to give him a welcoming ovation, and stopped before me. Gathering me in his arms he let the suits know that we were brothers under the skin. You can just see Bo Poke in the corner of the photo.

our daily walk through the countryside a boy sidled up to me and asked if I had liked the sausage. God, I thought, why couldn't someone like that have looked after my needs in the camp? But he didn't remind me of Yuri. And if boys didn't remind me of Yuri they were dead. I was thirteen now and Yuri had become an idealised figure in my mind. Any boy I met paled into insignificance when compared with my idol. I had already decided that I would spend my entire life alone. Or, alternatively, I would become very famous and rich, return to the forest, find Yuri and take him away. Rationally, I knew that Yuri would have left the forest by now but who wants to be rational when day-dreams are better?

The boy with the sausage said his name was Heinz, which didn't help his cause. One Heinz had already been too many in my life. The poor guy asked if I wanted more sausage. 'My father's a butcher and makes them himself . . .'

'Yes,' I said. 'You're all butchers!' and left him standing.

I never got used to the orphanage. Daily I went to the headmistress to collect letters from my parents and I wrote back to them immediately. I knew the teachers censored my letters so I tried not to complain.

One day a paediatrician who claimed to be my step-brother came to visit. My father had asked him to have a look at my heart and lungs. He took me to a hospital and did an X-ray to see if my TB had gone. He told me that I was on the mend but that my heart was still too small. I thought we would go back to the orphanage from the hospital, but instead he took me to his home for the weekend. I didn't like it there very much. He wasn't anything like my father and I didn't acknowledge him as my brother. I couldn't help wondering what he'd been doing while we'd been going through hell. When he took me back to the orphanage it was all very awkward. He asked me if I would like him to come again. I was fairly non-committal and he said to get in touch if I needed him, kissed me formally on the cheek and left. He did turn up again shortly afterwards and took me to his home for his son's first birthday party. He had a nice wife and in-laws but I thought I'd get on better on my own. The thought was always there – what did he do in the war? Where was he when our father suffered in Terezina? Had he been a member of the Nazi party?

As is usual when a lot of children of approximately the same age are together, there was a strict hierarchy in the orphanage. At thirteen I was no longer the runt of the pack. I had breasts growing and had learned a lot about survival. My major problem was the boys. Battling with the pimples of puberty and talking about little other than girls and their fantasies, they loved to display their machismo. I couldn't let them get away with all the crap they were saying and without thinking demanded to be let into their gang, the Lümmel Pack. They said I could join if I passed the initiation test. I don't think they really had one before the awful prospect of having a girl on the team reared its ugly head. Why I bothered I don't know.

They insisted that I was blindfolded and then led me to the ruins of an old granary, whipped off the bandage and thrust me towards the edge of a bomb-shattered floor. Across a pit of about three yards or so was a narrow metal beam. I didn't like the look of it and fervently hoped that I might be saved by somebody rushing on to the scene and driving us away.

The boys were delighted to see my misgivings and rolled around laughing, congratulating themselves on getting one over on the mouthy cow who was always putting them down. If I had been half as confident as I tried to pretend I was I would have laughed and walked away. But I'm not that brave. I stood over the abyss and tried to convince myself that if I got into trouble I could dive for the edge and avert disaster.

I took off my shoes. The boys were still taunting me, making jibes about girls being wimps compared with boys. That did it. I put my foot on the beam and tested it for stability. No problem there. Gradually I transferred my weight on to that foot. The boys were still at it. They even started throwing small chunks of plaster at me. I tried to ignore them and put the other foot on the beam. I wasn't going to make it. I stepped back to safety, thought for a moment, then lowered myself on to the beam in a sitting position.

The boys were quiet for a moment, stunned into silence. Then, angry at having been outwitted, they noisily protested that I had to *walk* across the beam and in addition introduced a new rule: I had to take off my clothes. I had been around enough to know that was testosterone talking and refused. 'That's it,' they said. 'You can't be a member.' It was my way out but I was too dumb to take it.

We reached a compromise. I would take off my frock but could keep my vest and knickers on. They eagerly agreed. I think they considered this a major erotic victory. Down to my underclothes, I got back on the beam and swayed dangerously. The boys, giggling and making smart-alec remarks, ran down the stairs to stand below me. I think they had some idea that they might be able to see up my knicker leg or something.

By this time all sensible thought had been replaced in my brain by the determination to prove to the boys that I was some sort of Brünnhilde. 'Don't look down!' I told myself. *Shit*! I thought. *I'll never make it*!

As I started walking across, something flew out of a

shattered room and swerved across in front of me. That did it. My arms windmilled ineffectually and I knew I was falling and that it was going to hurt. Even the boys were silent as gravity took over and I began to plummet. Plan B came into operation. Without much hope I launched myself towards the far side of the pit – and missed by a mile. The thought crossed my mind that I was a goner, that I'd never see my parents again.

The fall seemed to take a long time. Luckily I landed in the middle of a large bush, but the jagged end of a branch thrust right up between my legs and buried itself in my vagina. The pain was excruciating. And the blood torrential. The brave boys made themselves scarce, leaving me impaled and screaming.

I lay there, trying to come to terms with the pain. I wasn't dead, but was that necessarily a bonus? Every movement increased the torture. Again I contemplated death and hated myself for my stupidity in letting the boys goad me on.

At last I managed to extract myself from the bush. The bleeding had stopped but the pain was still horrendous and I couldn't move. I heard someone coming and managed to give a weak cry. It was Heinz, the sausage boy. Part of the gang, he had returned to the orphanage with the others but his conscience had forced him to come back to see how I was. He told me to lean on him and he'd take me back. I would be all right in a day or two, he reassured me. I screamed that I wouldn't be all right in a day or two. I needed a doctor – immediately! Even the screaming hurt like mad so I lay down and tried to come to terms with the situation. Heinz ran off and after a while one of the nurses from the orphanage came. She also wanted me to walk back to the dormitory so that the doctor could look at me. She gave up that idea when she tried to help me stand and I passed out.

I woke up in the hospital. The nurse made a joke about going to such extremes to lose my virginity but I didn't think it was very funny. I had some fancy stitches in very intimate places and they hurt like hell. By the time I got back to the orphanage the whole episode was public knowledge, but nobody talked to me about it. I suppose it was the nature of my injuries. It wasn't as if they could say, 'Can I see the scar?'

This adventure signalled the end for the Lümmel Pack. I was sorry about that. With a bit of luck one of the boys might have done himself a real injury!

Eleven

Shortly after my accident I was put on a plane and flown back to Berlin. The Russians were letting the convoys through again and the airlift was over. It was wonderful to be back with my papa and to schmooz with him again. I was still terribly aware that I was neglecting my mother. I sometimes threw my arms round her neck and said I loved her so much, and she would hold me in her arms and pat me comfortingly on the back. Then she would slap my bum and push me off to go to my dad.

After the airlift, everything got marginally better. Not good, but better. We had become used to the constant sound of bulldozers and the long periods without gas, electricity or water. In fact, we took the periods when any or all three functioned as a bit of a bonus – not to be counted on but wonderful while it lasted. There was still a stigma attached to being a Jew. What Hitler had started, by blaming the economic failure of the Weimar Republic on the Jews, died hard. Most of the Germans still attributed their poverty and hardship to the Jews. But we could cope with that. After Stutthof you could cope with anything.

The worst thing about returning home was that I had to

go back to school. This time I was sent to a girls' school. Although I learned a lot more and found studying quite interesting, I decided my life lacked excitement and that I should join another gang.

I'd heard that in the next road was a whore-house, which attracted a lot of American GIs. The GIs seemed never to learn. They would drive up in their jeeps, park, and as soon as the brothel door closed, the local boys would swarm over the car and, quicker than at a Ferrari pit stop, disappear with the wheels. It all seemed like good fun so I started sneaking off and hanging out with the lads. Their den was the ruined house on the corner where they could keep an eye on the bordello for business and make sure there were no 'Snowdrops' – as the military police were known because of their white helmets – around to spoil the fun. They'd meet there, hang out and smoke fags, stolen from the GIs' jeeps. I was still young and pretty skinny, but I was up for anything and could speak English, which was a great asset in post-war Berlin. I'd do my bit with the GIs and they would go through the 'Have you got an older sister at home?' routine before giving me chocolate and cigarettes or asking me how old I was, just in case. I was also the cover when the rest were doing their bit of filching. I wasn't too good at it. I was so focused on what was going on that I didn't keep a very good look out. One day I was busy watching the boys when they suddenly jumped up and disappeared down the road. Before I could get my brain in gear an enormous black man heaved me into the air by my jacket collar and asked me what I thought I was doing. I lied, said I was just passing and . . . the fact that I was holding several items recently liberated from his jeep was a little awkward to explain. Luckily for me, the GI merely told me to put the wheels back on his jeep. He must have been kidding. I couldn't lift them let alone get the screws back in. In the end he took pity on me and fixed them himself. He even gave me an orange. It was the first orange I'd ever eaten.

After this episode I still wanted to hang out with the gang but they had gone cold on me. What's the good of a look-out who gets caught? My life as a hoodlum was short-lived. I didn't seem to have what it takes to be a thief.

Our lives finally began to settle into a routine. Every Sunday after lunch my father would take me to the Gloria Palast, a cinema not far from where we lived. He would make a big production of putting on his suit to take his teenage *dotschka* to the cinema, which was always teeming with rowdy children. Most of the kids called him grandpa since they all knew him, but by now it was never malicious and it didn't bother him. He just winked at them. When I took offence on his behalf and wanted to attack them, he'd grip my hand hard so that I'd get control of myself.

The cinema was the first my father ever took me to. I had never seen a film before, and little did I know that films would become my life. The cinema was a whole new world to me. A world of make believe that I couldn't imagine existed. (At Stutthof I always tried to close my eyes tight and pretend I was somewhere else. But the sounds would still be there . . .) It was an altogether different world and what an incredible wondrous world it was. There were millions of make-believe lives to be part of: exciting lives and worlds I had never seen. I would ask my father all sorts of questions on the way home. And the following Sunday he had to go through the same thing all over again. I gave him no choice. Our big favourites were *The Jungle Book* and *Elephant Boy* starring Sabu, but I also loved Hopalong

Cassidy, Roy Rogers and Johnny Weissmuller.

Then my father became ill.

I was desperate and so was my mother. I refused to go to school. He had got uraemia, poisoning of the bladder. It seemed only a moment since we'd got him back – just five lousy short years. Nothing. I'd been without him for the same amount of time. I believed I should never again be able to live without him. He couldn't die. He meant everything to me. My mother thought she could will him to get better, but he had suffered too much. A lesser man would have been dead already but his athletic life had made him strong and he could bear more than most people.

Then came the awful day when an ambulance took him away. I cried, wouldn't let go of his hand. I shouted, 'No, no, don't leave me, stay here, Papa, don't go . . .' Matka said I was making it worse. When they shoved him inside the dark, black hole of the ambulance he looked towards the garden and said that he knew he would never come back. My mother went with him, but I was not allowed. I was told that I could visit 'tomorrow'. I hated those people in the white coats.

My mama came back very late at night with red, swollen eyes. She hadn't wanted to leave my father on his own in that place without a loving face by his side, but the nurses had forced her to go. She was tormented by the thought that he might die when she wasn't with him, while she lay sleeping at home. She didn't sleep all that night and we both got up at dawn and took the train to the hospital. He stretched out his arms and smiled when we came into his room. 'I want to come home . . .' he said. 'I don't want to die here. Take me home.'

The doctor said that although they couldn't do anything for him he couldn't leave. I had a fit and they threw me out. Because I couldn't keep my gob shut my poor mother had to deal with the hospital hierarchy while my father lay dying. In the end they let us into my father's room again and we stayed there all day. Papa kept mumbling that he had had no right to put us through all the horrors of the camp, that he should have seen it coming earlier, that he should have worked out something to save us . . .

Mama told him that it didn't matter now. All that was important was that he had followed his belief and had been proved right. He would have been responsible for the deaths of thousands of innocent people if he had given in.

He cupped my face in his big hands and told me that he would love me for ever. He knew he was dying but he wanted to comfort us. 'Promise me', he said, 'you'll never be a victim again. Ever! Promise.' I did, knowing already that it is easier to make a promise than to keep it.

Around midnight my mother told me to go home to get some sleep. I refused. I've always been glad I did although I hadn't really slept for days and was almost comatose. It was the last night I spent with my father. He died at dawn the next day. My mother held him close and whispered in his ear how much she'd always loved him. We stayed with him until they forced us to leave.

We came home late that day – 16 July 1953 – and lay together on the bed and cried for a long long time. He was the centre of our lives and now he was gone.

I sang 'Ave Maria' at the funeral or, rather, I was supposed to. But then I had an attack of tears and I couldn't breathe. I croaked through the song until I completely lost my voice.

Once the funeral was over I made my mother's life hell. I tried to kill myself. I just couldn't stand the pain. I still find it difficult to bear, so many years later. But then it burned in my heart like fire and I believed only a bottle of pills would make the agony go away. Only when I had swallowed them all did I begin to think about the misery I would cause my mother. How would she feel burying me too? In a daze I tried to get to the hospital to have my stomach pumped. Apparently I walked in the middle of the road and a car picked me up and took me to Emergency. They pumped the old pot out and saved me.

Mother was incredibly angry. I'd never seen her so mad. She hit me, slapping my face again and again. She had never done that before but I thought she was right to slap sense into my stupid brain. I begged her to forgive me. She knew the argument that would stop me from ever contemplating such a cowardly thing again. Did my father give up? she asked me. Did he ever, once, think that killing himself was the easy option? What would he think of me if he knew what I had done?

After my father's death everything changed. I didn't want to go to school. I wanted just to sit on the balcony, not get dressed, and think about him. Not putting on clothes was important because getting dressed meant saying 'yes' to life and the future. Not doing it was a sign of giving up. Going to school seemed useless and a waste of time. I wouldn't learn anything I didn't already know. My father had taught me everything anyway. He taught me about courage, love, the world, the stars, the universe . . .

Although I considered myself pretty switched on it was a view not shared by my teachers. They were constantly on my back, demanding that I should do better. It all seemed so unimportant. My mother was called to the school and told about my poor performance. When she told the headmaster that I wanted to be a surgeon, he laughed at her. She was so furious that she stalked out wordlessly.

Most of my father's family were in some branch of the medical profession and Mascha was determined that I should follow them. The fact that none of them had spoken to her since her marriage was hurtful, but she wasn't going to let their aloofness get in the way of her baby's success. She wrote to them and got a reply from the paediatrician I had met at the orphanage. Despite my cold behaviour when we'd met, he was willing to do what he could for me. I sat an examination and didn't do terribly well, but my stepbrother was a member of the medical school faculty and was able to railroad me through. I was offered a place in the school to which he was attached. It meant leaving my mama but we both agreed it was in a good cause.

I was accepted into the medical faculty as a probationer. Having gained my position through the back door, I was the focus of some resentment from the faculty and students. One day I arrived slightly late at a lecture. They were showing a film on vermin, so it was dark in the auditorium. Rushing to my seat I sat down, only to find something already on my seat: something furry and dead. I screamed. The lights came on and I found myself standing with a recently deceased rat in my hand. When I saw the beast swinging in front of my face, my screams tripled in intensity and, instinctively, I threw the rodent into the crowd. That started everyone else screeching in horror, especially the women, although most of them couldn't have known what they were screaming about. I didn't care. I stormed out of the place and that was virtually the end of my career in medicine.

Of course my poor mother was summoned to see the Dean. He got all sniffy and told her to take her wretched daughter out of his wonderful establishment. No mention was made of the fact that someone had deliberately put a rat on my seat. Dear old Mum still thought I had a career among the bedpans and pleaded for my reinstatement, but the Dean was unyielding. Matka, however, would not give in. She went to see the *Bürgermeister* – mayor – and he used his influence to get me reinstated.

The next semester was Pathology. The professor put a rat before me and said, 'Dissect!' Only I was given a rat. I went potty once more and was duly thrown out again. Even my mama didn't try to get me back in. Thus I did not become a surgeon.

Twelve

Being booted out of medical school, however undignified the departure, didn't traumatise me. I had realised almost as soon as I'd put on the obligatory white smock that it was not for me. What I wanted, although I'd never confided my secret dream to anyone, was to be up there on the screen, a fainting heroine rescued by Sabu the Elephant Boy or maybe a sultry female pirate mixing it with the likes of Errol Flynn and Douglas Fairbanks Jnr.

My regular reading, apart from *War and Peace,* which I read again and again, were the film journals that were freely available in Berlin, courtesy of the GIs. I read about how this star was discovered on a farm or the other in a drugstore, how Sam Goldwyn had never intended to cast Virginia Mayo but asked the casting agent for the wrong woman. Once he had her he was too bull-headed to admit to being wrong and she became a leading player. There were dozens of happenstance stories that resulted in the big time. Why shouldn't it happen to me? Hadn't I been a right little entertainer in the camp? What tougher audience could you get than Nazi guards? The more I thought about it the more I convinced myself that there were powerful men out there just looking for me.

'Hey, you, kid!' Cecil B. De Mille would say to me as he climbed out of his Cadillac. 'I want you to star in my next picture. I'll make you a star. What d'ya say, kid?'

I confided my dreams to my mother and instead of banning me outright from pursuing them she took the chance to practise a little blackmail – or should it be called psychology? She told me she would support my efforts if I first learned to do something that would be of use if the acting thing didn't work out. To my horror she suggested I learn to type. I considered the idea a great waste of time. Cecil B. had never discovered a star in a typing pool.

The following morning Matka plonked a typewritten tract in front of me and said nothing while I read it. By the time I had finished I knew what it felt like to hear your death sentence read out in court. In bright, flowing text the paper enumerated all the wonderful things you could do with your life once you had received your diploma from the Memmert Academy of Shorthand & Typing. Somehow book-keeping sneaked in there but since I was hopeless at maths it was the first casualty of my new, sensible life. 'Waste of time,' Herr Memmert told my mama after a few lessons. 'Waste of money.'

I sat in a row of girls doing the ten-finger typing exercises. I thought of the theatre and wanted to weep. The school was close to the train depot and I watched the *Stadtbahn* come and go, knowing it went to where the theatres were. What would become of me? I couldn't just go and work in some bloody office. I wanted to be an actress. I was convinced I'd be good at it.

The day came when I was presented with the diploma that guaranteed that my dancing fingers would be a major asset to any profitable business. I showed it to Matka and she began to put her mind to the question of who would employ me.

'Hold it!' I said to her. 'What about being an actress?'

She looked at me as if I had told her a dirty joke. What did I want with being an actress when I could be a secretary?

To be fair to her, she didn't put up too much opposition. Getting a job as a secretary at that particular time was almost as hard as becoming a Broadway star. So Matka suggested that we visit some of the theatres that were opening up all over Berlin, mainly to cater for the American dough-boys with more money than artistic appreciation. It didn't seem odd to me to appear at the theatres with my mother but it certainly did to a lot of the sleazy entrepreneurs of the time. They would brighten up considerably when I arrived, tarted up like a *Mikado* extra and starry-eyed. Their libido generally got a bashing when I stepped aside to reveal my mum. Some even took me aside and suggested I got rid of her and returned later that night to get down to some real entertainment. It was the sort of offer you got every couple of steps on the streets of Berlin if you were over nine, with no obvious VD scabs, and laid any claim to having some tepid blood in your veins. I've always been up for a compliment but I wanted to be a star, not some round-heeled floozy in a café theatre.

I was a quick learner and after being thrown out of one or two of the better-class theatres I realised that I was supposed to be able to stand on stage and convince a sceptical director that I had something an audience wanted to see.

In a battle for survival, I'd back my mother against anyone, but for advising me on the thespian art she just didn't have the right background. There wasn't a lot of theatre in the dressage ring she had inhabited before the war. The only person I knew who had even a wind-up gramophone was Haneli.

I thought it was wonderful how Haneli had survived

the war with her lust for the good life intact. When I first contacted her and said I would like to visit her, she was full of enthusiasm, but on hearing what it was all about she cooled off a little. She wrote a letter to my mother and asked her if she supported my becoming an actress. When Mascha wrote back and said that we had an agreement that if it didn't work out I would get a sensible job, Haneli was overjoyed.

Hanusia had now moved into a new flat. It should not have taken long to get there had Berlin buses not had to negotiate the gangs of workmen who were still rebuilding the city. Instead of a journey of half an hour, however, it quite often took half a day. Because of this, it was decided that I would spend the weekends with Haneli. She was happy about that. Her family had been murdered in Treblinka and she was all alone. One night when we had already gone to bed and turned out the light, Hanusia told me what had happened when the Nazis came to take her away. My uncle Utz had defied them and stood in front of her, daring them to kill him first before he would let them get his wife. They just shot him. Then they raped her and left. She tried to kill herself but a neighbour got help and saved her life.

Hanusia spoiled me. She'd rustle up wonderful titbits, like blinis with sour cream, borscht and piroszki. Sometimes it was mashed spuds – I'm obsessed with potatoes – with her very special tomato sauce, and she also knew a man who baked black bread, which I loved.

Sometimes we would go to the Hunting Lodge in Grunewald, a forest in the middle of Berlin, and we'd hear great concerts. We loved listening to Rachmaninov and Tchaikovsky, and, naturally, I adored Elgar. I learned Tchaikovsky's Violin Concerto by memory although I couldn't play the fiddle, and Rachmaninov's Second Piano Concerto. We had the most ecstatic times.

We also went to the theatre. There wasn't a play put on in Berlin during this time that Hanusia and I didn't attend. It began to come home to me that being an actress was a bit more difficult than just standing in front of a camera and saying whatever nonsense came into your head. Reading had always been a source of great pleasure for me. But the scope had been limited. I'd read only Russians: Tolstoy, Turgeniev, Gorki, Dostoevsky, Gogol and of course Chekhov. I loved Chekhov. Haneli changed all that. She introduced me to the classics and modern plays. She made me slog through Shakespeare, Goethe, Schiller, and everything she thought would help me to make my way as an actress. It was Haneli's enthusiasm that carried me through. At night we would lie in Haneli's big bed and read through the programmes of whatever we had just seen and she would make outrageous comments. She would also question me about what I claimed to have read the previous week and if she didn't like my answers would insist that I reread whatever it was and take it in this time. I learned that whipping through a book was not the same as reading it slowly and thinking about it. I still take a long time to read and I love just sinking into a book and turning the pages. When I put it down there's a melody that lingers on, and I often mull over scenes and imagine how I would play them in a film.

I am also very affected by nature, as my father was. Trees are my first love. I hate seeing them cut down. There's something so sad about looking at a giant, standing there, impervious to the weather, being felled by a little pygmy with a chain-saw. It's one of the sounds I hate most in the world: the roar of a chain-saw, then the dry crack of branches, like the snapping of bones, as the majestic being crashes to the ground.

Animals I'm a bit more ambivalent about. I'll eat anything that moves without the slightest compunction, but I can't bear to see animals, and especially birds, in cages. Haneli shared my feelings. Nevertheless, for some reason, on one of our Sunday outings, we ended up at the zoo. It was almost closing time. It was cold and most of the mums and dads had abandoned the teddy bears' picnic and gone home for *Pfannkuchen* around the fire. We stood there looking at the poor animals padding mindlessly up and down in the cages. Before I had time to think I ducked under the barrier. I don't know what I thought I was doing but without any regard for the damage I might do, I made my protest. I unlocked several cages before I was caught red-handed by one of the zoo attendants. While my freedom was curtailed, the animals in the cages I had opened just looked at me and made no attempt to liberate themselves. I was taken to the police station and charged with a public order offence. Haneli pleaded for me but I think she was a bit too well dressed and confident to get sympathy from the ill-paid police.

Once again my mother came to the rescue. As soon as she heard about my trouble she travelled across town, went to the zoo and pleaded with the authorities not to prosecute me. She told them terrible stories about our lives, promised that she would keep a close watch on me and never give me the chance to do anything so stupid again. By this time, still at the police station, I was terrified. The police had told me I could go to prison for years for my offence, so when my mother appeared I agreed with whatever she said and didn't even think of trying to share my views on animals in cages with the zoo keepers or policemen. I grovelled to the zoo proprietor and I grovelled to the police. And they decided that as nobody had been hurt and I came from a troubled background, the incident wouldn't be taken further.

My mama was a bit frosty with Haneli for allowing me to go berserk. Poor Haneli, it wasn't her fault. She had tried to stop me but when I'm in full flow I won't be denied. Matka couldn't be mad at Hanusia for long and soon everyone was friends again. However, this misadventure did have a knock-on effect: Matka said it was time either to get a job as a secretary or to prove that I might have a career in the theatre.

I went to every crappy little room that was making a hash of even masquerading as a theatre, with no success. At my mother's insistence, I also approached the more conventional venues. I turned up at the Schiller Theatre, believing my bit of Chekhov would have them putting on plays just for me. I did my piece and everyone rolled around. It was pleasing to get a reaction but I thought it a strange one for a straight scene out of Chekhov. The director was quite kind, saying that it was the first time he had considered the comic possibilities of that particular scene and that he would like me to come back later – maybe in a year or two. The other theatres also seemed to think my interpretation of whatever scene I gave them wasn't exactly what they wanted. Some said it nicely – others weren't so sensitive. Every time I came home Matka would question me and when I told her what had happened would go quiet and set to with some unnecessary housework. I could see the stenographer's chair looming larger by the day. Eventually, with all other options exhausted, I thought, 'Sod it, I'll try the best' and made my way to the Berliner Ensemble.

Thirteen

The Berliner Ensemble, founded in 1948 by Bertolt Brecht, was already world famous. The only disadvantage to working with the Berliner Ensemble was that they practised their art in East Berlin, which was still accessible at this time but not exactly a holiday resort.

Already the dross of communism was beginning to build up in East Berlin. In the West everybody was struggling to get back to some sort of normality. Now that the street battalions had gone and the professionals had moved in, the city was beginning to look better by the day. In the East they seemed to be working to a different tune and though the work battalions were still cleaning bricks and filling in pot-holes with rubble they appeared to work without joy or enthusiasm.

In the East were also Russian soldiers. It was the height of jingoistic communism, with an entrenched belief among the comrades that before long the mighty Soviet would rule the world. They were very mindful of what the Nazis had done to their country and the terrible death toll they had meted out. Individually the soldiers were quite sweet: they had a strong sense of home and duty, and didn't need a lot of encouragement to whip out a photograph or tell you about the folks they had left behind. Danger came when they were together. As helpful and understanding as they could be when they were solo, *en masse* you soon learned to walk another street.

Predictably, Matka wasn't keen on my venturing through Checkpoint Charlie. But I didn't listen. I reasoned that a lot of the folk I had met in the partisan camp had claimed to be Communists, including Kuragin – and everybody loved him. And after all, it was the exact opposite of fascism.

I thought long and hard about the best way to present myself at the theatre. Should I write first and beg for an audition? Or should I just turn up and astonish them with my virtuosity? The downside to writing was that I would have to list my qualifications for the job and say what acting I had done before. Turned down by every other theatre and getting a laugh out of Chekhov didn't seem to be the right sort of recommendation somehow. So I decided just to turn up and let my natural charm and overwhelming talent speak for me. I wouldn't give them the Chekhov. It was time to box clever. I would wing it and claim my piece was by some obscure Polish writer, so nobody could bang on about 'misinterpretation'.

I arrived outside the theatre, walked past it and reconsidered. Now I was there, just the sight of the dirty old place was enough to get my stomach doing bungee jumps and my legs feeling like perished elastic. I walked back and looked through the door. Gloom. The only colour was provided by inspirational tracts on theatre nailed up by the local Communist party.

I walked about fifty yards up the road, screwed up my courage and stalked back, swinging through the entrance before I had a chance to change my mind. A man stood in the lobby. I hadn't counted on anyone being there and was immediately overwhelmed by fearful confusion. I made out I had just dropped in to pick up a pamphlet but when the man sniffed and turned to go into the theatre, I summoned all my courage and gave a cough that caught his attention. He smiled encouragingly.

'I'm here to see Frau Weigel,' I gasped. The man asked if I had an appointment and I gurgled something in reply, giving a sickly smile. He looked at me for a moment or two, told me to hang on while he found out if she was in and pushed through the door. He came back just as my nerve was failing me and I was about to leg it up the road.

Frau Weigel would see me.

She seemed incredibly small but came towards me with quick, large steps. She reminded me of my mother, except that Matka was twice as tall. Although she seemed hard as nails she was, in fact, soft and direct: no nonsense. It was her voice that captivated me: she sounded like Marlene Dietrich. And of course she was one of the best actresses on stage at the time. I tried desperately not to be intimidated but came as near to fainting without actually flopping out as it is possible to get. So far so good. She was wonderful and very gruff. She asked what I wanted. I had pulled myself together now and worked up a sort of hysteria. This was my big chance. If I muffed it my entire life would be 9 to 5 in a swivel chair. I said I wanted in.

'Well,' she said. 'You don't lack chutzpah.'

I took it as a compliment and asked if I could show her what I could do.

She waved her cigarette around and stopped me. 'You're an actress?' she asked. Again I was non-committal. 'And I thought you were after the job making *Muckefuck* for the cast.'

The small misunderstanding about making ersatz coffee was soon dealt with and I was asked to pop up on stage and do my bit. I did a piece which I pompously called 'Home from the War' by Witkiewicz.

Of course, she realised I was having her on. She knew every tiny bit of Witkiewicz and 'Home from the War' was not one of his works. Why hadn't I invented some name? I kicked myself.

To my surprise and relief, Frau Weigel let me go on and even told Otto, the lighting man, to put me in a spotlight. I played a woman whose husband comes home from the war to find his wife taking part in the oldest profession to save the life of her child. She is sorry and he is sorry, and the whole thing was a travesty. But Helene didn't roll in the aisle, laughing uncontrollably. Tickled by my brazen nerve, she asked me if I could do anything else. I told her I could do Chekhov but that I preferred not to as I didn't like the German translations, which made his plays into high drama.

'What do you think the plays are?' she asked in an amused tone.

'I think Chekhov is very funny, bringing out the funny side of the people he writes about,' I parroted.

She lit another fag and told me to get on and do 'my' Chekhov.

'My' Chekhov must have coincided with 'her' Chekhov because she let me stay. I was a member of the Ensemble.

My first job was to brew *Muckefuck.* It wasn't what I had in mind but eventually I would get some walk-ons and even the occasional line. What did I care? I had made it. Now I could listen and learn, and was at last in the setting where my amazing talent could blossom. I might be the tea-girl today but that would only make it so much more poignant when they hung the traditional gold star on the dressing-room door.

I lived with my Auntie Fidi, my father's sister-in-law, in her flat on Lenin Allee. Once a week I would borrow a bike from one of the carpenters and visit my mother. They were painful little interludes but I felt under an obligation. The pain was due not just to the continuous attempt to convince Mama that I wasn't descending into a life of debauchery but to the checkpoint. Every time I went through it I was searched by the *Volkspolizistinnen.* They were much worse than the *Vopos*, their male counterparts. The women invariably made me strip naked. It was very frightening and reminded me of the degradations of Stutthof. There was no clear definition of what you could and couldn't take through the checkpoint. One day coffee would be all right if you took only a small amount and promised, before Stalin, that you didn't intend to sell it. Then the next day you might be stopped by a woman who had decided that coffee was an effete capitalist drink that should be confiscated. Clothes were another chancy item. Matka was always terribly aware of the favour my aunt was doing me and insisted I took her presents, very often clothes. Invariably, guards would snatch them away and throw them on to a heap in the corner. Sometimes they would even take those I was wearing if they thought I had too much on. At first I tried to protest but I soon learned that the more you did so, the more you got stopped and the longer the search took.

The frustrations of the checkpoint, Mama's constant harping about living away and the deteriorating quality of life in the East began to irritate me and I considered giving up my new job. I soon changed my mind, however, when one of the actresses decided that she had had enough and was going to escape to the West. With one female less I reckoned I might be called up for a proper part in the next production . . .

Perhaps the actress had known something because, not long after she returned to the West, the borders were closed and the Berlin wall rose up. I could no longer go home to see my mother even once a week.

My mother was frantic. I played it cool and assured her that, as a theatrical star, I was safe from any interference from the East German authorities. That didn't exactly reassure her but I didn't take a lot of notice. Whatever the consequences, I wasn't going to give up my big chance in the world's best theatre.

Emboldened by my newly acquired status as an Ensemble player, however minor, I relaxed and was soon giving anyone who would listen the benefit of my experience. Otto, the lighting man, was a particular fan. He was old – at least forty – and though he would sometimes come on to me, I found him quite easy to control and felt safe with him. With his uncritical attention I soon worked up a spiel that included not only thoughts on acting, directing, scenery and publicity, but a more dangerous monologue about the powers that controlled the land. My theme ran along the lines that the East German government consisted of a load of morons who had no artistic appreciation. Political schooling did not moderate my views. Every week a commissar gave us a little lecture on how lucky we were to be looked after by our big brothers of the *Volksrepublik*. We were all supposed to sit and nod dutifully, and then wish the comrade farewell and get on with our work for another week. Everybody understood it was just a duty call. Except me. I began to rant on about the amount of time wasted on political schooling. The teachers were a bunch of cretins anyway. It would be much better if we were just left alone. No one argued with me. No one agreed with me. They were too smart. The nearest I ever got to encouragement was from Otto and he was really only interested in running his hands over my developing body.

Inevitably, I went a criticism too far and the incumbent

stool-pigeon told the Cultural Officer, who told the *Volkspolizei* and before I knew what was happening I was marched off to the local *Vopo* HQ. I wasn't even thought worthy of a ride in the back of one of their big black limos. At the station I was put through the routine: first I was left sitting by myself for hours, then questioned by a bored woman about my family, friends, where I lived, what I thought about the Americans. By this time I was thoroughly worried and wished Matka were with me. She was good at fielding these sorts of questions. With each answer I felt I was digging a hole for myself. I was made to wait another eternity and then was interviewed by a man in uniform. He asked the same questions but with a lot more menace. There was more sitting in a little dark room and another interview, this time with a suit, who rapped out his questions without waiting to hear what I had to say. He seemed to be set on proving I was a pure anti-red, Soviet-hating capitalist. I was soon terrified, convinced that he had already armed a firing squad.

I was again removed to a cell, where I huddled in fear until a civilian woman came in and to my utter surprise told me I could go. At the front desk I found the reason for my release: Helene Weigel had been in to bat. She had convinced the police that I was some sort of imbecile with a suicide fixation and they had agreed to release me into her custody. She left me in no doubt that if I didn't shape up I would be out of the Ensemble. I grovelled and promised eternal fealty, and that my mouth would be as mute as marble. Helene showed she had a sense of humour by giving me the part of the mute Kattrin in Bertolt Brecht's *Mother Courage.*

Fourteen

I stood in the wings feeling nervous. It's not every day you're called upon to pull the chestnuts out of the fire for a major theatrical company. Of course, the rest of the cast didn't exactly see it that way but I was appropriately impressed with my belief. I knew the nervousness would pass. All the top actors admitted to nerves before a performance. It was expected and only proved what a magnificent job I was going to do playing the mute Kattrin.

I could see Otto sitting in his little cradle in the flies. He had been a great support. The American magazines made a big thing about leading players not associating with the crew but, until that moment, I had been more crew than player and it was hard to play the *grande dame* with your fellow workers when you're sweeping the stage or slopping out cups of *Muckefuck* to the cast. But, I reminded myself, that was yesterday. My time had come and Otto would have to face the sad fact of life that our cosy little relationship was over.

I looked around the grim, jerry-built set and felt my destiny. It didn't matter that the back of the theatre was almost wholly constructed from timber scavenged from the bombed-out buildings of East Berlin; nor that the

Communist administration, in spite of their vaunted championing of the people's theatre, refused to give assistance to the struggling company. All that mattered was that I had made it. Finally, I was going to stand in front of the footlights and show what I was made of.

As I prepared to make my entrance I was aware that someone had come through from front of house and was talking to Otto. I knew it was about me. Otto was nodding and staring at me as if trying to make up his mind about something. I dismissed him from my thoughts and was attempting to focus on what was happening on stage when he touched my arm and drew me back a little. I was annoyed. It was this sort of thing which set me apart from the other, more seasoned, members of the cast. I would have to have words with him about over-familiarity. Before I could say anything he put his mouth close to my ear. 'The *Vopos* are out front,' he said hoarsely. 'They want to speak to you.'

Thoughts of resounding stage success were instantly replaced by alarm. My recent brush with authority had been enough to shut me up for a week or two but since my status had been enhanced I'd again found difficulty keeping my thoughts to myself.

Overwhelmed by feelings of panic, and images of the *Volkspolizei* closing in on me, I gathered up the voluminous skirts that I wore for my part as Kattrin and bolted through the stage door. I had no clear plan. I just knew that another trip to the *Volkspolizei* HQ was not going to be as easily resolved as the last.

Outside the theatre, the absence of street lighting and the terrible state of the roads and pavements were a mixed blessing. Though I didn't fall immediately into the hands of the *Vopos*, I was soon lost. Tears formed in my eyes but I managed to choke back the self-pitying sobs which were trying to force their way through my chattering teeth. I began to run again but a broken paving stone soon sent me sprawling. I knew I should rest and take control of myself but there was so much adrenalin burning in my veins that I pushed myself to my feet and rushed on.

From the darkness lights blazed out, completely blinding me. I didn't have to be told that they came from a police car. Hiding in the dark and trapping individuals in their headlights was one of the *Polizeis'* little party pieces. Depending on how frustrated they felt, they would then either search their victim and let him go, arrest him or beat him up. There was also a fourth alternative for solo girls but that was the least of my worries: I was a State criminal and would finish up in the Gulag archipelago if I were caught.

As the car rolled forward my eye was drawn to a straggly hedge on my left. A voice barked out, 'Stay where you are!' and I heard the terrifying whine of a dog being temporarily restrained. The thought of those wicked canine teeth and great slavering tongue snapped my synapses into overload and my knee-jerk reaction was to dive out of the revealing light into the sheltering bushes.

As I hit the undergrowth I knew I had made an ill-informed decision, for beneath the branches there didn't appear to be any ground. Rolling downhill at an increasing velocity I began to wonder if I wouldn't have been better off in a nice warm cell. But I didn't have the luxury of choice. My hurtling body burst from the shrubs, slid painfully down a rocky incline and splashed into the icy waters of the River Spree.

For a moment the huge Kattrin skirts acted like a life-jacket and kept me afloat, as I found my voice and screamed, but then the saturated clothes began to drag me down. My boots, full of water, felt like anchors. The thought crossed my mind that I should get rid of the sodden gear but the idiotic concern that I would have to explain to Helene how I had ditched some of her precious costumes just to save my paltry life crossed my mind and I hesitated.

By this time the police were hanging over the bank, shining their torches and shouting stupid instructions, as if I didn't know I was in the water and in trouble. Every time I managed to struggle to the surface it became clear that the torchlight was falling further away. I was in the grip of the notorious River Spree current and being swept to my death.

I managed to relieve myself of Kattrin's skirts. The boots were not so easy, however. In the dark, swirling water, submerged most of the time, I could only manage to free one foot.

It was at about this time that I decided I was going to die. I wish I could say that I faced the possibility with dignity and calm acceptance. Unfortunately I can't. All I could do was scream, cry and splash frantically around.

The policemen's torches were soon nothing more than pinpricks in the black night. Other dots of light on both sides of me confirmed that I had drifted out into the middle of the river. I was freezing, and panic and fear had exhausted me to a point where I could hardly be bothered to kick my legs in an effort to keep my head above water. I thought about my mother. Would she be devastated and blame herself for letting me leave the security of home? The cold water made my head feel as if a steel band were being viciously tightened around it and my temples were about to cave in. I was vaguely surprised that my legs and arms were still feebly functioning – they seemed to have no connection with my brain.

The panic had gone now. I just felt terribly sad, although I don't think I actually considered the premise that I was about to die. That didn't seem to come into it.

My brain just seemed to be divorced from my body and accepted the fact that one was going to be separated from the other. I can't say that my life rushed before my eyes but it was as if I had a grand overview. It was all there but I was no longer a part of it. I felt myself drifting away and let it happen.

Suddenly I saw flashing light. The light was the tunnel into the next world that I had heard people talk about. I looked hopefully for my father who, I was sure, would be there to meet me. But the light kept going on, off, on, off ... Vaguely, I thought, 'Someone is attracting my attention. What for? I'm drowning.' Only I wasn't and hadn't – so far.

I decided to live and fight. I started swimming with the very last energy I could pump up. I was *not* going to drown in a German river and kill my mother too. Hysteria was my friend and lent me the strength to kick for the flickering torchlight. When I reached the steep bank it was paved stone and I had no idea how to get out of the water.

I heard shouting, English voices. 'My coat! Grab my coat ...' Now I could see a coat being shaken in my direction but I couldn't reach it. Then I clutched it but it slipped away. I had to get out of the water. I had to reach the coat. It came down closer. Someone was lying on the ground now, shaking the coat at me. I mustered up my remaining energy and seized the fabric, which threatened to twist out of my grip. 'Don't let go or you'll die' beat like a mantra in my head.

Hands reached down and took hold of my arms, dragged me out of the river like a waterlogged kitten and dropped me on to a concrete path. I didn't feel a thing. There were three men in GI uniforms – two MPs and a young lieutenant – bending over me. They kept asking me questions but I was so full of Spree water that I couldn't hear a thing. They gave up and stowed me in the back of the car. The lieutenant found a blanket and enveloped me in it, wrapping his arms around me to try to stop me shivering and to transfer a little much needed heat. I loved him instantly. I mumbled something naff and promptly passed out.

I regained consciousness to the sound of an American voice, straight out of a movie, telling me, 'It's all over, everything's okay. Just drink the whisky and everything will be perfect.' I was too tired to reply, the tiredest I have ever been, and promptly fell asleep.

The car stopped outside one of the typical big, ugly Berlin apartment houses. I was manhandled up the grim, badly lit stairs by two of the men. One of them rang a bell and at once the door opened to reveal a grinning over-made-up lady. The better looking of the two troopers explained the situation and I was escorted to a room with a big bed in it. Other brightly made-up ladies removed the rest of my costume and dumped me in a hot bath. After that I fell into bed, where I regretfully recalled that I hadn't said thank you to the kind Americans.

When I woke it was light. I sat up and looked around. The decoration was a bit gaudy and had seen better days, and in the bathroom I noted the many bottles of perfumes and bath salts, all with flashy American labels.

Back in the bedroom, I sat on the bed and wondered what would become of me now. I reasoned that I was in West Berlin so I could go and see my mother. However, the only clothes I had were the sodden stage wardrobe, minus one boot and a skirt. Before I could work myself up into a sweat the door opened and a woman in her early forties came in. She was neat and small, and not overly friendly. I explained my dilemma, but she wanted only to know if there was anyone she should contact to let them know where I was. I thought she was pretty cool. There was I, a mysterious stranger, yanked out of the river at death's door and brought to her in a squad car by a trio of Yanks and all she wished to find out was if there was someone she could telephone. I told her about Matka and how she could be contacted through a neighbour. She nodded and suggested that if I wanted something to eat I should go to the kitchen. I was ravenous so I drew a blanket around my shoulders and followed her.

The apartment was largish but, like most flats of that period and in that time, gloomy and badly in need of repair. The woman led me through to the kitchen, put a knife, some black bread and cheese in front of me, and left. I was into my second sandwich when a young girl came in and introduced herself as Nelli. She told me she'd been there when the Americans had brought me in. I told her my story and she was suitably impressed. Other women came into the kitchen, so I had to tell the tale again. They all thought it was hilarious.

I was beginning to get the idea that my rescuers hadn't dumped me in a seminary for young ladies. The women's speech was too colourful, sprinkled with English swear-words that they could have picked up only by frequent and intimate contact with the forces of occupation. I was too prudish to ask them what they did for a living, but they soon told me anyway. I was in the greatest little whore-house in the West – well, West Berlin, anyway.

I thought it was terribly exciting. The girls started recounting fantastic stories about the tricks they had pulled and I sat there, bug-eyed, screaming with laughter. It was the best therapy I could have had and within the hour I'd forgotten how terrified I had been the night before.

When my mother walked in, the room fell silent and, feeling guilty by association, I hastily borrowed some clothes and followed her out into the decrepit street, without daring to look back. Matka wasn't exactly talkative as we made our way across the city. When we got home she insisted that I take off my borrowed finery and go to bed. It sounded good to me. For one thing weariness had hit me again and for another it put off the hour of reckoning with Matka.

The next morning she brought me a cup of tea. She was in a better mood now. She gave me a hug, held my hand and sat beside me on the bed. I knew what was coming – I could see typewriter ribbon in her eyes – but I wasn't worried. I had thought up what I believed to be a cunning scheme.

At the Berliner Ensemble, I'd overheard some of the actors talking about the Burgtheater in Vienna. I hadn't paid much attention because I'd assumed that I would be staying with the Ensemble for the foreseeable future. Now that that had all come to an abrupt end and the office door was in front of me, it was time to clutch at clouds. So far, I hadn't impressed Matka with my life-style, so I knew I had to be a bit devious and decided to tell a slight fib. Well, a whacking great lie. I told my mother that in East Berlin I had been approached by a representative of the Burgtheater to go to Vienna for an audition. He had practically guaranteed me a job, I assured her. I don't suppose she believed me for a minute but I think she was getting bored at home so she let me persuade her that Vienna was the answer to all my problems – and said she would come with me to the audition. That really hit me between the eyes. I'd hoped merely to distract her from the secretary idea until something better came up. Before I knew where I was, I'd been swept up in my own web of deceit.

We didn't have much money to spare so we decided that we would take to the road and hitch-hike wherever possible, and hoard what money we had for whenever the going got too tough. It meant travelling light. We packed a few bits and pieces, put our pennies together and made our way to the entrance to the Avus, the motorway leading to Helmstedt, the American–Russian control point. At first I received plenty of offers of lifts but the drivers suddenly had to be elsewhere when I produced my mother. We even tried the standing-behind-a-tree ploy. I'd get a car to stop and then she'd come out. It didn't work. Before we could get in the driver would drop the clutch and the car would speed off.

Finally, a milk truck stopped for us. At lunch-time we drew into a busy truckers' caff, loud and cheerful, with beer and cigarette ash like a wet sponge carpet on the floor. Suddenly there was a lot of shouting and laughter. Matka asked a driver what was going on and he told us a bloke at the bar had bet a hundred marks that he'd swallow a live mouse. Our driver was up for that and tried to get my mother to chip in but she hated betting. I think she thought life was enough of a gamble without taking on side bets.

Everyone craned forward to see what was happening. A young, good-looking man was holding a grey mouse by its tail, displaying it for everyone to see. I forced myself to watch. Someone banged on a tin plate and the show began. The man held the wiggling mouse high above his head and slowly lowered it into his mouth. Everybody was shouting and laughing. The poor mouse seemed to know what was coming and made a last desperate effort to get away. Too late. The man put it in his mouth and then walked around the yelling audience with the still wriggling tail hanging out. I felt ill. Seeing the effect he was having on me the young man turned to give me the finale. The tail disappeared as the mouse slid down into his stomach. That did it for me. I puked all over his boots and ran outside.

Matka came after me and said that the driver of the milk

truck wanted to get on but perhaps we should wait a while until I felt better. I croaked that I wanted to go home. I felt too sick to go anywhere. Mascha nodded solemnly and put her arm round me. 'Right!' she said with an air of finality. She didn't have to remind me what I was going back to but I kept seeing the tail disappear in the man's mouth and retched and retched again. So that was the end of the Burgtheater.

It was a long time before we found a ride back. There seemed to be no one on the road crazy enough to want to go to Berlin. Then it started to rain and the few cars that came along refused to stop for two sopping-wet passengers. Eventually a trucker took pity on us.

As we waited at the border at Marienborn to get the truck's load checked, the driver started talking about the war. He'd been at Sobibor concentration camp. Matka told him a bit of our experiences and they talked all the way back to our home. The driver asked if he could visit when he next came to Berlin but we never heard from him again. I don't think my mother minded. She wanted nothing to do with those years. Neither did he, I suppose. Talking about our past opened the floodgates of memory for Mama and I never heard her mention them again. She didn't want to hear others talk about it, she didn't want to be reminded. She locked it up in the recesses of her brain and threw away the key.

The next day I tried to hide from my mother by again staying in bed. Eventually, she brought me a cup of tea and sat down beside me. She asked me how I was and I said all right. I asked her how she was and she said she was fine. She didn't push it. I guess she thought I had agreed to fall back on my diploma and type for the rest of my life. As daunting as the prospect was I was beginning to think it was the only option.

Mama drew in a deep breath – and the doorbell rang. We looked at each other, startled. Someone ringing the doorbell was a bit of a novelty. Matka got up and answered the door. The US lieutenant who had fished me out of the Spree stood on the doorstep with a bunch of flowers and a shiny cake tin with a picture of Father Christmas on it. He'd rescued me once more.

Fifteen

We were married six months later, in May: a white wedding with a white carriage and horses. It had created a bit of a problem since my husband-to-be was a Christian and I was not attached to any church or synagogue. When one mentioned faith in God to my mother she'd get up and leave the room and I wasn't far behind. My husband-to-be and I had one or two rows over the God question but I let him see a few pictures that were for ever engraved on my brain . . . After that, my future husband left me alone about religion, but he still wanted our union sanctified and whatever he desired I wished him to have. It made no difference to me. My wedding was great fun, though. We had a hilarious ceremony with a vicar who stuttered – in a mosque. Not a lot of people can say that.

As we prepared to leave on honeymoon, everything packed into the car, I started to say goodbye to Matka and suddenly I couldn't go. She stood in the doorway and looked pathetic and unhappy, and terribly alone. I told my husband that we'd have to stay. He thought I'd gone off my rocker. We had a brief discussion, *sotto voce*, and he suggested that we took her with us. That's the kind of person he was.

Although Mama pretended for a while that it was a bad idea and she would be fine on her own, she eventually gave in and joined us in our '49 Oldsmobile. We travelled around Italy, visiting Rome, Venice, Pisa, Viareggio – where I was crowned Queen of the Night in a beauty contest – Sorrento and Sicily. Early each evening Mama would claim to be tired and leave us to dine alone, though I often wondered how tired she really was. She loved the trip madly, and so did I.

On our return I immediately began teaching myself to drive, practising in our driveway, and passed my driving test three days later. I thought I was a natural and should be a racing driver. That would be a smashing career, I told myself, better than acting as it wouldn't involve learning lines. I practised racing on the autobahn and out of boredom started going to Helmstedt in the car. At the checkpoint I would exchange my Lucky Strike cigarettes for rotten Russian *papirosi* and chat with the soldiers in Russian. It gave me a real buzz to talk to people who were in many ways regarded as the enemy. I found I related to them more easily than a lot of the officers and wives I met in camp. I would race back to pick up my husband from his barracks for dinner. I'm sure he thought my Russian control-point rendezvous were rather naff but he indulged me and joked about my being a 'secret agent'. I'm not sure which side he thought I was on, or why. My fraternising with the future enemy didn't seem to do any harm and it kept my Russian in top gear.

I liked being married and decided the time was right to have a baby. I wanted to see if I could be as good a mother as the one I had. But before I could put my plan into action we learned that my husband was to be transferred to America. 'Don't you worry,' I told my mother. 'You'll come and join us soon.' *When I have my baby*, I thought, *you'll have to come.*

My husband was stationed in Fort Carson, Colorado, and I was delighted with our new life, so different from my earlier experiences. We were allowed to rent a flat anywhere in the vicinity of Fort Carson and took the most glorious apartment overlooking Pikes Peak. From the large french windows there was an astonishingly beautiful view of the snow-capped mountain, a little puffy cloud at its peak. I took my husband to the Fort at six every morning, then went to the commissary, bought food and cleaned the flat. In the afternoons I would go down to the river and read Shakespeare, and wonder where I would have been if I hadn't been fished out of that other river by my knight in a shining patrol car.

Shortly after we moved to Colorado I started feeling sick and to my delight Doctor Kennedy confirmed I was having a baby. I sat on the stones in the Garden of the Gods and gave thanks for this great gift to whom I was going to dedicate my life. From that day on I felt I was finally a complete person.

Politically, things were going badly with the Russians. Following the Bay of Pigs débâcle in Cuba my husband was constantly on stand-by with his unit in Florida, keeping watch for possible Soviet manoeuvres. I was terrified. I fretted that my baby could be without a father before it was even born. I couldn't bear to be in the apartment without him and decided to go to a shack we rented in the mountains near the little village of Silverton until the baby was due. I took long walks through the snow and the forest, which reminded me of the partisan camp in Poland, and sat in the shack by the fire, eating steaks and salads. I had all the books I'd always wanted to read and lived for my growing baby.

One night, a week before the baby was due, when I was watching *Rawhide* and Rowdy Yates was about to be hanged, my waters broke. I didn't panic. I'd worked for a gynaecologist for a short while and had learned one or two things about childbirth on call-outs. I rang the hospital at Fort Carson and they sent an ambulance to come and get me. However, it continued to snow and when they reached the pass it was impossible to get through. They had to send for a snow plough. By the time they'd cleared the pass I'd followed in my mother's footsteps and had my baby virtually by myself. They got there just in time to cut the cord. They showed her to me and I swear she winked at me. I called her Steffanie.

My husband was still away and couldn't get back to us until Steffanie was three days old. When he arrived we celebrated, delighted with ourselves and our daughter, and he took us straight home. We sat on the balcony and I showed Steffanie Pikes Peak and the snow and the valley and the river and she giggled, then I tucked her up in the crib, with a silk heaven over it, which I had made for her.

Her poor dad, who was a captain by now, had to be away a lot but he loved the army. It meant a lot to him to be successful and gain promotion. He had gone to paratrooper school because he had been afraid of heights. I was not lonely, however, because Mama had come to visit us. She was potty about little Steffka and we travelled around sightseeing. She loved it.

Matka had been with us only a couple of months when she fell ill. She had the most horrendous stomach pains and couldn't keep anything down. I had no idea what to do and the doctors couldn't tell us what the problem was. We had millions of tests done at a Denver hospital but to no avail. When things eased a little Matka decided to go home. I told her that given time they'd cure her in America but she was adamant. I missed her and hoped desperately that she would soon get better in her own home and come back to us.

My husband was transferred to Aberdeen Proving Ground in Maryland. We decided to drive all the way there from Colorado in the Oldsmobile. It was one of the most wonderful trips I have ever made and we always thought of it as our second honeymoon. We lived on the base in a little house of our own in the way I'd always dreamed of: mother, father and little *dotschka*.

Alas, it was not to last. Steffka had just learned to stand up and taken her first tentative steps and I was besotted with her incredible achievement. That night my husband declared that he had volunteered to go to Vietnam. I couldn't believe what he had done. How could he go to war when he didn't have to? It was so stupid. He told me that I didn't need him now I had the baby. I thought that was unfair since he was never there anyway. The army seemed more important to him than we were. We had a blazing row. Things were said that couldn't be recalled. He said he'd be back and I said probably not. He said, wait for me and I said certainly not! I had been so delirious playing happy family that I hadn't recognised the fact that my husband had become an extra. Without doubt, Steffanie had become the leading lady. But then he was a soldier and he obviously wished to do some soldiering. It left us with nowhere to go. We decided to write and to review the situation in two years' time when his tour of duty was over. Shortly after he left for Vietnam.

With my husband gone, there seemed little point in staying in Maryland. I packed my things, strapped Steffka in a car seat beside me in the Oldsmobile and went in search of new pastures. I still had the acting bug and decided to have another shot at pursuing my dreams.

I had read in one of the trade magazines that the Playhouse was putting on a series of plays. The Playhouse was what is called in America a 'stock company', the equivalent to Rep in Britain. It seemed like a good place to start. I gave the director all the crap about my exploits as a lead player with the Berliner Ensemble, casually mentioned my Chekhov with the Schiller Theatre and waxed extravagant with the truth about my connection with the Burgtheater. I don't think that impressed him half as much as my ready acceptance of the miserable wage he offered.

My high moment was playing Blanche du Bois on tour. That sounds pretty exalted. 'Tour' conjures up a grand procession through the theatres of America. In fact, what we did was duck and dive through any old hall or decaying auditorium that would have us. The Playhouse was so strapped for cash we even had to provide our own costumes and I certainly had no funds to waste on digs so I frequently lived in the theatres where we worked. Predictably, it all came to a sticky end. I'd been with the Playhouse for seven months and had been paid for about four of them, which just about covered Steffanie's baby food. She was talking now and trying hard to have a meaningful conversation with her idiotic mother. I'd asked the owner of our latest venue whether he minded if I slept in what was laughingly called my dressing-room. He'd volunteered to install a couch and on the first night, after the show, came round to see if everything was all right and to invite me out to dinner. His friendly demeanour paled perceptibly when I brought Steffanie along. After the meal, he made some mumbling reference to coming back to his place but Steffka was out on her feet so I cried off. He drove us back to the theatre with bad grace.

The next evening there were more people in the cast than in the auditorium and the proprietor, in an ill-tempered outburst, blamed the company and railed that it was against fire regulations for me to sleep in the theatre.

I was amazed at the turn-around. I suppose he had expected to get more out of our association than a peck on the cheek and a thank you.

I moved into a local boarding-house that I couldn't afford. I begged the director to give me some of my back pay but he didn't have it. He couldn't even pay for my accommodation. It was the end of the road. When I left the boarding-house on the Friday I made sure I had everything with me. I reckoned I wouldn't be allowed out with my cases the following day unless I threw some dollars on the counter. It meant that I would have to let the company down on the Saturday but I didn't care. 'The show must go on' is a great standby in Hollywood movies but when you haven't been paid for weeks and you have a baby to take care of, it sounds pretty daft.

Friday night saw seven people in the audience. I tried to tap the director again but he wasn't having a good time and got a bit shirty with me. Hadn't I seen the house that night? Seven bloody customers! How did I expect him to pay me out of a lousy $14 take? I didn't argue. I went back to the dressing-room, picked up Steffka and drove to our lodgings to collect my final bits and pieces. I felt a real shit promising the landlady that I would pay her the next day. She was a kindly soul and gave us a generous dinner before we went to bed.

At two o'clock, which I supposed to be the perfect hour for a moonlight flit, I crept quietly down the stairs, threw my things in the boot of the car, installed Steffanie in the carry cot on a nest of pillows and let off the handbrake. Luckily the drive led down to the road which sloped towards the highway and the State line. I switched on the engine after a hundred yards or so and put my foot down. I figured I would be in another county and another jurisdiction before my landlady woke up to the fact that I had reneged on the rent.

But that was only one of my problems. What should I do? As always, I called my mother for advice. She had recovered from her stomach infection by now but, as ever, was worried about me. She hadn't been too happy when I'd admitted to leaving my husband so, naturally, I had since played up my success with the Playhouse. It wasn't easy now to paint a scenario which left me looking good and also explained my predicament. Not surprisingly, Matka told me to go back to my husband. It wasn't the solution I was looking for. My husband was in Vietnam so as far as I was concerned there was no husband to return to.

Back in the Oldsmobile I headed east, until, with a sinking heart, I felt a tyre blow. As the car came to a stop, I remembered that I hadn't had the spare tyre repaired following the last puncture. I sat at the side of the road and tried to work out my next move. As far as I could see in any direction, nothing was stirring. I put the car in gear and drove slowly with the deflated tyre on the soft sand at the side of the road. Several lorries passed and blew their horns but nobody stopped. I even began to pray that a police car would come along. I hoped I was far enough away for the little matter of an unpaid lodging bill not to get in the way of salvation.

Through the heat haze I could see something at the side of the road. A gas station or a store, I hoped. It turned out to be something even better: a heap of tyres. There was a sort of totem pole with wheelhubs nailed up it surrounded by a pile of second-hand tyres. Sprawled on them was a young Indian boy of about thirteen. He was playing it cool. He didn't move when I stopped a couple of yards away from him and climbed out of the car. When I asked if the tyres were for sale he did manage to raise a flagging eyelid, and slowly sat up to cast an expert eye over my deflated wheel.

'Five dollars.' He was obviously too exhausted from sitting up to waste words.

I nodded. It would knock a hole in my paltry reserves but there was no alternative.

The boy picked up the nearest tyre to hand and, without getting up, rolled it towards my car and held out his hand for the money.

I was surprised and getting annoyed. I didn't feel like being jerked about by a lad. 'Aren't you going to fix it?' I snapped at him.

He looked a bit surprised, rose lethargically to his feet and ambled over to the tyre, peering at it as if seeing it for the first time. 'It doesn't fit,' he said, as if I were to blame. At this moment Steffka decided to stand up on the seat and smile down at the boy. The presence of a baby seemed to do something for him for he turned back to his pile, but after a brief hunt for a suitable tyre, he shrugged his shoulders. 'We haven't got one,' he said cheerfully.

The heat was getting to me. I sat on a tyre and fought back tears. This was stupid. Fancy getting all tearful over a bloody tyre, I castigated myself, but the hint of tears worked.

The boy looked along the track that ran at right angles to the road and thought. 'I think I have one back at the yard,' he said. 'Would you like me to get it?'

I nodded wearily.

'Look after the stand,' he commanded, as if there was a queue of people lining up to buy his threadbare wares, and loped off along the lane. I lifted Steffka out of the car and made myself comfortable on the tyres. I was beginning to mull over my options, or lack of them, when a little girl in an oversized blue frock appeared. She stood a little way off and stared. I tried smiling but she wasn't in the market for smiles. I turned Steffi to face her. That didn't make a mark either.

'What is it?' I snarled.

The girl ran off a little, stopped, said I was to follow her, then sprinted away at a great rate.

The 'yard' turned out to be an auto graveyard. Everywhere you looked there was a rusting giant. And at least thirty dogs stretched out in the sun. They flickered an eyelid as I passed but that was the extent of their curiosity. Before the walk I had felt tired, now I was so exhausted I wondered if I was hallucinating, for from all sides it seemed that there were pairs of sun-glasses leering at me.

An elderly Native American with long grey hair stood in front of me and looked me over. 'Hey, you want a tyre?' he said. Why else would I be hauling my aching carcass around in the heat of the day, I felt like snapping, but I kept my thoughts to myself and nodded.

The old man walked away and shouted, 'Woman.' In response, an elderly woman poked her head around the door of the nearest corrugated-iron shack. He jerked his head towards me and walked off.

The woman strolled over, looked at me and waved me to a car seat by the side of the shack. She went towards the door and stopped on the step. 'Ya wanna eat?' she asked.

I nodded, then hesitated. I remembered that half my reserves were needed for the tyre I had to buy. 'I'm afraid I haven't any money,' I mumbled primly. She made a little explosive sound with her lips and went into the shack. I sat there miserably and tried to outstare the sun-glasses that were all turned in my direction. After a few minutes the woman came back and thrust a plate of rabbit and bread at me. I took it gratefully. The little girl in the blue dress followed her grandmother out with a glass of milk and some home-baked biscuits for Steffi. I wanted to cry, it was so unexpected.

The grey-haired man came back. Now that I was eating

his food he felt that introductions were in order. 'I'm Johnny Running Bear,' he said tersely.

'Ingrid.' I wanted to add 'Victorious on horseback', but I thought better of it. I held out my hand, but he wasn't prepared to go that far.

'Give me your keys and I'll bring your car in.'

Hold it! I thought. *Nobody knows I'm here. At least the car on the side of the highway is a sort of bookmark*. Then I thought *Who gives a shit* and gave him the keys.

I stayed in the reservation for nearly six weeks. Once the initial wariness had dissipated we got on like a tepee on fire. They were wholly uncritical and never once asked me how I came to be on the road with ten bucks, two punctured tyres and a toddler. On the other hand they were happy to tell me all their troubles. I had to agree that they had a bad deal from the government but although I never let on, I felt that a lot of their problems could be solved if they lived more in the present. While I was with them, as far as I was aware, they didn't make one sale from the scrapyard. The women, who were supposed to make touristy things like belts and moccasins, never seemed to finish anything and didn't have a market to sell them to if they had done. When I left they gave me various presents, one of which was a belt. I was really touched. Later I found a label on it: Made in Taiwan.

A cousin of Johnny's lived off the reservation and had worked out a better way of making a living. Every week he would turn up with a Volkswagen Combi full of would-be wranglers. Johnny would meet them with some horses at the top of one of the pony trails leading down into the Grand Canyon. I dearly wanted to go with them but I was already living off my hosts so I didn't like to suggest it as I knew they would let me go even if it meant taking one less paying guest. Then one day they had a no show. Johnny was going to leave the horse behind so I decided it was time to let him know that I would love to go with him. He nodded and I was in.

When we reached the top of the trail I had second thoughts. Johnny's woman, who was actually named 'Woman', had fixed me up with a woven basket for Steffanie to ride in, which I wore slung around my shoulders. Looking at the steep path, fears rose at an alarming rate. What if the horse stumbled? What if it was stung by a horse-fly? What if I just fell off? Nobody seemed to be interested in my problems. I cursed myself for having adopted such a tough image, for having pretended I could do everything for myself. Now nobody could see I needed some cosseting.

To my enormous relief, the descent passed without incident and we arrived on the bank of the river near nightfall. There was a well-used barbecue pit, a rough corral for the horses and strategically placed logs to give us the feeling that we were a bunch of tough guys out for a ride and living off the land. Tents were slung up for those who preferred them to a sleeping bag and the canopy of stars. I opted for the stars.

The guide built a fire and started cooking. I wished I could have taken my jeans off and sat there with nothing on. My legs and bits were killing me. I wanted to moan a bit and share my aching bum with the others but they all looked a bit sorry for themselves. I thought of Matka and kept schtum. My back was also sore but the Indians kindly set up a backrest for support and soon the aroma of roasting meat made me feel better.

After supper, the Indians went off to collect more firewood and the other wranglers retired to sleep. I moved close to the fire as it was getting cold now that the sun had gone down, and cuddled Steffanie, my face warm and glowing from the embers. Suddenly the logs shifted and a thousand golden stars spiralled up into the dark sky. In the flames I saw the face of my father. He looked at me, a soft, gentle smile on his face. Tears poured from my eyes. I lifted up my baby and showed her to him. He nodded and winked at me. Then he was gone.

I cried and hugged Steffi, and in my excitement began to hyperventilate. When Johnny came back he could see something had happened. He put his big hand over my nose until I began to breathe more normally. 'You got a problem?' he asked, not unkindly. I wanted to tell him but his cousin was standing by his side so I just shrugged and they both went off. Johnny brought me a tin cup of hot coffee and sat on the log beside me. He didn't say anything but I was bursting to share my experience and blurted out what I had seen. He dropped into his trading-post Indian pose and simply said 'Indian Magic' before going to snuggle down into his blanket. I guess he thought I was a little weird. Maybe I was.

I spent the rest of the night thinking about what my vision meant. It seemed to be telling me that there is life after death, there are folk in the hereafter looking out for us. I took comfort in the belief that Steffanie's grandfather would keep her safe.

In the morning I felt terrible. My buttocks had stiffened up, my back was quite obviously pounded to smithereens in several places and my biological clock told me it was still the middle of the night. Johnny didn't want to know about any of this. He had a schedule to keep. Day one: down the trail. Day two: ride along the Colorado river bank to camp two, spend afternoon swimming, taking photographs and hire a canoe and paddle around in the shallows. Day three: back up the trail. My bum and back just had to lump it. I tried to be a little trooper and not complain but the occasional sigh insisted on looking for sympathy whenever Johnny or one of the guides was close enough to hear. That night I dropped off to sleep as the sun went down and woke up when Steffanie was calling for attention the next morning. It was an early start and by nightfall we were standing at the top of the pony trail waiting for the horse boxes and Combi to arrive. The trip up had been worse than the trip down and I promised myself I would never get on a horse again. When Johnny was giving his customers his honest Indian spiel and touting for dollar bills in his hat I gave him the dead eye. 'Squaw no likum hard saddle?' he asked. I agreed.

It was time to move on. I still didn't have any money but Johnny donated a couple of nearly new tyres and Woman made up a hamper of bread, dried meat and fruit. I hated to leave. My time with them had been very therapeutic. They had no agenda. If things didn't turn out the way they expected they would shrug philosophically and blame it on the great Manitou or the government. I worked out that the great Manitou got the blame if the weather was bad; the government for everything else. Although their problems were not wholly the fault of the government I did feel they received a raw deal and when my life had settled down again I wrote a letter, based on what I'd seen and the stories they'd told me, to Lyndon Johnson. He was obviously horribly embarrassed to be brought to task because he never wrote back.

In the car I studied the map. I had decided to return to Europe. New York airport seemed an awfully long way off. I looked in my purse: $7 and some small change. If I spent $2 on some milk and a big box of cornflakes I would have enough petrol money for about 300 miles. I knew it was useless but I had to do something.

I set my sights on New York and hit the highway. Coasting downhill, accelerating carefully and keeping the speed down got me about a third of the way. I pulled into a gas station, filled her up and then went through the 'I left my purse at home' routine. I left Steffi's push chair as security and promised to be back before the hour was up. Another trusting American citizen I had gibbed. I took a note of the gas station and promised myself that as soon as I sorted things out I would send the money. Sadly I never did.

My tank ran empty again before too long. I was also starving. So far I had held on to my wedding ring. To sell it seemed so final and an act of betrayal. But I had come to the spot where you either give up or you put everything on the line. My mother had always given her all and it had got us through much more dire problems than not having fuel in the tank. Her answer would have been to get a bit of tubing and siphon what she wanted out of an army jeep and hang the consequences. I'd lived in polite society for too long to want to try that, so it was the ring or nothing.

I found one of those shops with a window stashed with forlorn musical instruments and lethal-looking weapons. The ring was a broad band of twenty-four-carat gold. My husband had paid over $70 for it. A fortune. I was offered $10. I argued and the offer was raised to $12.50. Without concluding the deal, I stomped out of the shop and sat on the ground beside the Oldsmobile. What were my options? The only other thing of value I owned was the car. I ran it into a sales forecourt. The salesman looked as if I came with a bad smell attached. I looked at my heap expiring there and could see his point. It didn't sit well among the highly polished cars. I told the man my troubles and wished I'd thought to wash the heap before trying to persuade him what a wonderful bargain it was. He scrutinised it with the sort of look on his face that said that only finding a secret cache of diamonds in the glove compartment could make him interested and said he wasn't in the market for a '59 Oldsmobile at that particular moment. A man of sense. He followed this up, however, with the suggestion that he might be in the mood to change his mind if I returned later – after he had closed up shop. I didn't turn him down on the spot. I didn't know how I might feel about the offer if I couldn't get a better one before nightfall.

By the middle of the afternoon I was left with two alternatives if I didn't want to get old in a suburb of Little Rock. I could either renegotiate my deal with the second-hand car dealer or accept $12.50 for my wedding ring. The coin came down on the side of the wedding ring. I divided up the spoils: $2.50 for immediate food; $5 for petrol and $5 for emergencies. I reckoned it was probably enough to get me to the airport and there I would be on the doorstep of Europe and anything could happen.

I just made it to the airport. For the last hundred miles I concentrated on conserving fuel and refused to answer the question nagging at the back of my mind: what would I do when I reached my destination? When I at last pulled up outside the airport doors I was instantly warned to keep moving. Livid, I begged, promised, lied, showed my baby and grovelled, but to no avail. The official directed me to a car-park.

I refused to waste money on parking so I drove around the back of the airport where there was a row of cabs and drew in behind them. On cue, a uniform came over and told me to move on. Only taxis were allowed to park in that spot, he informed me. Again I began arguing and pleading, until eventually one of the cab drivers came over, listened and finally suggested that I should be allowed to stay there while I got myself together.

The cabbie introduced himself as Emile, a refugee from Algiers, and squatted down beside the car to play with Steffanie. At last I felt I had found a friend. I blurted out all my trials and tribulations, how desperately I needed to get back to Europe where my brother was dying . . . If I didn't get back all his money would go to his girl-friend . . . and such rubbish. Seemingly unmoved, he continued playing with Steffi, but when I eventually ran out of steam he came up with a simple suggestion: 'Sell your car.' He got up and walked around it. 'Clean it up and you might get a couple of hundred for it.'

I nodded.

He went across to his cab and took some rags and a bucket from the boot. He filled the bucket at a standpipe, came back, threw a cloth to me and started sloshing water down the car. I was glad of the action. It made me feel I was getting somewhere. A couple of other drivers came across and helped with the shine while Steffanie had a wonderful time stamping in the puddles.

I must admit that the old jalopy didn't look too bad cleaned up. But what now? Emile parked the car by the side of the cabbies' rest room and got one of the other drivers to take me up to the terminals. I felt like a devotee of Hari Krishna hanging around the concourse and approaching incoming passengers. I expected to be arrested at any moment but I guess the presence of a toddler at my side kept the cops from being heavy. I had more or less given up on finding a tourist wanting to buy my car when a big blond German, his blonde Frau and four blond children hove into sight. They were my meat! I gave them my best German and a tale of my plight that could have won me an Oscar. They were obviously a bit worried that I was pulling a scam. I explained that even as we spoke the car was in the official care of the airport authorities who had given me permission to sell on the concourse. I took them out, stuck them in a taxi, took them to Emile and let him explain what a wonderful bargain they were getting. He got me $250, enough to get me where I wanted to be. We tucked the family aboard and waved them off.

Quickly I shoved Steffka and the few paltry belongings I had been able to hang on to into the back of Emile's cab and he took us back to the terminal. I threw my arms around him, grabbed Steffanie and hightailed it to the information desk. I wanted to get away before the Germans changed their mind and came back.

The only plane out in the next hour was going to Madrid. Well, it was Europe. I could always walk from there if I had to . . .

I plonked my money on the counter.

'Madrid – one way.'

Sixteen

I sat there crying, feeling a bit of a fool. All around me people were screaming and shouting. Off to the right a band was playing enthusiastically and there seemed to be only me and the poor bull in the middle of the arena who weren't having a good time. I assured myself that this was all necessary as part of the indoctrination programme I had set myself. I was in Spain so the thing to do was to blend in and, as I could see, Spaniards were potty about bullfighting. At the least it was certainly better than sitting in the flat in Calle Dr Fleming, a flat that I couldn't afford, and fretting.

When my flight had landed at Madrid airport I'd been down to my last $10 again. I didn't speak a word of Spanish so the taxi driver had taken me to Calle Dr Fleming, where most English and American expats congregated. I'd taken a short rent on a one-bedroom apartment and had been delighted when my next-door neighbour, a photographer called Caesar Lucas, had introduced himself by coming over with a bottle of wine and two glasses. His English was good, so I was able to mine him for information, such as what work was available. At this time Almeria was just about the busiest film location in the world. I told him about my vast theatrical experience and he promised to introduce me to several actors staying in the apartment block.

The next time Caesar came round he invited me to the bullfight in the Plaza Monumental, where he was going to take photographs. He was as good as his word and from my first-class seat I had a close-up view of a dumb animal being sliced up alive, then bleeding to death when the matador pierced its lung instead of severing its spinal column. As I sat there bawling my eyes out my new-found photographer friend was busy snapping away.

The Spanish love a *dolorosa* and the next day my photograph appeared on the front page of Spain's leading national newspaper, *El Pueblo,* where it was spotted by Ana Mariscal, one of the top directors in Spain at that time.

Mariscal called the newspaper and asked if they knew where she could find me. They did. I was invited to lunch and asked to do a screen test for her film *Los Duendes de Andalucia*, which was starting almost immediately. Not wanting to look good fortune in the face, I hardly dared to point out a rather glaring problem: I couldn't speak Spanish.

'I don't care,' said Ana Mariscal. 'I want you for my picture. You're perfect for the role of the boozy nympho-maniac American, who has a passion for bullfighters! We'll dub it. As for the screentest, Fellini just gets his actors to count – one, two, three, etc. – instead of speaking proper lines. If it's good enough for Federico Fellini, it's good enough for Ana Mariscal. Learn the language as you go along.'

That was it. Steffka and I went to Seville and I began my first movie. I learned the lines phonetically, which was quite ridiculous. My pay was equally ridiculous, especially after all I'd read and heard about film stars and their fees. All we could afford was one room in a hotel for Steffka, me and the nanny I'd been forced to employ to look after her while I was working. Steffi was a bit of a restless sleeper at this time and kept falling out of bed. No matter how I strapped her in, I'd hear a mighty bump in the middle of the night. I obtained a bed with sides from the hotel but still she managed to fall out. Meanwhile I'd sit in the bathroom half the night trying to learn my lines.

In the morning I would arrive on set with my speeches firmly embedded in my brain, only to discover that, for Ana, the script was merely a starting point and my lines had been changed. I thought that was extremely unfriendly of her. Some of the other actors tried to help me, mouthing my lines so that I could get through them. Everyone thought it was hilarious.

I realised it would be easier if I could speak Spanish fluently, so I befriended Maximo, one of the best-looking English-speaking extras and a law student, and asked him to be my teacher. Learning Spanish soon became my passion. I had to be able to converse, to have a say in what was going on. Maximo and I took every opportunity to practise. He was unbelievably sweet and helpful, day and night, but at that point not interested in me as a woman, I think, which made it all the more hilarious when the Guardia Civil arrested us for indecency in a public place. We were sheltering in a doorway, practising my next speech and the Guardia thought we were having naughties. They let us off with a fine but we were more careful in the future where we practised our Spanish. Maximo was an excellent teacher and I picked up Spanish so fast Ana was quite baffled.

Los Duendes de Andalucia was about bullfighting and was shot entirely on location in Andalucia. We started filming at the Bodegas Domeque where the sherry comes from. The leading man was one of the top toreros in Spain,

Victoriano Valencia. He was a cheeky sod but he was also a fabulous matador, which means that he killed well, without agony for the poor bull. Before the film actually began shooting, we were invited to a tientadero, a small bullfight in a village, where Victoriano dedicated the life of the bull to me. Not yet initiated in the art of the sport, I did not appreciate the honour he had done me and I think I offended him by not applauding with vigour. Later, at dinner, I was having one of my rebellious moods and instead of chatting to the great matador as he wanted me to, I made a fuss of one of his sidekicks. I was beginning to distrust Spanish men and their attitude to women. However, I did learn enough about *torear* during the film to appreciate the fantastic courage, art and sport in bullfighting.

Filming in Spain at this time was pretty much a free for all. There was no proper union and hours of work were what you worked. There was a great camaraderie among the actors, although this was not extended to the crew. They were regarded as the bailiffs' men and best kept on the outside looking in.

There was a lot of night shooting on *Los Duendes de Andalucia.* At times I used to be quite desperate to get back to the hotel to see my baby wake up. I would drag in as the sun was rising, give Steffi lots of cuddles and tell her how much I missed her, have a romp and then I'd have to go to bed. Maria, the nanny, would take Steffanie out into the Andalusian sunshine to play so that I wouldn't be disturbed. Maria was from Santander in the north of Spain and, when she'd applied for the job as Steffanie's nanny, I'd been shocked by her resemblance to Fräulein Gloge, the woman who had looked after the children in the *Kinderschuppen*. Maria had a similar hump, the same gentle nature and I knew that I could trust her with my child. She was quite strict. She would make me go to sleep after a short interval of playing with my *dotschka,* saying that there would be plenty of time for messing around when the film was finished and I would be out of a job.

The filming meandered all through the winter. The Spaniards find it a great surprise every year when winter comes. They are a little like the Brits in that respect. Every year it snows in England there's chaos. The Spanish are equally surprised that it gets cold in winter. I hate the cold. I started wondering if that film would ever wrap. We went to Córdoba, Huelva, Granada and the Hotel Don Pepe in Marbella.

It was rumoured that the ex-President of Argentina, Juan Domingo Perón, had put up the money to build the Don Pepe and while we were filming there he came to see how things were going. That evening he invited the cast to dinner. His arrival was the best-staged production the hotel had seen since the filming started. He was dressed in a white suit with a red carnation and was smoking a cigarette in a holder. His hair was dyed jet black and was at odds with his elderly face.

Perón talked to the men first, putting them at ease, then moved in on us poor females. Rapport with Perón was instant and was surely what had kept him in power for so long. He did the Latino's thing over my knuckles and gazed, enraptured, into my eyes. Formalities over, he called for champagne. I thought he was wonderful. He flirted outrageously but without getting heavy. I kept as close to him as I could without actually getting into his jacket and he seemed to be amused by this.

We spoke at first in Spanish but my vocabulary was rather limited so we attempted English, but as his English was little better than my Spanish we resorted, much to my annoyance, to communicating in German. Perón was charming. I felt that anything I said to him mattered, that

I was important. I tried to get a conversation going about the revolution in Argentina that had got him kicked out of the country, which was certainly not the most sensitive topic I could have chosen, but he took it all in his stride and skilfully led me on to other, safer, topics. Around ten o'clock Perón said goodbye to everyone individually and invited us to call on him at his residence in Puerta de Hierro whenever we were in Madrid.

The film wound down slowly. I looked forward desperately to having more time with Steffka. When it was finally a wrap I picked up Steffanie and Maria and caught a sleeper to Madrid. In the train station we had our breakfast and discussed our next move. The cameraman on *Los Duendes* was going straight on to a new film and had told me to ring the production company, Zurbano Films, at once. It was decided that no time should be wasted. I would go and knock down the doors at Zurbano Films while Maria took Steffanie and looked for somewhere to live. We would meet later, with good news, we hoped, at the Café Guijon, a place famous for catering to film stars, which I now felt entitled to frequent.

When we met a few hours later, Maria had done her bit and found us a flat which would be available the next day. My tale wasn't quite so positive. I had got through the main gate of Zurbano Films but hadn't been able to see the man who counted. I would have to return the following day.

In the morning, with Steffka on my hip, I sauntered into the director Nieves Conde's office and gave him the full treatment. I think he was so stunned by my entrance with child that he developed a speech impediment. I launched into my spiel at once while he was still off-balance and it worked. He gave me the job on the spot. I was delighted to have my film actress status so quickly confirmed.

Steffka and I danced down the Grand Via to tell Maria the great news.

I was anxious to see the flat Maria had rented. Typically of her, she had taken one of the most expensive apartments in town. She always liked the best things in life. It was one of the larger flats in our old block on Dr Fleming and had two bedrooms and a balcony, which I adored. The rooms were furnished just to my taste, with panelled wood, carved Spanish wooden furniture and Persian rugs. It was gorgeous. We booked out of the hotel where we had stayed overnight and took a cab to our new domicile.

As we drew up to the building the actress daughter of Charlie Chaplin, Geraldine, walked out of the lobby. We had met only a fortnight earlier in the Don Pepe. She had also been making a film in Marbella and we'd become friendly in the week we'd shared the hotel. It was fantastic to find that we would be living in the same building. A lot of American actors and directors lived there, including Jeffrey Hunter, who in due course 'adopted' Steffanie, Bob Fuller, Stephen Boyd, Burt Reynolds and Marc Lawrence. The building had a restaurant, a concierge, a switchboard, maid service and a pool on the roof. I told Steffka that we would be happy here no matter what and that I'd work my socks off to pay the rent.

A week later we were on our way to the Sierra Nevada. The film was called *El Sonido Prehistorico*. Everyone who was anyone in Spanish theatre or film – plus me – was in that movie. There was Jose Bodalo, Lola Gaos, Arturo Fernandez, Soledad Miranda, Antonio Casares and, for the American market, James Philbrook. I can't remember much about the film or the other players, but it was great fun, especially learning to do Zorba's dance. Nieves Conde, the director, was not very inventive or demanding, but he did come up with a new, and cheap, line in monsters. We had an invisible dinosaur! On top of the terrible haircut I was given, I think I was quite bad in the film, didn't have a single good line to say and what I did say came out all prissy and naff. Of course, Lola Gaos stole the show. She had the best part and also did the best job.

While we waited for our scenes Lola and I cooked up all sorts of plots. We schemed that she would bring me into the Teatro Nacional de España, and I would translate *Mother Courage* so she could take it to the hierarchy of the company and get it put on with her as the lead.

Back in Madrid I still seemed to be on a roll. The Sam Bronston Studios were about to make a film called *A Funny Thing Happened on the Way to the Forum* with Phil Silvers and Zero Mostel. Richard Lester was directing. I had a friend who had already been cast and put in a word for me. I couldn't believe my luck. However, when I turned up for the audition, expecting the red-carpet treatment, I found myself in a cattle call with about a hundred other hopefuls. This wasn't for me. Wasn't I a star? Hadn't I just done two films back to back?

With the help of my accent, which made me stand out, I wangled a part in *A Funny Thing . . .* Though small, it was worth it for the great time I had on set with the two stars. They were both fantastic to me and we shared many jokes, but my horsing around didn't help when it came to the final edit and most of my scenes ended up on the cutting-room floor.

Seventeen

It seemed to me that my future might well be in Spain, where apparently I could walk from role to role. To perfect my language skills I insisted that everybody spoke to me in Spanish. I listened only to Spanish radio and read Spanish newspapers, books and magazines. It put Maria's nose out of joint a little as she wanted to practise her English, but I was the breadwinner paying her wages so I put my foot down and before long I was chirruping away like a native.

With the help of Maximo and Maria I undertook the translation of *Mother Courage*. I didn't hold out much hope that Lola Gaos would be able to persuade the Teatro Nacional to put it on and was decidedly gobsmacked when I was asked to pay the resident director a visit. In Franco's Spain the egalitarian message of the play could have spelled real trouble, so he was taking a bit of a chance. I hoped I might be given a speaking part but news of my near performance as the mute Kattrin in the Ensemble must have leaked through and they wanted me to reprise the role. Or it could have been that my Spanish wasn't as good as I thought and a silent part suited me best. Whatever, in the end I was happy to be appearing in Spain's National Theatre.

My work in the theatre, though furnishing a regular income, could not support the three of us, so I started moonlighting. *Dr Zhivago* was being filmed nearby so I breezed into the production offices and offered my services. I was given several parts, which staved off poverty for the run of the play, but nothing that was going to lead to a glittering career. On set I met some incredible actors such as Rod Steiger, who was wonderful to me, Tom Courtney, who had one of the best parts in the film, and Omar Sharif, who thought he wasn't good enough in his role, and worried that he didn't look like a Russian doctor. Julie Christie was not allowed make-up and made up for it by eternally putting on more mascara. The most exciting part for me was watching David Lean at work. Since I didn't have a single demanding line, I had ample time to observe the great director and I was repeatedly impressed by the calmness with which he handled the daily dramas. He treated everything and everyone with great restraint, never got riled or lost his cool. The greatest outburst of temper I witnessed was when he raised his voice just a little and said, 'Please, gentlemen, can we just keep it down a little?' I understand he lost his rag completely in an incident with Judy Davis on *A Passage to India*, but that's another story.

I loved working on *Zhivago* for every day brought something new. The most memorable of my five roles was when as a gypsy I danced around the pot-belly stove on the train. The rest were the sort of parts where you sit in the cinema and say 'That's me' but before you can get it out the image has long gone. It was paying the rent, though, and for that I was grateful.

Dr Zhivago wrapped in Madrid at the same time as *Mother Courage*'s run came to an end. I wasn't really worried. To cover our rent I picked up jobs from the big film companies, parts which might have been called glorified 'extras' by the uncharitable but I didn't see it that way. When the lack of cash was most severe, I worked as a stunt-rider in Almeria. Even though I hadn't learned to ride I galloped like Zorro, pulled the reins to the left as I was told and was thrown to the ground, my head an inch from a rock. A couple of times I worked with Charles Bronson before he was a star. Charlie and I would sit under a solitary tree in the middle of nowhere and eat our sandwiches. He'd mumble that he'd never get anywhere in the movies with a face like his and I would tell him that with a face like his he'd become a star.

Although there was plenty of work, I began to realise that, in a world dominated by the English and by Hollywood, Spanish films would not get me far. I resolved to pay less attention to my Spanish contacts and to focus on the American studios. With this in mind, when I heard Orson Welles was making *Chimes at Midnight* in Spain, I was determined to be in it. I had long been an admirer of Welles. He seemed to typify everything that was great in the film world.

Setting up a role in the film proved difficult, but I wouldn't let it rest. I met one of the minor players, a man I had been quite friendly with on *Los Duendes*, and though he couldn't put in a word for me he did offer to introduce me to Mr Welles.

He invited me to dinner at the hotel where all the cast and Orson were staying. Mr Welles appeared with his coterie of yes-men and commandeered two tables not too far away from where I sat. I nudged my companion. Now was the time for the introduction. We could get up and casually pass Mr Welles's table on the way out and he could say, 'Ah, Orson, I'd like you to meet . . .' I would do the rest. But my companion insisted the timing would be better after we'd eaten. I couldn't think of food at a time like this so I focused on Mr Welles, giving him the full treatment: flashing eyes, a glimpse of leg, cleavage and any other part of my anatomy which might interest him and get me invited to his table. Welles talked, smoked and drank non-stop, and took no notice of me squirming around like an epileptic octopus with tentacles hooked up to the national grid. At last even I realised that I wasn't getting anywhere. It was going to have to be the full frontal assault. I stood, shook everything into place and did a Rita Hayworth across the floor.

I was practically shoving my belly-button on to the end of his cigar before he noticed me. And then he wasn't particularly inviting. 'Yes?' he said tersely.

I painted on a smile and dropped my voice an octave. 'Hi, I'm Ingrid Pitt.'

'Good for you!' he said and went on talking.

Mortified, I quickly considered my options. If I slunk away everybody in the restaurant would know it, especially the creep who had brought me. It would also bring on a hot flush for years to come. On the other hand if I stayed and Mr Welles persisted in rejecting me even the sous-chef would know about it. I thought of Matka. She always played for the positive and said sod the humiliation.

'I'm an actress. I'd like a part in your film. I've always admired you . . .' It was all coming out wrong. I was gushing.

Welles stopped talking, looked ahead for a couple of seconds, then turned slowly towards me. He looked me up and down with an expression that told me he wasn't very impressed. 'If you are a professional actress you should know that there are certain channels. I do not give auditions when I am having dinner. I suggest you give your résumé to the casting director.' He nodded dismissal and turned back to his companions. Smiling brightly, I acted as if he had been charming and gracious, and went back to my table.

The next morning I went to the casting office as soon as it opened. I told the secretary that Mr Welles had told me to see the casting director. The use of the hallowed name got me through the door, where I repeated my story. The director wasn't as easy a pushover as the secretary. He excused himself and went out of the room, where he probably phoned Mr Welles because when he came back his attitude had changed. All the main roles were cast, he told me, but there was a walk-on as a hooker. The fabled Welles sense of humour I guessed. My immediate reaction was to tell him where to stick it but I double-guessed my mouth and kept it shut. After all, it was Orson Welles and it was an American production company. Marilyn Monroe had started with nothing more than a minor role and look at her, I told myself. I said I'd take it. He looked a little startled. After all the bullshit I had been giving him about my wonderful career, he'd expected me to flounce out. And I should have.

Orson might have been my idol, but I soon faced the fact that he had feet of clay. I couldn't do anything right for [illegible] called that, was nothing, yet he was determined to humi[illegible]e me. He swilled back at least two bottles of brandy a day, was never seen without a massive cigar in his mouth and, not surprisingly, stank. He was also unbelievably crass. When, a glutton for punishment, I told him again that I had always admired his work and dreamed of working with him, he opened his flies and invited me to put my hand inside. The end came when the second assistant told me that Mr Welles wanted to see me in his hotel room. Full of reservations, I knocked on the door and he called, 'Enter!' I looked around but there was nobody in the room. Then the door to the bathroom opened and Welles came out in his underpants. Without so much as a salutation he grabbed me and manoeuvred us towards the bed. I fought back but Welles only laughed. Finding some strength in the fury that flooded my veins, I heaved at him and he tripped and fell on to the bed. As I rushed to the door, he shouted out that if it weren't for bloody women men could still play happily in their caves . . . ! I didn't hang around for my severance cheque.

When I told Lola about my escapade she screeched with laughter at the thought of skinny little me being suffocated under the whale-like form of Welles. After she calmed down she said she was surprised that I had taken it so badly. Hadn't anyone ever tried the bedroom ploy on me before? I had to admit it was not the first time I had had a man face me in the altogether but what had hurt was that this was a man I had admired hugely and had never expected to be so coarse. The pomposity of that statement was enough to have Lola in stitches again.

Eighteen

When I got back to Madrid I was astonished to find my husband waiting for me in the flat. It was two years since I'd seen him. His stint in Vietnam had come to an end and he was visiting us before returning to Asia for a second tour of duty. I was devastated by this statement. Steffka sat on his lap and played with his medals while I became terribly morose. After my run-in with Mr Welles, my husband seemed so safe, so normal. Perhaps I was wrong to drag my baby around and deprive her of a proper home. But what kind of life could my soldier offer us? To volunteer to fight in Vietnam not once, but twice . . .

I begged him not to go back and tempt fate, but he just smiled his slow smile. 'I don't belong in your movie life,' he said.

I've not got much of a movie life here, chum, I thought, but I'd just told him how fabulously I was doing and dared not change my story and sob on his shoulder.

He asked me if I could stop and go back to the States to play army housewife. I knew the answer to that, as I did to all the questions we would argue over that evening. I was sure that Steffka would grow up without him.

We were a funny bunch in the bed that night, him

holding me and me holding Steffi, and no one got much sleep. He told me stories about Vietnam and I gave him my six pennyworth about the war being a crime motivated by big business. He left the next morning. I was unbelievably sad. He'd given me the most wonderful gift of my life – my little girl – and I'd taken her away from him. I kept wondering if I wasn't incredibly selfish and bloody stupid.

Troubled by these considerations, I took Steffanie to Retiro Park, where we played in the sand, fed swans and, in the afternoon, went to a circus that had just arrived in town. Steffka thought she'd had a wonderful day but I was depressed. I couldn't forget the brief visit of my husband who'd become a stranger. Our daughter never even asked where he'd gone or whether he'd come back.

In the evening I didn't feel like cooking so we went downstairs to the restaurant and had dinner. Most of the actors who lived in 42 Dr Fleming were there. There was a lot of work about in Spain at that time, and they all were in a very positive frame of mind and soon cheered me up. By the time we went up to our apartment I had relaxed and was feeling better.

Lying on the coffee table were the divorce papers my husband had brought for me to sign. It was all so final. I put Steffka to bed, then sat in a chair half the night thinking. When the sun came up I was able to accept the consequences of the decision I had already made on the night of his visit. I spent another day in the park with Steffanie but this time my mood was defiantly happy.

I'd heard about a forthcoming film called *El Beso en el Puerto* (*A Kiss in the Harbour*), so went to see my agent and, not trusting him to do his job competently, sat in his office prompting him while he sold my various attributes to Ramon Torrado, the director, and Arturo Gonzalez, the producer. Together we persuaded them that I was the ideal female lead to play opposite Manolo Escobar, one of the biggest pop stars in Spain at the time.

We had enormous fun shooting in Benidorm and the film was a great success. It played next to Richard Burton's *Beckett* in the Grand Via of Madrid for three years. The music was also fabulous. For years afterwards if I went into a restaurant the band would strike up the signature tune, 'El Porompompero.'

Manolo introduced me to a producer from the main Spanish television station. He was putting on a variety/chat show and was looking for a presenter. I convinced him that I would be perfect. The show was called *Aqui España* and although the format wasn't too original it worked. On each show, I would present a piece about what was going on in Spain and in the entertainment industry, introduce a guest, usually a singer or a visual entertainer – no writers – and then sit back while the guest entertained the audience. It was a sort of Des O'Connor with a few *olé*'s thrown in. One of the guests was Julio Iglesias. I thought he was terrific. At dinner after the show I asked him what his plans were. He didn't seem too sure and thought he might have a future as a footballer. I told him it would kill the velvet in his voice and he fell about laughing. With my usual reticence I told him he was daft. 'You should learn to sing in English, go to America and conquer the world,' I said, and recounted how I had taken on my first Spanish film with a vocabulary of '*sí*' and '*no*'. I must have inspired him because he went to England and spent two years singing in a pub in Kent learning English. And just look at him now.

Fernando Rey was another guest who got my lip about learning English. Less than a year later he played second lead in *The French Connection* opposite Gene Hackman. I like to think it had something to do with me.

*

Although I talked about taking on Hollywood, I saw my future in Spain. My blondeness and intriguing accent, and the fact that I could now play in Spanish, English, German, Russian, Italian and French, was a great help. My resolution was only slightly shaken when a fey bullfighter read my hand and told me I would soon leave Spain and find success in England. He warned me to be extremely careful because someone who would claim to be my friend would cause me a great deal of harm. It was a ball-park prognostication but, within its limitations, it turned out to be pretty accurate.

Rumours had been floating around for some time that the Spanish were going to form an actors' union. Nobody had taken the threat seriously. In Almeria the Americans were doing one film after another, sometimes two at a time. The locals were making fortunes. Anyway, I reasoned, what with my TV show and the work I was still getting in the theatre, I would be above any nastiness – such as slinging out foreigners – that a union might try.

At this time I seemed to be able to do just about anything I wanted. I'd now bought a big American Dodge and hung around with a torero who, a touch flamboyantly, called himself 'El Zorro de Toledo'. Tino Sanchez was handsome and stimulating, and believed utterly in the big future all the *cognoscenti* predicted for him. He was the spitting image of Yuri and it wasn't long before I found myself ferrying him and his *quadriga* (team) around. He called my Dodge his *coche de quadriga* and I found it all madly exciting.

At a bullfight in Ondara, near Valencia, El Zorro, assuring me I'd be in no danger, insisted I went into the arena. Unfortunately, the horse I was riding had been struck by a bull on his previous outing and was extremely nervous. I tried to preserve a little decorum and not throw my arms round its neck for stability. Things only got worse when the bull came into the arena. My mount began to jig about, which only served to attract the attention of the bull. As it started to come our way, the animal took off with me hanging on grimly, trying to smile and praying that someone would rescue me. To my relief the *banderilleros*, as is their job in a bullfight, distracted the bull and allowed my horse to make for the gate. In the forecourt the terrified beast stopped so abruptly that I finished up hanging round its neck and practising my newly acquired vocabulary of Castillian swear-words. The poor horse stood shaking and sweating, and I knew exactly how it felt. After that I didn't mind wearing the *traje campera* and prancing about in front of the crowd but no one ever got me on the back of a horse again.

Spain was changing. Even I noticed it. The work at Almeria was drying up and non-Spaniards were getting the cold shoulder when they turned up for local films. I persevered, imitating an ostrich, until I received a letter from the newly formed Spanish Equity union saying that my work permit had been revoked, though I would be allowed to fulfil any contract I currently had in place. My *Aqui España* contract was on its final month and the one with the Teatro Nacional hadn't been renewed so I knew it was the end.

I didn't want to alarm Matka with my woes, but when I rang she caught my vibes instantly. She thought it was a love affair gone wrong and I didn't disillusion her. In a way she was correct: my love affair with Spain was over. Once more I wondered whether I was doing the best for Steffanie and reviewed the options open to me. First there was my husband. In spite of coming to Madrid to give me the divorce papers he had made it clear that if I could just accept that he was a soldier and had to do soldierly things we could be reunited when he got back from the war. Now that he had become a major there would be more money, better housing, a chance to give Steffka the sort of education she deserved. I had turned him down but it wasn't too late. If I wrote and told him I was coming back at the end of his second tour in Vietnam, was happy to give up my dreams and make a new home for us, I knew he would do his best to forget the last three years.

Then there was my mother. After all the things she had done for me why couldn't I make her happy for a few years? Go home, take a secretarial job, spend the evenings playing with Steffanie, looking after Matka? It would all be so easy. Except that I never wanted to live in Germany again and wouldn't do it for anything in the world. I hadn't the courage or fortitude to walk away from the grasshopper life I had made for myself and do something as unselfish as dedicating myself to the two people I loved most in the world. I snuggled in bed beside Steffi and decided that I would make a decision in the morning.

For the next day or two I dragged Steffka around Madrid. I think I was hoping someone would offer me a job that wouldn't upset the union pundits. I knew it was a vain dream. When, on the second night, I returned home to find an ornate envelope in my mailbox, I tore it open and read: 'His Excellency, President Juan Domingo Perón, invites you to dinner at Puerta de Hierro.' On the back in biro was scribbled, 'Sorry about the short notice and formality. Blame it on my secretary.'

I looked at the date. The party was the following evening. I badly wanted to go to dinner with Perón. For one thing he had been such good fun in the Don Pepe and for another I was sure there would be plenty of high-rollers there who might be able to reveal a way out of my short-term difficulties.

Perón's residence, Puerta de Hierro, was not at all what

I had expected. It was quite small and other than one tiny photograph of Evita, in a niche with a candle burning before it like an icon, there was no evidence of her. I met Isabel, Perón's new wife, who was mousy but kind and gentle, and we talked about this and that but had no real point of contact. She had been a folkloric dancer before she met Perón and seemed nice and uncomplicated, and obviously totally adored her husband. Lopez Rega, Perón's *eminence grise*, was there, silent and threatening in the background. A few Spanish dignitaries were present with their wives and two Argentinians, who apparently had been in Perón's government. One, Luis Sojit, was to survive through to Perón's next administration and be very helpful when I went to live in Argentina later. The meal was *asado* – barbecued meat – cooked, in the tradition of the great outdoors, by our host who was splendidly apparelled in *bombachas* (gaucho trousers), check shirt, with a wide silver-adorned *rastra* (belt) around his waist. I tried to make some contacts but it soon became obvious that the Spaniards were there out of duty and the others were more interested in buddying up to the ex-President than opening some magical door for a down-and-out actress. By the end of the evening I was beginning to wish I hadn't bothered to come.

When everyone started making moves, I was at the front of the queue but before I could get out of the door Isabel asked if I would come back the following week. She was a film buff and wanted to talk movies with me. This was more like it. After all, Perón was credited with flying the *coup* with countless millions and was currently the owner of some very expensive property on the coast. Perhaps I could interest him in backing a few projects I had salted away. He might also be able to sort out my problems with the unions. I said I would love to see her again.

As good as her word, Isabel rang. This time there were

only Luis Sojit, Isabel and Perón at the dinner-table. Isabel prattled on about films and I told her some stories about actors and directors, most of which I'd picked up from fanzines and the actors passing through Dr Fleming. But when they waved me farewell I was no further forward than the day I first went there.

The following morning I had another leap of faith when Isabel phoned to ask if I could meet her at Horcher's for blinis and caviar. A car came to pick me up and I walked through the door of my favourite Madrid restaurant bang on the hour. Isabel was already there – without Perón. Good, I thought, girl-to-girl. This time I was determined to be more direct but before we could get beyond opening pleasantries, we were joined by some friends of Isabel. It soon became obvious that I was in the middle of some sort of monthly hen party. Everybody was talking clothes, food, husbands and wallets. 'Wait for it,' I told myself. 'They'll all go in a minute and there'll be just me and Señora de Perón.' But Isabel was the first to go, taking me completely by surprise or I would have finagled my departure at the same time.

I returned to Dr Fleming completely demoralised and preoccupied with the question of how I was going to pay another month's rent, so when the telephone rang and I was told 20th Century-Fox was on the line I was certain it was a wind-up. Before I could tell the joker to get lost and slam down the telephone, he mentioned an American writer-friend of mine, Mike Stern. Mike had insisted on taking some of my photographs with him when he returned to the States and now Fox wanted me to do a screen test.

Nineteen

A stretch limo picked me up from LAX and whisked me to the fabled Beverly Hills Hotel. There was a bit of a kerfuffle at the reception desk. Evidently the room had been booked in my writer-friend's name but that didn't seem a problem. Blithely I followed the bellhop out to one of the little cluster of bungalows. The room was splendid, all I had imagined it to be. I was a little surprised that so far my benefactor hadn't arrived to welcome me, but this was LA: everyone was busy-busy-busy! I spent some time looking at everything, found a little bar, helped myself to a small bottle of champagne and went out on the patio to enjoy the scenery, luxuriate in the tiny bubbles bursting against my nose, the warm sun dappling down between the heavy shards of the palms and the undeniable fact that I had made it to the City of Angels, the city of dreams.

Having rested, I decided it was time to get my act together, to unpack and let the studio know that I had arrived. I opened the huge, sliding-door wardrobe in the walk-in dressing-room and, to my confusion, was confronted with a row of suits. I checked the drawers: shirts, socks, the usual men's gear. I guessed my American writer-friend was looking for a pay-off for his charitable act but when I rang reception they explained that the room, although booked by Mr Stern, was in the name of someone I did not recognise. I was his guest. This was turning nasty. It looked as if I was the victim of a pimping raid on foreign shores. I slumped on the bed, my hopes in ruins. How could I have been so daft? I castigated myself. Like a dumb cow I'd shut my mind to the possibility that I was being imported for anything other than my talent. Why hadn't I insisted on getting an official letter from the studio?

I rang Fox. No, there was no screen test scheduled in my name. Yes, the man was one of the money men behind the company. No, I couldn't have his address. I pushed. The woman said that he was at Beechcraft in Santa Monica buying an aeroplane. He was due back that evening. She was curious and asked me why I wanted to get in touch with him. I had the impression that she had guessed pretty accurately our relationship. I hung up, rang for the bellboy and demanded another room. How I was going to pay for it didn't enter my head.

My new room wasn't a patch on my old one but in the Beverly Hills Hotel they're all not to be sniffed at. I lay on the bed and wondered furiously how I could make this terrible situation work for me. The telephone rang. It was my blind date. I recognised that nothing would come from meeting him with steam hissing out of every orifice so I cooled my temper and agreed to meet on neutral ground in the Polo Lounge.

My date was straight out of the make-up cave for ageing Don Juans: face-lift, stomach belt, Persil-white teeth, slicked-back rug and a suntan that had little to do with anything in the solar system. Just to make sure that he had covered all the points of bad taste he was wearing the sort of outfit that would have looked too young on a twenty-year-old. He flashed his bleached dentures and told me that there had been some terrible mistake. Unfortunately the screen test had been cancelled due to factors beyond his control but he was sure that if we could be friends he could talk to any one of a number of highly placed tycoons who would love to help me out. Understanding only too well what his idea of friendship would involve, I told him sweetly that he would have to pick up the tab for my room and food until I was able to sort out something else and that if he saw Mike he should tell him that if he ever crossed my path again he would be singing soprano before nightfall. Slightly amused, but more bored with the whole business, he agreed to my demands, got up and walked off without another word. I went back to my room and hoped he wouldn't renege on the deal later.

The next morning I was sitting by the pool when a telephone call came through for me. The waiter plugged in the instrument. I thought it might be Maria who had taken Steffanie to Santander to give her a little holiday while I was away but it was Mike Stern. He apologised profusely and, before I could slam the phone down, asked if I needed some bar work. It took Mike a while to calm me down. He swore that he would get me something more worthy of my talent as soon as possible. Meanwhile, waitressing was the time-honoured way of getting started in Hollywood. Two days later I was cooking.

I hadn't travelled 10,000 miles to work in a restaurant but the rest of the staff were nice, all with dreams of making it big in LA-LA Land, CV and scripts always at hand just in case a producer or director walked in. I was soon fed up with cooking spaghetti and offered to make plum cake. It was my father's favourite and before long became the favourite of the customers. Later I added Polish cheesecake which got me a lot of accolades but no nearer to my goal.

The Spaghetti House did at least throb with the fat and famous. None of them so much as did a double-take when this fabulous blonde primped and gushed and served her plum cake, until one day Willy Wilder, Billy Wilder's brother, walked in. Willy loved my plum cake and soon started to stop by to chat with me in German. One day he invited me out to lunch and began to tell me about a film called *The Omegans* that he was going to shoot in the Philippines in only a month's time. Would I like to play the lead? he asked. I sat there and looked at him. A film shooting in four weeks, with no leading lady? It was not credible. The only explanation was that Willy was just like all the others. I burst into tears. Willy sensitively guessed at the reason for my outburst and hastily assured me that the offer was kosher. I was just what he wanted for the lead.

Willy's wonderful offer meant that I could go home at once and be with Steffka again. He gave me an advance on my pay to cover expenses and soon after I got back to Madrid the script arrived with a return ricket to Manila. I had, stupidly, put myself in a vulnerable position but, through determination and amazing good fortune, I'd won the day.

Twenty

The rain was so intense that I couldn't see my hand six inches away from my face. I was staying on a houseboat with nothing for company but creepy crawlies and the fear of headhunters, who I'd been told lived in the nearby mountains. I'd quickly asked for some bodyguards for my houseboat and kicked myself for insisting on special quarters when I could have stayed with the rest of the cast and crew in tents.

The only American actor on the film was Keith Larsen, husband of Vera Miles. Willy's wife was there and the crew, camera and sound were American but the rest were local luminaries.

We'd spent a couple of weeks in Manila, where I'd been able to ring Steffanie and have long chats. I had trained her well to cope with our separations. She knew I had to provide for us and she was always glad when I landed a job but she made certain I knew that she missed me. I would give her things to accomplish while I was away and, sure enough, the minute I returned, out came the books or drawings, depicting her mother in the funniest shapes and forms, doing what she went away to do.

Film-making is hard work and you don't want to be

preoccupied with small details and worries. On every film I've worked on someone has looked after me and made life tolerable. On *The Omegans* I had a Filipino dresser, Cabrera, who was prepared for everything. During filming I had to lie in the Pagsanhan river for hours, day after day, covered in leeches. Cabrera would put me in the swimming pool at the end of the day and with a lighted cigarette burn them off me. One couldn't be prissy or he couldn't do his job.

On the few occasions I wasn't used, I'd borrow the jeep and race through the jungle to the nearest phone to call Steffanie. Invariably she and Maria would be out. I'd leave message after message with the *telefonista* and, feeling as depressed as hell, motor back to location.

Once the film was wrapped, all I wanted was a quick flight back to Spain to be with Steffi. I had to stop over in Hong Kong, where I decided to go for a walk to see something of the fabled city. Flush with my film pay I decided to buy myself a piece of jewellery to commemorate the journey and picked out a beautiful jade ring. The jeweller warned me against buying it, saying it was bad luck to buy jade for yourself but I gave him a gentle raspberry and wore it from the shop.

The next morning I began to wonder if the old man hadn't been right. Just before I left I checked my belongings, only to discover that my travellers' cheques were missing. I had left them in my room when I'd gone out the previous evening. I notified the management (who informed the police) and the issuing bank and, in a decidedly bad mood, took the hotel limo to the airport. Half-way there I discovered I had left my jade ring at the hotel. I told the driver to check in my luggage and caught a taxi back.

Having retrieved my ring from where I'd left it on the bathroom shelf, I hailed another taxi but the traffic was murder and, to my horror and frustration, my plane left without me – but *with* my luggage. Politely, the airline supervisor told me that it would be waiting for me at Tokyo airport, my next stop-over. It was hours before the next flight and I kicked my heels around the airport, particularly irritated because Toshiro Mifune, Japan's superstar in Kurosawa's hit movies, whom Willy had introduced me to in Manila, had promised to pick me up at Tokyo airport and take me to dinner. I wished I'd just left the bloody jade ring and caught my scheduled flight.

When I landed in Tokyo I enquired about my luggage, only to be told that the flight that had left without me had not yet arrived and was believed to have disappeared over the Mongolian mountains. It was never to be heard of again. If I hadn't gone back for the jade ring I would have disappeared with it. The engraving on my ring was 'Be Lucky'. When Steffanie turned eighteen I gave it to her so that she should be as lucky as I was that day in Hong Kong.

On top of everything else, Mifune was not there to meet me. He had been told that the plane was missing and decided I was a goner. I got on the phone to him and told him that reports of my death had been grossly exaggerated and that I wasn't due out until the morning. He came and picked me up, and we went out on the town. He was incredible. Everywhere we went he was treated like royalty. I was a bit miffed. I got elbowed aside in the fans' eagerness to get at the great Japanese star. Early next morning he took me back to the airport. We promised to keep in touch.

I was aching to get home, nearly physically sick with longing. When I arrived in Madrid, I was almost glad I had lost my luggage. There was nothing to stop me rushing straight through customs. Steffanie was standing with Maria at the barrier, grinning and waving her favourite teddy bear at me. Like a fool I burst into tears, grabbed her and sobbed down her neck. She let me get over the worst of it and then, practically, suggested we all had a Coca-Cola. She had just discovered Coke and thought it was the answer to any problem. I don't think she realised why I was weeping and couldn't stop. I'm a very lucky old bat!

Most of the actors who had lived at Dr Fleming 42 had left. By 1967, no more American films came to Spain. I didn't care. I considered myself an international actress now. Well, I had just done an American movie for a Wilder. If you said it quickly enough, Willy even sounded like Billy. There were still some Americans in Dr Fleming and they were impressed.

Marc Lawrence, who had stayed in Spain, introduced me to Milo Frank, who worked for Cinerama. They were starting production on *Krakatoa – East of Java* with Diane Baker, Brian Keith, Rossano Brazzi and Maximilian Schell. I hoped Milo might be able to offer me something on the film but since they already had Barbara Werle, there was no way they could work another blonde white woman into the script at that late stage. In spite of this Milo and I became staunch friends. He kept telling me that I should move to Hollywood but I prevaricated, playing with Steffi, making up for lost times.

When Milo returned to the States he continued to write, phone and nag me to get my head in gear. There was a lot of work in Hollywood and he was in a position to see that I got my fair share. As the bank balance was not balancing very successfully, I decided I'd better drag myself to LA for the second time.

I sobbed all the way to the States. Everything I did seemed to take me away from Steffanie, but I couldn't possibly take her with me until I had sorted out what I was going to do. I took a short-term lease on a flat in 2000 Doheny Drive, just a stone's throw from Sunset Boulevard and the Spaghetti House where I had so recently been a cook. I'm afraid I exaggerated my fortune outrageously there, but nobody seemed to mind. I just prayed that I could get something set up very soon and not have to face the humiliation of begging for my old job back.

On his home territory Milo wasn't quite the big shot he had been in Spain but he did get me an agent, Walter Kohner, and gave me some introductions. Everything was definitely on a better footing than on my farcical previous visit.

I was still missing Steffanie desperately but couldn't afford to bring her to join me. I knew Steffka was safe with Maria, but that didn't stop me worrying, especially as I had been forced to move them to a new flat in a less salubrious part of Madrid.

One night I dreamed that Steffanie had fallen down the elevator shaft. The dream was so vivid I couldn't ignore it. Half out of my mind, I rang the telephone operator and demanded to be put through to Madrid immediately. She chewed her gum and told me there was a six-hour delay. I became so hysterical the operator switched me through to the supervisor to whom I recounted my dream. She was probably into dreams for, having tried to reassure me that it was all going to turn out for the best because dreams always worked in opposites, she agreed to have my call prioritised. It still took nearly half an hour and by that time I was fit to be tied.

When the telephone finally rang I knocked it to the floor in my eagerness to pick it up. For a moment I thought I'd broken it but then I heard Steffanie's voice. She'd just got back from play school. I dread to think of the state I would have been in if nobody had answered the phone. Hearing Steffi's voice patched me together instantly. I might be an absent parent but I was determined not to unload my guilt on my baby. I made out I had just phoned in the normal way to see how she was and what she was doing. She asked me when I was coming home and I told her that I'd just found a new job and when I was paid I would send for her and Maria. She took it all in her stride and passed me on to Maria, whom I begged to get a gate installed across the kitchen window that opened into the elevator shaft so that Steffanie couldn't possibly fall out. I didn't tell her why but she promised to have it done immediately. When I finally hung up the New York supervisor rang and said, 'A'right there, sugar?' What a fantastic woman! I don't know what I would have done if I hadn't been able to hear my baby's voice right away.

The job I had landed was a TV series called *Dundee & the Culhane* with John Mills. I played the 'perk' for a travelling judge in the Old West with a gun-slinger as bodyguard. Ralph Meeker was the local star. It was great working with two old pros like that. I love Westerns and this one was tremendous fun. Between shots I learned to play poker for sunflower seeds. Or I thought I learned to play poker. I was to find out very soon that playing for sunflower seeds is a whole lot different from putting your hard-earned cash on the line.

I was worried by the level of violence in LA. Every day the papers were full of reports of muggings and shootings. Everyone seemed to carry a gun and when one of the continuity girls on *Dundee* was attacked with a knife as she parked her car one night at the supermarket, I decided it was time to learn to protect myself. I had a friend who was a stuntman-cum-actor and he was studying karate at the great Nishijama *dojo* (gym) in Hollywood. I decided to enrol.

Karate was extremely good for me, for my peace of

mind especially, and it was an excellent way to while away the boring lonely days when I wasn't working. As usual I went OTT. Every moment I could spare I was working out and doing *katas*, which are a series of choreographed stances and movements laid down by Funigushi, founding father of Shotokan karate. I put so much effort into it that I was graded in no time.

Nishijama's *dojo* was an 'in' club, frequented by the stars. Even the King, Elvis Presley, was a regular visitor. Like everyone else I was in awe of him and worked my butt off to get noticed. Elvis would arrive with a group of mates, most of whom seemed to be highly proficient in karate. He would work out, bid an expansive farewell and leave. I tried to persuade Nishijama to introduce me to him but he wasn't keen as he recognised that one of the reasons Elvis came to the *dojo* was to get away from people pestering him and to relax. I was almost at the point of walking up to him and saying 'Hi, I'm Ingrid. Fly me!' when Nishijama asked me to do a *kata* with Elvis. I almost fainted. Elvis was very good; I was awful. Still, he didn't seem to be too upset and I worked out with him on a few other occasions. He was a black belt at this stage and I a brown. On each *kata* I wanted desperately to make an impression and pushed hard, until one day I went too far. Elvis wasn't expecting it and his counter was more forceful than I'd anticipated. He caught me flush on the breast. He could see he had hurt me and stopped immediately. He apologised and I said it was all right – 'What's a poke in the boobs between superstars?' *Sensei* Nishijama instructed us to carry on. I guessed that discipline was everything and you didn't stop a *kata* because some broad with ideas above her station got her tits in the way. I think Elvis was embarrassed. Then I got another job and didn't go to the *dojo* for a while. I never met Elvis there again. It was such a shame because he was very good. I enjoyed his stage performances a lot after that because he used the karate movements of the *katas* in his act. I watched him in action in Las Vegas at one of his great shows. He asked me to stand up and announced that he would sing 'Love Me Tender' to Ingrid Pitt – which I thought was out of this world . . .

My next job was in *Ironside*. I was playing an escaping Soviet Olympic swimmer and the day hadn't started well. Standing around in a swim-suit waiting to do my water nymph bit for the cameras hadn't improved either my temper or my health. I wanted my bed, a superheated water bottle and a balloon of brandy. Just as I was about to make my wish come true and have a really early night the telephone rang. It was Ralph Meeker. I hadn't seen him since finishing *Dundee & the Culhane* about a month earlier. During the series we had become quite friendly. He now told me about a poker game that was going on at the house of the legendary Hollywood stunt co-ordinator Yakima Canutt. He wanted to take me along. Yakima was particularly famous for the bench-mark super-stunt with John Wayne in John Ford's *Stagecoach,* the one that Harrison Ford reprised in Spielberg's *Indiana Jones and the Last Crusade* when he went under the lorry and came up over the back. The last thing I wanted was to go out and be sociable but I was still at the stage when I believed that if you stuck close to the successful some of the gilt would rub off, so I let Ralphie persuade me and was waiting on the stoop when he arrived.

Yak welcomed us casually and led us through to his conservatory. Several men in various stages of bogus Western gear were sprawled on chairs already playing cards. They rose reluctantly to their feet and made patronising sounds in my direction, then switched the big welcome to Ralphie and did cowboy things, which were meant to signify that he was a real, paid-up Yahoo. I wasn't paying much attention, however. I was still trying to get my mind around the fact that I had just shaken hands with one of my all-time favourite film stars, John Wayne.

The boys settled down in their seats and made room for Ralph, who seemed to have forgotten me. I was feeling awful. Not only did I have the flu, I was being overlooked. I found myself relegated to the sideboard to pour drinks, while the Duke exacerbated my irritation by referring to me as 'little lady'. I wasn't anyone's 'little lady' and I was grumpy enough to want to prove it. So, after serving drinks for the umpteenth time, I slumped into a vacant chair next to Yakima and demanded in. They were all a little surprised, but then so was I. The only poker I'd played had been on the set of *Dundee* while we were waiting to be called and Ralph had been bored enough to teach me the rudiments of the game. As I waited for my cards I could see that the Duke wasn't particularly happy about the 'little lady' not knowing her place and guessed that Ralph might be in for a man-to-man later.

We were playing for table stakes and I didn't want it to appear as if I were on the breadline so every dollar I had was in front of me. But not for long. I tried desperately to remember what Ralph had told me about not 'chasing bullets' or 'filling holes' but still I lost. All the pressure wasn't doing my headache any favours and it had shifted gear to migraine. I felt sick and had difficulty seeing the cards.

While Ralph and the other men ignored me, Yak made sympathetic sounds as I slid towards bankruptcy. After a while he excused himself and went out to water the sage bush. When he returned I was sitting with a pair of fours and another in the hole. Yak stopped behind my chair and gave me an encouraging nod as two other players jacked in their hands, warned off by my pair. Only the Duke was left in and he was using phrases he had picked up from his films, like 'I guess I'm just gonna have to go with that, little lady' and 'Just what have you got hiding in there, little lady?' Truth was, I didn't know. What I did know was that I was down to my last couple of dollars and if Big John didn't see me I was finished. Yak gave me an understanding smile and made a noisy performance of sitting back in his seat. Big John looked at him, surprised that he was being so clumsy. Yak pointedly picked up his chips and dropped them on to the table, then looked at my pathetic little remnant of a week's wage. The Duke got the message, gave me a lopsided smile and drawled, 'I guess you got me dead to rights there, ma'am' and tossed his cards on to the table. I beamed. In one game I'd gone from 'little lady' to 'ma'am'.

Yak scooped up my winnings and emptied them into my lap. Nobody said anything but I got the feeling that no more cards were to be played until I had done the decent thing, croaked a good-night and stumbled off to bed. Ralph begged off taking me home and a taxi was called.

As Yakima stood with me in his hall making polite one-sided conversation, he suddenly appeared to have a brainwave. 'Get in touch with Brian Hutton. He's doing a film in Austria and there's a great part for you in it.' He told me to ring Hutton at MGM and to use his name as a reference. I was grateful. I needed to get into a proper film. The taxi pulled up at the door just as the Duke came into the hall. He feigned surprise to see me leaving but I could see he was relieved. He shook my hand once more, gave one of his well-practised smiles and opened the door for me. 'Real nice meeting you. I hope Hollywood's good for you, kid,' he said, then went back to the boys.

Twenty-One

Using Yakima Canutt's name was magic. Brian Hutton saw me at his MGM office the next morning. My laryngitis hadn't been helped by the night before so I just smiled and pointed to my throat, croaked, laid my favourite photograph on his desk and wrote 'HEIDI' all over the picture. He got the drift and five minutes later I was outside with his London telephone number in my pocket and a promise that he'd talk to me when I arrived in London, where he was casting. I told myself it meant nothing. He probably said the same to anyone who bearded him in his den but to my delight a few weeks later when I rang his London number he remembered me instantly. I didn't know how to ease into the subject so I blurted out what I had to say. 'I've finished *Ironside*. Shall I come and see you about Heidi now?' I made it sound as if I would be passing through London anyway. He told me that he was always pleased to see a pretty girl.

On the plane to London I bumped into Stephen Boyd whom I'd known superficially as a successful actor in Madrid. By the time we got to Heathrow Stephen and I were getting on like a house on fire. I told him about my forthcoming audition and he wished me luck. He was going to do *Shalako* in Almeria with Brigitte Bardot and Sean Connery, and said there was still one part uncast that would be perfect for me. He offered to introduce me to Euan Lloyd, the producer, but I'd already decided to go for Brian's film, *Where Eagles Dare.* Before we parted at Heathrow we arranged to have lunch the following day.

In the morning I telephoned the Winkast Production office and asked for Brian. His secretary told me that I'd just missed him, he'd gone to Austria to look at locations. I laid it on thick: Brian had told me to come for the part of Heidi – I had flown all the way from LA where I had been filming – that sort of thing. She sounded bored rather than impressed but she took my number and promised to get him to ring me as soon as he returned. I hoped it would be soon. I had booked in at the Hilton around the corner from Tilney Street where the production office was and it was expensive.

The first interview for the part of Heidi took place in Brian's office with just him and Elliott Kastner, the producer. Brian was certainly impressed but the producer was non-committal. I guessed he had people lined up for the job and resented me butting in. Brian told me they had to see a few others before coming to a decision but I was definitely on a call-back. Financially, this was the worst scenario. If he had told me I didn't have a chance I could have tried to get the part in *Shalako*, although Euan Lloyd was talking to Honor Blackman's agent by then. The call-back promise left me in limbo. Fortunately, I didn't know that there were 300 hopefuls up for the part and Hutton intended to look at every one of them. Then there were all the other parts to cast and locations to fix.

Days turned into weeks and my meagre coffers were badly depleted. I thought of doing a moonlight flit but there was no obligingly sloping driveway or nearby State-line to offer a way out. I told Stephen Boyd of my plight and he instantly offered to lend me whatever I wanted but I didn't want to feel obligated. I gave myself until the end of the week, when I would have to throw myself on the mercy of the Hilton manager and see if he could sort out how I was going to cope with my bill.

On Saturday Stephen rang and invited me to join him at a party at the Pair of Shoes, a club next to the Hilton. It meant a good meal, at the least, so I agreed. Stephen wanted to play poker. In the plane I had been a trace colourful with the description of my game with John Wayne and Ralph Meeker, so he asked me if I wanted to sit in. Before I could think it through, my mouth said 'yes'. *What the hell,* I rationalised after hearing what I had said. *I'm finished on Monday whatever happens.*

Predictably, my meagre pile disappeared at a rate that meant there wasn't going to be a second hand. I felt such a fool. I was saved by the boss of the casino, who invited Stephen and me to have a drink with him. He took us to a little area he kept for entertaining his personal guests and we had some champagne. I didn't really enjoy it. I had so little money left that I realised I would hardly be able to feed myself over the weekend, let alone settle the hotel bill. Our host asked me if I had tried craps. When I said I hadn't he led me down to a table, gave me £50 of credit and left me to do my damnedest. I asked Stephen what I should do. He said shoot the craps, so I did. And won £800. A fortune in 1967. I was so excited that I wanted to continue. It seemed to me that if I could pick up £800 with a few throws of the dice a fortune could be mine without breaking into a sweat. Stephen was adamant. He forced me to watch as some of the high-rollers lost fortunes. It made me realise how incredibly lucky I had been. I thanked the casino proprietor and went back to the Hilton, where I immediately paid my bill. I was much too excited to go to bed so we checked in at the 007 Disco and twisted the night away.

The next morning the telephone rang at nine o'clock. I could hardly unglue my eyes. This was partly due to the fact that I hadn't come in until nearly four-thirty and partly because I'd been lazy and not taken off my mascara. Mascara in the Sixties was applied by the trowel. The call was from Brian's office at MGM. Could I get round there for a screen test that afternoon? I was fully awake in seconds. I showered, went downstairs to the beauty salon and ordered the full treatment. If I didn't get the job it wouldn't be for lack of effort.

I had no idea what I was going to do for the test but neither had Brian. He asked me just to talk to him on camera. To calm myself down I did a bit of personality stuff first, which was naff as hell but it relaxed me. It obviously worked because I landed the part and when I did the movie Brian wanted me to do the lines exactly as I'd done them for the screen test. I've still got a copy of it. Very sobering. But Brian must have liked it.

I didn't want to fall into debt again and I was missing Steffka desperately so Brian told me to go home to Spain while problems with the Home Office and Equity were sorted out. Back in Madrid I was tense with worry. One moment I thought everything was all right and the next I would be in despair. To try and buck myself up one day I went to the beauty salon below the apartment for a shampoo and facial. I had my head in the basin when Steffka rushed in and shouted excitedly that the production office was on the line and they wanted to know if I could go to London immediately. The hairdresser was still standing with the rinser in her hand when I was half-way up the stairs to my apartment.

Steffi and I in a London cab. We decided to leave Spain and make London our home.

With Theo Cowan, my press agent, and the man he should never have introduced me to, George Pinches.

With Jon Pertwee in *The House that Dripped Blood*.

With Roy Ward Baker, director of *The Vampire Lovers.*

With Peter Cushing in a PR shot for the launch of *The Vampire Lovers*.

Meeting Farah Diba with Christopher Lee at the Persian Film Festival.

Relieved, after my first solo cross-country flight.

Next page: Countess Dracula

With five times world motor racing champion Juan Manuel Fangio. With everyone treating us like lepers in London it was nice to have someone like Fangio welcoming us so warmly in Argentina.

Tonio with the black, red-tasselled beret of the *dorminadores* (horse-breakers).

Asado at an *estancia.*

At the press conference to announce *El Ultimo Enemigo. Left to right:* Emilio Perina, Tonio, IP, Orlando de Benedetti, Gunter Jeanee.

Tonio and I returning from 'exile' in Uruguay.

Steffka in Argentina.

At Gaston Perkins's *estancia* 'La Corona'. *From right to left:* Gaston Perkins, Robin Ellis, IP and Tommy, Gaston's son.

In *Smiley's People* with Kurt Jurgens.

With Donald Pleasance in *Hanna's War*.

As terrorist Helga in *Who Dares Wins*.

In *Wild Geese 2*.

On the jury at a film festival. I love attending film festivals and in particular meeting my fans.

Steffka.

My two protectors.

Photo by Martin Spaven

Twenty-Two

London was under a deep blanket of snow when I flew into Heathrow Airport. My instructions, over the phone, had been to take the studio car to Borehamwood to be fitted out with my Heidi costume, then return to the airport for the flight to Munich. Because of the snow, however, London was at a standstill and it wasn't possible to go to Borehamwood and back in time for my flight to Germany. If I had been more sure of myself – and had signed my contract – I would have plonked down in London and let the studio sort out the problem. However, well aware of the difficulties the production company had encountered getting me a work permit, I was terrified that someone, somewhere, was going to get cheesed off with the trouble I was 'causing' and shout, 'Pay the silly cow off and get someone else.' It happens more often than you think. So I did the Judy Garland 'the show must go on' bit and told my driver to let Elliott Kastner, the producer, know that I would knock something together in time for the shoot the following day, and boarded the flight to Germany.

In Munich the weather was slightly better than in London but not much. I had to wait for Alistair MacLean's wife to arrive from Hamburg and we were whisked away to Salzburg. At the hotel I went to my room and wondered what I should do. I was in the first shot the next morning and no one seemed the slightest bit interested in what I was going to wear. The bits and pieces I had were all right for the basic outfit but I needed a waistcoat and a blouse. I couldn't get hold of anyone in the hotel and dashed out in a blind panic wondering where I would buy the missing items. When I returned from my shopping spree in possession of a velvet waistcoat and a blouse that needed urgent cutting and sewing, the third assistant was waiting in the hotel. He gave me a call sheet and was faintly amused that I was keen on sewing my own blouse.

As I gathered up my things to go to my room, a voice said, 'Hi. You must be Heidi.' It was Clint Eastwood. He looked good lounging against the bar, a shot of bourbon in his hand and his well-practised lopsided grin activating the lines around his eyes. Clint had been there for a couple of weeks and was getting bored. I told him I had to go, I had a lot of work to do before the morning. He told me to forget the work and come to the Bambi Ball in Munich with him. God, what a temptation. But no, my blouse needed cutting and stitching, and I was not going to be in trouble on the first day for not having my costume sorted out. I don't think he believed me.

The next day I was driven out to the Schloss Adler. Everywhere there were German lorries and Nazi uniforms. The atmosphere of the war had been so faithfully recreated that I had difficulty not believing I was back in my childhood nightmare and I began to have trouble breathing. I gave myself a good talking to. This was my big chance. The Germans had destroyed part of my life – I mustn't allow them to squash me again. I concentrated on the actors. There was Donald Houston and over there Ferdy Mayne. Brian Hutton was up on a crane directing the carpenters on the orientation of the helicopter that was to be blown up later. My little deception worked pretty well. Only occasionally did I have a moment of panic, but I was able to handle that.

In spite of the cold the shooting went well. I got on wonderfully with Clint Eastwood and Richard Burton, and Brian Hutton was a dream to work with. For some reason, however, Mary Ure seemed to resent me from the start. What she had to fear I don't know. She was the ranking star and I was an unknown. I found out how much rank she had when I went to the hairdresser a blonde and came out some sort of mouse. Mary had demanded to be the only blonde in the film. Our relationship wasn't improved when her husband, Robert Shaw, turned up on a flying visit and flirted with me. I knew it meant trouble and tried to discourage him but it was almost as if he was deliberately winding Mary up, for when we were alone together he was polite and amusing.

Robert Shaw wasn't the only wind-up merchant on the scene. One day I walked into one of the rooms in the castle that were being used as Green Rooms. It was dark and dismal. Suddenly there was a lot of yapping and a couple of dogs darted out from one of the big leather armchairs in front of the fire. Dogs frighten me and I automatically kicked out. The outraged face of Elizabeth Taylor appeared around the side of the chair. I had heard she was on an imperial visit but hadn't met her – or her pets – until then. It was not an auspicious start.

Richard didn't help the situation by jumping up and putting his arm round my waist to draw me over to the fire. 'This is Heidi,' he said, without removing his arm. 'She's the local spy.'

Elizabeth's face twitched in what I took to be a welcoming smile so I stuck out my hand and said, 'Pleased to meet you.' She shook my hand limply and as I stepped back Richard slipped his arm round me again. I didn't know what to do. Richard had always been friendly but so far, beyond a brief handshake and a slap or two on the set, our relationship had been non-tactile. He was trying to get a rise out of Elizabeth. Not wanting to be involved in his game, I suddenly remembered I had to be somewhere else. Elizabeth never became a bosom pal but I think she understood that I was being used to make a point and thawed out a little later.

Location shooting all but over, we were due to fly back to London on a special chartered flight. There remained just a few tidying-up shots, showing the bus ploughing through the snow to take the Brits to the airfield and safety. Unfortunately, Brian's luck ran out by one day. There was a big thaw overnight and all the snow melted. It had to be painted in on the neg and cost the company an extra million pounds.

Arriving back from location, Elliott Kastner gave a lavish party at the Dorchester. I only had time for Alistair MacLean. He told me riveting stories, like how Elliott got him to write the script for the film since he didn't write the book until after *Eagles* was released. He complained about the literary world not reckoning him as a writer. At the end of the party we debated half-jokingly running off together – alas I had a film to finish and he had a wife . . . Inspired by Alistair I began to think seriously of getting something published myself. I wasn't needed much on the set so I parked myself back at the Hilton and started writing children's stories. They soon lost their appeal and being confronted with the Nazis on a daily basis I commenced writing a screenplay based on my mother's experiences during the Holocaust. Later I sold it to director Johnny Hough – who still swears he intends to produce it. Much later I wrote the book *Katarina*, based on the same story, and it was published by Methuen.

Time was also hanging heavily on Clint Eastwood's hands. He was used to television series and Spaghetti Westerns, which were shot at high speed. Clint hated the days hanging around for a thirty-second set-up. One of the reasons he had taken on the film was that he wanted to get a British motor cycle. Elliott Kastner had promised him his pick. Clint had kept his twitching foot off the kick-start so far, but twiddling his thumbs on set he could resist no longer. I wasn't mad about bikes but who could resist an offer of a ride with Clint Eastwood? We took a few turns around the parking lot and then, one day, convinced that I was as nutty about motor bikes as he was, Clint rang me at the Hilton. 'Hey, dove, fancy a ride around a circuit?' he asked.

I agreed before I could think about it. While I dressed I mulled over the word 'circuit'. I soon found out what he meant. Clint had discovered that you could take your own bike around the circuit at Brands Hatch. He was excited. I was trying to think of a way out. The trouble is that I'm too much of a coward to take the coward's way out. Clint did a few exploratory laps, then came back to the pits. Resignedly I swung my leg over the saddle and was struggling to put on my helmet when my prayers were answered. Elliott Kastner stormed up to us in a fury. He ranted on about insurance while Clint unsuccessfully smothered an enormous grin. Kastner then turned on me and accused me of leading Clint astray, while behind him, Clint gave me a cheeky smile and continued to act like a naughty schoolboy.

Towards the end of shooting Elizabeth turned up at MGM Studios in Borehamwood where we were filming interiors. There had been a lot in the papers about this fabulous diamond Richard had bought her. For some reason she seemed to want to show it off. She had the whole shooting match laid on for her unscheduled visit:

photographers, security guards, outriders. I guess she was making a point – but I'm not sure what it was. We were all gathered around admiring this huge rock. Elizabeth slid it off her finger and proffered it to me. 'Want to try it on, darling?' she said silkily. Ah! That was her point.

I wasn't about to make enemies so I slipped it on my finger and said lamely, 'Do I have to give it back?'

She smiled even more brightly and said, 'Of course you do, darling.'

It was the first time I had really understood what subtext meant. She was still under the impression that I was after Richard and the stunt with the diamond had been devised to put me in my place. I pushed the dialogue further: 'Aren't you frightened someone might steal it?'

'That's why you have bodyguards, darling.'

Match point, I think.

Elizabeth's big moment was undermined when Clint rushed in and shouted that his wife Maggie had had a baby. That was the end of work for the day. Everyone decamped to the Thatched Barn a mile up the road and champagne flowed freely. At one point a runner from the studio appeared with the request that we return to the set forthwith, to which Richard resonantly replied, 'Bugger off!' He was in his element, having a hell of a time. I was all for going back but he swung me on to his lap and said, 'You're not going anywhere. I've not finished with you yet!' I could feel Elizabeth's piercing violet eyes trying to burn holes in my brain but I had been at the champagne for long enough not to care.

Peter O'Toole turned up – he had an instinct for this sort of bash – and he and Richard, drunk as skunks, bawled Shakespeare at each other, much to the amusement of everyone else, until they were both so pissed they could hardly remember their names, let alone the Bard's couplets. Clint seemed a bit bemused by it all. I don't think he was a big drinker and can never remember him being the worse for wear. Clint always treated me like a gentleman, never making any improper advances.

In spite of the truce that I had managed to negotiate with Elizabeth, Richard still tried his hardest to give the inaccurate impression that something was going on between us.

Perhaps Elizabeth would have been mollified if she had been in the back of Richard's Roller after the last day of proper shooting. We were all a bit depressed, as is often the case when filming's over. For a few brief weeks or months everyone bonds closely, then the last page of the script is scored through, the sets are struck and everybody goes off to make new bosom pals and promises of lifelong friendship. I was sitting between Richard and Clint, and wondering if I would ever be in such august company again. The mood was sombre but also almost sacred. Then Clint leaned forward. 'Shall we tell her?' he asked Richard. Rich was slumped in the corner, almost asleep.

'Tell me what?' I asked.

'Might as well,' Richard mumbled.

'What?' I demanded.

Clint grinned. He had a mischievous sense of humour. 'Richie and I had a bet,' he said mysteriously.

I was getting exasperated. 'What sort of bet?

'Who'd get you in the sack first,' Richard said, joining in the fun.

I knew they were only teasing me. I wanted to giggle but kept a straight face. 'Who won?' I asked innocently.

That floored them. They looked at each other, then burst out laughing. I wonder if they sorted it out later?

Where Eagles Dare was Elliott Kastner and Alistair MacLean's most successful movie. I think Brian Hutton's direction contributed to its success, as did Ron Goodwin's fantastic theme tune. It has become a classic, one of the best war films ever made. I am proud to have been part of it.

Twenty-Three

I sat at the window of my twentieth-floor suite in the Hilton and looked out at the scene below. Across the road in Hyde Park the Household Cavalry were out exercising their horses. In Park Lane red buses and London cabs cruised up and down endlessly. I thought of my father and his love of England and decided I didn't want to live anywhere else. Steffka, however, was still in Madrid. She had come to London for a couple of weeks at Easter and we had rushed around sightseeing, but now it was June. I had to see her.

I rang her and asked how she felt about living in England. She was excited by the prospect, although neither of us thought about the fact that she was now a Spanish speaker and there would be a lot of catching up to do when she attended an English school. Maria was also surprisingly willing to come to London, amazing me as usual with her positive attitude. I went to an estate agent, told them my requirements and caught the plane to Madrid to help pack up our belongings. At last a decision had been made. I would no longer have to stay awake all night wondering what my next move should be. Any doubts that I had made the right decision were quashed by an incident in Spain.

We decided that we were going to have a combined home-coming and farewell party, and invited several friends and a couple of American film technicians, who for some reason were still working in Madrid. Just before everyone arrived, Maria suggested that we probably wouldn't have enough wine. She was going to fetch some but as she was in the middle of cooking dinner Steffanie volunteered. She was five now and used to running errands. The wine shop was just across the plaza. I was a bit doubtful but I hadn't been around much lately and didn't want to knock back the confidence she had built up living with Maria. Steffi scooted off and I watched her from the balcony. I grinned down at her and waved as she stopped and turned suddenly, but she didn't look up. She was staring at something at the bottom of the building, which I couldn't see. Suddenly there was a bang. I knew instantly that it was a gun shot. Breathless, my heart thumping in my chest, my head spinning, feeling helpless at my sixth-floor vantage point, I watched and prayed for what seemed like an eternity. Slowly Steffanie looked up at me. She was unhurt.

I screamed, 'Run! *Run into the house! Run*!'

She ran and I rushed to the lifts to gather her close to me. Through our sobs, I asked, 'What happened?'

'A man fell down after the bang . . .' she said, confused, not knowing what actually had taken place. I pulled her into my arms and rushed to the flat. Without letting go of her I hauled the suitcases from the wardrobe and started packing.

'What are you doing, Mama?' she asked.

'We're leaving Spain. *Now*!'

We later learned that the shot had killed a man walking through the colonnades alongside the building. It was one of the first political killings by ETA, the Basque

Separatists, in Spain. It horrified me utterly that my child had been so close to a murder. I didn't care that the estate agent in London hadn't had time to find us a place to live. I wanted to leave Spain immediately. Poor Maria was left to sort out everything but I felt I had no choice. I couldn't bear to think of Steffka in danger.

We arrived at the London Hilton that night and stayed for a week before renting an attractive flat in Barkston Gardens in Kensington. It was just for a year but I assured myself we'd have a house organised for ourselves by then. Maria joined us a couple of weeks later and we felt whole again.

I went to Las Vegas for the press showing of *Where Eagles Dare*. I was on such a high that when Kohner, my American agent, called me in my luxurious suite and said I had a TV series on offer I just turned it down. Me, with an international blockbuster film, and they were offering me TV! No one at that time who had just done a massive action film for MGM would consider TV. It was movies I wanted.

From Vegas I went to the Persian Film Festival in Tehran, where I met the Shah and Farah Diba. A lot of us had flown out from England, including Christopher Lee. At dinner my friend Baharam Soltani told me that Christopher Lee's godfather, Eric Swift, had been one of the prince's tutors years before and asked if Christopher and I would like to come to Isfahan to visit his palace. He wanted to show Chris the many pictures of the prince with Christopher's godfather. I'll never forget walking the long corridors of the palace with Chris and Baharam, looking at the many photographs. Christopher Lee is one of the most erudite and entertaining people I've ever met. He has a beautiful voice, full of expression, and has the most incredible tales to tell, many about his exotic family.

Back in Tehran, a couple of 'heavies' came to my hotel. One of them dangled a velvet bag under my optimistic nose, then emptied its contents into the palm of his hand. 'Diamonds!' he exclaimed. 'From his eternal Highness, the Shah Reza Pahlavi. He asks the pleasure of your company for dinner tomorrow night at Golestan Palace. Please, will you do him the honour and accept his gift? There will be just the two of you. His Royal Highness awaits most anxiously your reply.'

I was still young and juicy, and easily insulted by someone offering to pay for their entertainment, so I came over all pompous and told them to get lost. The mistakes of youth!

Christopher was obviously the main man with the brains so I stuck close to him and we enjoyed a lot of invitations. Gregory Peck and Sergei Bondartchuk, the Russian director of *War and Peace,* were also in the party. Gregory kept mistaking me for Lee Grant who wasn't even there. I wasn't amused and so he continued doing it to wind me up. Bondartchuk gave me the opportunity to parade my Russian. I tried to get him to talk about the making of his film, *War and Peace*, my favourite picture of all time, flattering him outrageously. Though incredibly polite, he was obviously unimpressed.

The Iranian Festival Committee took us to the Shah's sister Shams's palace. An illuminated glass dome in the middle of the desert, from the bus it looked like a SciFi set. We had travelled for hours and finally pulled up at an ugly, barbed-wire gate where we were put through the third degree. The barbed wire and the guns of uniformed soldiers boarding the bus were unnerving me and I asked to be taken back to my hotel in Tehran. Our guide smiled a lot, and tried to reassure me that the questioning was routine and that everything would be all right.

'Yes,' I said, 'I've heard that crap before.'

We had to relinquish our passports before advancing through more barbed-wire fences across wasteland towards the lighted dome in the far distance, where we were greeted by yet more armed guards. I guess the revolution that dethroned Shah Reza Pahlavi a few years later wasn't as unexpected as it seemed at the time.

Things picked up when we entered the dome. There were beautiful trees under a perspex roof and birds flying around. A massive staircase covered in thick red carpet and fat golden rope balustrades led to the upper floor. The sumptuously dressed servants gave out gold goblets and kept the champagne flowing. Tired of 'ooing' and 'aahing', I grabbed a plate of finger food and joined Gregory Peck and Sergei Bondartchuk on one of the steps of the wide staircase. We'd hardly spooned the caviar before a servant came along and told us not to sit there. We tried to ignore him but he got quite huffy and accused us of being so uncoordinated that we'd spill something on the carpet. We thought it pretty funny. Here we were, buried in the sort of opulence you could only get with the Arabian Nights, in the land of the Persian carpet, and we were being warned off dribbling on the mat.

Back in London Bondartchuk came to my house for dinner. The old smoothie told me that I cooked the meanest plate of borscht he'd eaten in his life. He invited me to study at the Soviet Film Institute in Moscow where he was one of the top instructors. Although it would have been a fantastic experience for me, I couldn't possibly go to Moscow. My big mouth had got me into trouble already in a Communist country. Now I was a mother and wouldn't take the risk. I smiled and said I had absolutely no time to study in Moscow. I was working, working all the time.

Twenty-Four

Where Eagles Dare was well and truly behind me now. I had moved into a little mews house in Carmel Court in Kensington with Steffanie and Maria. I was getting bags of publicity, and invitations to premières and other less salubrious events, but no work. I regretted giving my agent in LA the raspberry when he had suggested TV work but hadn't the guts to ring him and do some world-class grovelling. My London agent seemed to have forgotten me as well. I had taken him for all the wrong reasons. For one, he was Mary Ure's agent, although he emphasised that since he had Robert Shaw on his books he had been obliged to take her on. That he could be so ungallant should have been enough reason for me not to join his agency. Especially since I could have had Jimmy Frazer who was a total treasure. It's a big mistake to use the head instead of the ticker. It didn't work and I was stranded with someone else's man who didn't give a hoot about me. I've never forgiven myself for such a terrible error of judgement.

But that just paled into the embroidery compared with the lulu I was about to make. Theo Cowan, my press agent, introduced me to a man who appeared to be the answer to a wanna-be superstar's prayer. He seemed to be kind, persuasive and reasonably influential in the business. And all he professed to want was friendship. It seemed too good to be true. I should have trusted my instincts. George Pinches was the booker for the Rank Organisation cinema chain, which at this time commanded more than half of the screens in Britain. If George, on behalf of Rank, gave you the cold shoulder it was very cold indeed.

George and I seemed to rub along fine. He swore he just wanted to be my friend and didn't put any pressure on me to step up the relationship into anything more meaningful. He was also hugely sympathetic about my work-permit problems. The temporary work permit I had for *Eagles* had long expired. I wasted a lot of time sitting around at Immigration in Holborn trying to convince bored civil servants of my love for England and the Brits, and my desperate need to stay. I just couldn't impress anyone. George suggested I went to see the greatest lawyer of them all, Lord Goodman, to tell him about my father's successful years in England and his subsequent refusal to put his scientific knowledge to work for the Nazis. His Lordship tried to work something out on my behalf but for another year I struggled on with the Home Office, spending a day each month trying to secure my status. When it seemed that there was nothing left that I could do to stave off deportation George came up with the perfect answer: we could get married. I would get a passport and we could live separately but happily ever after. I wasn't sure. I liked George, but not enough to marry him. What if I met someone who swept me off my feet and became the love of my life? It wouldn't be a problem, George promised, we'd just get divorced.

Eventually, when the deportation order became more threatening, against my better judgement, I agreed to the marriage. Our future was mapped out at a Sunday lunch in the country. I would give my attention to my work without all the nasty little side issues that day-to-day life served up. George, with his influence in the industry, would look after my career. He would live in Dolphin Square near the Houses of Parliament and I would live in Richmond, Surrey. I would continue to attend premières and business dinners and play his acolyte, but we would keep the marriage secret.

I'm sure George entered into the agreement with nothing but good intentions but, like a prospective lover promising passionately only to want a feel, George's attitude changed as soon as we walked out of the Register Office. Unfortunately mine didn't. It was to prove a salient point on a domestic battleground for a long time.

Although I carried out my part of the deal to the letter, and was there, lipsticked and hairdressed to the nines, whenever George needed a partner for a party, George always wanted more and the pantomime became very boring. Every sentence he said was full of innuendo and spite. And I wasn't exactly being inundated with film roles, either. Instead of helping my career, my liaison with the Rank film booker seemed to be scaring potential employers away. I couldn't understand it, especially as George was always telling me about all the strings he was pulling in the background to assure my superstar status.

In spite of our messy on/off relationship, I did feel sorry for George for it was clear that he pandered to my every whim and promised me everything, while I gave him nothing but reluctant limited companionship. He also appeared to have no real friends. We were never invited to anyone's home and he even admitted that if he were to lose his job, no one would ever talk to him again which, as it turned out, was a frighteningly prescient statement.

One year Disney invited us to the Oscars. When we

arrived at the hotel it was the old game again: only one double room was booked and the hotel was full . . . I told him that if there wasn't a room for me I was getting the next flight back to London. A vacant room was mysteriously made available.

The Oscars should have been a joy. I love that sort of thing. Instead, it was a nightmare with George in a particularly ugly mood making disparaging remarks all the time and trying to make me feel small. I was sullen and didn't speak even when spoken to. I've always regretted not being more conciliatory. I could have been more gracious but clearly whatever there had been between us as friends had long been ruptured and discarded.

When we returned I tried to keep out of George's way but he reminded me of our bargain and salted the pot by telling me about a film called *Gemini* which he had negotiated for me. Later, when George and I had one of our vicious rows, the producer, Arnold Barber, sent a big bouquet of flowers with a note telling me that he was sorry but George had demanded that I be dropped from the cast . . . George asked me to come with him to Monaco for a Disney convention and reluctantly, on the proviso that I could bring Steffanie, whose birthday was imminent, I agreed.

At dinner one night we ran into Jack Kelly, Princess Grace's brother. He came over all gallant, ignored George completely and rabbited on with a highly fictionalised account of the dates we'd once had. I could see the steam coming out of George's ears but I was beginning to enjoy myself and did nothing to cool the situation. Jack invited me to join Princess Grace's party at New Jimmy's, down on the seafront and, as there was no way George was going to leave me alone, he came along as well.

Grace was wonderful. We talked babies and I told her

that I had Steffanie with me. She instantly suggested that I brought her to tea the following day, Steffi's birthday, to meet Princess Stephanie. I was so excited I woke Steffka up when I got back to the hotel and told her my great news. We would have tea at the palace on her birthday.

At breakfast the next morning, however, George told me that the Disney people had heard about Steffanie's big day and had organised a party at the Hotel de Paris where we were staying. I reminded him of the invitation to the palace and how rude it would be to cancel it but he scotched that straight away: we were there for business. I was furious.

The Disney party turned out to be pretty marvellous, however. There was a big cake and all the Disney characters sang 'Happy Birthday'. The only discordant note was me. And I was making enough discords to drown out the Wigan Colliery Brass Band. The journey home was sub-arctic. I desperately wanted to say something that would make us mates again but neither of us knew how to step down.

Back home the situation didn't improve. George didn't send around lorry-loads of roses and I wasn't going to ring him. It was this sort of atmosphere that brooked no good to anyone.

I was hoovering when the phone rang. A voice said it was Federico Fellini.

'Of course you are!' I snapped, willing to believe that George had put one of his mates up to the call so that he could relish my disappointment when nothing came of it.

'No rrreally, Ingrriiid. I want you to come to Cinecittà and make a test for me. Will you do that?'

I said 'You hum it – I sing it!' or something equally stupid and hung up the phone. It rang again.

'If you don't believe me, ring me in Cinecittà and see if

it is not me who rang you. I have seen a picture of you and want you to be in my new film, *Amarcord*.'

'Okay, give me the number,' I said.

'Everybody knows that number.'

'Well, I don't.'

He gave it to me and I began to wonder if maybe he was telling the truth. So I dialled Rome – but couldn't get through. I tried a couple more times with no luck, so carried on cleaning. He rang again. I decided that if he was that persistent maybe I should believe he was who he said he was and we made arrangements to set up a screen test.

I arrived in Rome at the Parque di Principe full of trepidation. Was this going to be another Beverly Hills Hotel fiasco? When I saw the massive bouquet of flowers Fellini had sent, I felt a bit better.

Fellini arrived at the hotel first thing in the morning. He kissed my cheek, plonked himself on the sofa and pulled me on to his lap. Sensing that I wasn't too happy, he gave a big laugh and let me get up. Before I could get to the storming out and packing stage he confirmed that a screen test had been arranged for the following morning and I was appeased.

I arrived at Cinecittà the next day and was pounced on by a make-up man. Italian make-up men who play for the other team are a race apart. They prance and mew, and do outrageously camp things. That day's campness seemed to centre around my make-up – I looked ridiculous. I crept on to the set and waited for the Maestro (as he was referred to by everyone) to do his nut. He came over, looked at me from different angles, nodded approval and directed me on to the set. The test was hell. Every other second somebody shouted '*una cozza tecnica*' and rugby scrums formed around whatever piece of equipment was misbehaving. They'd scream into each other's faces until they'd had their fill of halitosis and then they'd start again.

I wanted to know something about the character I was to play – we thespians have to have our motivation right or we feel we're not being taken seriously – but Fellini said: 'Just count numbers in any language you like, *cara*.' I was stunned. Surely there was more to acting than counting numbers. Not according to Federico Fellini. He saw himself as a highly motivated shepherd and actors as moronic sheep. He's probably right but it was a bit caddish of him to make it so obvious.

At dinner that evening he asked me how long it would take me to get fat.

'Fat? What sort of fat?'

'Bloody fat,' he said.

I didn't like the sound of that. For once I used my head. 'Do I get fat before or after I sign a contract?'

He looked pained and said until he knew what I looked like fat he could make no promises. I was a svelte nine stone and planned to stay that way – unless a juicy enough carat was slipped into my financial diet. In the end I didn't get the part and it went to Sandra Milo. I believe she was probably always going to get it as she was in most of Fellini's films. I spent a couple of days sightseeing various production offices, signed an agent and caught the flight back to London and Steffka. I wasn't too put out. I hadn't got the job but at least someone serious was looking at me.

George, predictably, was furious. Fellini was beyond his control and where I was concerned he had turned into a control freak. For the sake of peace I played down the trip. When he simmered down he told me that we were going to a première. Like a good little girl I asked when. Anything to keep the peace. As it turned out it should have been one of those times when bells rang, buzzers buzzed and lights ignited the sky.

The film was *Alfred the Great*. At the party afterwards I sat next to Hammer Films supremo James Carreras. I hadn't a clue who he was and I'm sure he didn't recognise me either. Gradually, however, it dawned on me that he was an active producer, a rare species indeed in the British film industry at that time. He hadn't a chance. By the time he left I had his card next to my heart and he had promised to see me at his office the following day.

The next morning I had a hell of a time trying to make up my mind what was the best thing to wear to get a movie mogul to discuss long-term film contracts. As the grimy winter daylight struggled to take over from the night I came to a decision. It was snowing so I needed something a bit glam but winterproof: Russian boots were a must and a maxi-coat and wide-brimmed slosh hat to keep out the draught were *de rigueur* in Sixties London on Wardour Street. As I left and looked up to the window to wave goodbye, Steffanie was standing there, giving me a Churchill victory sign.

I arrived at Hammer House and ascended the stairs with confidence. 'This', I assured myself as I stood before the big double doors, 'is my lucky day!' I threw them open and went in. Where there should have been a twittering receptionist just waiting for my grand entry was a vacant chair. For a moment I didn't know what to do. Then an inner door opened and a secretary with a broad smile and bouffant hair came into reception. I told her what I wanted and she looked surprised. Evidently my arrival wasn't the big event I had anticipated. Jimmy Carreras hadn't even told his secretary. She excused herself and went back through the door. I stood there, the snow that had collected on my coat and hat thawing and dripping around me. I felt my confidence ebbing away and prepared myself for the worst, but when the secretary came back the news was good: 'Mr Carreras will see you now.' I thanked her profusely and didn't care if I was overdoing it. At the same time I was pumping up my own ego. Back to plan A.

Jimmy was sitting at his desk. Around the walls of his office were pictures of him with various celebrities.

'Hello, Colonel Carreras . . .' I said brightly and with a practised movement I swept off my hat and let my carefully prepared hair tumble around my shoulders. Act one. Another deft movement rid me of my maxi-coat. I tossed it negligently on to a chair and let him get a crack at the skimpy sweater and even skimpier micro-skirt I was wearing. He didn't bat an eyelid when I slunk across the Axminster and hitched a thigh on to the corner of his desk. I'd seen Brigitte Bardot do the same thing in *La Parisienne* and I'd earmarked it for just such an occasion. He was a perfect gent and didn't fall about laughing. Now I was perched on the corner of his desk I wasn't quite sure how to continue. I was saved by the secretary appearing in the doorway and asking if I would like coffee, which gave me a chance to unhook my gam and sit in an armchair.

Jimmy thought for a moment or two, or maybe he was just making sure he could talk without laughing, then offered me three roles. I nearly fainted. Three films? 'No,' he said carefully. 'One film – three roles.' Only faintly disappointed, I nodded encouragingly. The film was based on a Sheridan Le Fanu short story, 'Carmilla'. It was about a vampire lady with a penchant for biting impressionable young girls, was called *The Vampire Lovers*, and was to start shooting in a month's time.

Back on the street, the awful winter weather had changed to halcyon summer. I floated along, bought a copy of 'Carmilla' and wafted home, high as a kite.

Twenty-Five

Becoming part of Hammer Films was like being welcomed into a family. I was very aware of it as an institution and was honoured to join the ranks of luminaries who had made their mark there.

Hammer Films' publicity department decided to go to town: 'The new face for the Seventies!', 'Queen of Horror', 'The most beautiful Ghoul in the World!' I was thrilled and wallowed in it. I probably should have been cool and cynical. Unfortunately when they handed out attitudes, cool and cynical wasn't – and isn't – in my bundle.

Jimmy Carreras, Michael Styles and Harry Fine – producers of *The Vampire Lovers* – were fantastic to me and Tudor Gates's brilliant script combined with Roy Ward Baker's solid, imaginative and tasteful direction made *The Vampire Lovers* the best of all the many adaptations of Le Fanu's short story.

Roy was fabulous to work with. Before filming actually started we met a number of times at my mews house and discussed the way I should play the part of Carmilla. Roy patiently guided my thinking until we both knew exactly what we were aiming for. After that, filming was a doddle.

The film involved nude scenes. I'd never done the full-frontal bit before but I was proud of my body and not too reluctant to show it. Madeleine Smith, who played my second victim, had also kept her gear on in front of the cameras so far. She was a little more apprehensive but saw the relevance and agreed to get it off. Nevertheless, we both had reservations, especially as we weren't too familiar with the producers, so I spoke to Jimmy and asked him if we couldn't have a closed set: the producers and other non-essential personnel could go to London and see rushes. He agreed at once.

When the day came for me to shoot the scene in the bath, I came out of my dressing-room clad in nothing but a white towelling dressing-gown held loosely in place over my naked body. As I walked down the corridor Harry Fine and Michael Styles, the excommunicated producers, were coming towards me. They looked so depressed and miserable that I felt guilty for having robbed them of their fun. We were just about eyeball to eyeball when they looked up, and I knew what to do: 'Whee!' I threw my robe open to let them see what they were missing. They certainly went off with a renewed spring in their step. It's so easy to make men happy.

I discovered that when you're naked on set everyone is terribly nice to you and looks after you beyond the call of duty. This is particularly the case when you're doing a bath scene, which I seemed to do a lot of at Hammer. Is the water hot enough? Is the water too hot? Are the towels in the right place? How about the light? Are people leering? Would you like some cognac? They're terrified you might lose the mood or – God forbid – want to get dressed. Jimmy had sent champagne to the set, and Madeleine and I indulged ourselves.

Not everything went smoothly filming *The Vampire Lovers*. When the time came to kill the Kate O'Mara character, who believed I loved her and was unaware of my vampire tendencies, I first slung her on to the floor, knelt to take her in my arms and smiled down at her. As the camera moved in close and I displayed my fangs inches from her neck, suddenly out popped the fangs, straight into her cleavage. Time and again we had to do the scene and the bloody things sprang out like exocet missiles homing in on her breasts. I could feel myself beginning to lose the mood but, determined to be a pro, I told Kate I was going to kill her with or without fangs. That didn't help the situation much. Kate was helpless with laughter. Roy was unbelievably patient but I wanted to get it in the can. I'd seen the clapper boy chewing gum so I called him over, took it out of his mouth, stuck the fangs in with it and killed her – clean, quick – and she laughed no more.

I met Peter Cushing for the first time on the set of *The Vampire Lovers*. I was having my wig fitted when the hairdresser warned me that Cushing was doing terrible things to me on the set at that very moment. In spite of the red light I stormed into the studio and saw, way over in the distance, a man holding something like a cabbage in one hand and swinging a sword in the other. 'Swish' it went – and I realised I had just had my head cut off. The censor cut this scene from the film but it was a hell of a way to stage an introduction. I let out a startled yelp and Peter rushed over to me and introduced himself.

'My dear, how awful to meet like this.'

I forced myself not to come up with a smart-arsed reply like, 'I feel a bit cut up too.'

We became great friends after that. On my father's hundredth birthday I had champagne brought to the set to celebrate. When Peter heard what the party was about he invited me to dine with him and his wife Helen in the Thatched Barn. After dinner the *maître d'* brought a cake, covered with candles, on which was written in icing sugar 'For Ingrid's Papa'.

Helen knew Russian quite well and we used to write short letters to each other after that, using Peter as postman. Then, all of a sudden, she fell terribly ill. The illness – it was cancer we found out later – raced through her poor thin body with such force that in three months it was all over. Peter seemed never to recover from her death. Some time later I met him by chance in Whitstable. That afternoon in a café he told me that he couldn't go on living without Helen. I thought I had to talk him out of doing harm to himself, although I know if it happened to me I'd feel the same. What is the use of living without love?

The House that Dripped Blood was another film for 1970, a vintage year for me. It was made by Amicus, Milton Subotsky and Michael Rosenberg, a sort of ersatz Hammer. In fact, one of the best known photographs of me as a vampire is from the film. It was in four parts. I had wanted the first, but after a lunch with Peter Duffell, the director, and Jon Pertwee (whom I knew from a *Dr Who* episode 'The Time Monster'), Jon talked me into doing 'The Cloak'. He made it sound such fun that I immediately said yes. 'The Cloak' was the last story in the film and a comedy. It was great to see the audience leave the cinema with a giggle.

After *The Vampire Lovers* I considered myself a part of the Hammer stable, not exactly in the same class as Michael Ripper, of course, but a paid-up Hammerite none the less.

When I heard that they were setting up a new film I was all ears. I discovered it was to be a film about Elizabeth Bathori, the biggest female serial killer of all time and a relative of Vlad Tepes – the Impaler. That was enough for me and I called James Carreras immediately. 'Now, Jimmy Darrlink!' I said. 'I must have the part of Elizabeth Bathori. Please, give it to me and you won't look back!'

Silence.

'Jimmy?'

'Hang on a minute, darling, I have to think about this. Peter wants Diana Rigg to play her.'

'Sod Peter, whoever he is. I want it, Jimmy, give it to me. Please! Anyone else would be wrong for the part. Only I can play it right. I simply have to have it!' I whinged.

'I'll tell you what – if you can convince Peter that you're right for it, you can play the Countess,' Jimmy said slowly, thinking on his feet.

'Who is this Peter? What does he do?'

'Peter Sasdy, the director.'

'Who's the producer?'

'Alexander Paal. They're both Hungarians – like the Countess . . .'

Peter was fantastic and very approachable. He invited me to lunch at the Gay Hussar in Soho and I convinced him that he had to have me. When I have a cause, I have the nerve to win the war.

Everything about *Countess Dracula* was perfect. The script by Jeremy Paul was excellent, giving the old Countess a lot of depth, and I was sure I would shine in the role. I made my mother come and stay, and I studied her way of speaking as she had the kind of voice and intonations I thought the Countess would have had. I gave her the sort of croakiness that Eastern Europeans have when they smoke and drink a lot of vodka. After each take I would rush to the sound man and listen to the play-back. I was happy with the result.

Sasdy and Alexander Paal were less so. They had terrible rows in Hungarian on the set. The atmosphere was almost unbreathable at times. In the end I couldn't stand the constant bickering any more so I got a friend of mine, a fellow countryman of theirs, to teach me some Hungarian swear-words. The next time they rowed I appeared at the top of the stairs. In colloquial Hungarian I shouted: 'Do be quiet, you carry on like shitty little gnomes. We're losing time here . . .' They were shocked. They thought I had understood what they had been saying all the time.

Alexander Paal was a brilliant stills photographer and did sessions with me at his studio in London at weekends. The best photos I possess from my entire career were taken by him.

Apart from Sasdy's and Paal's arguments, filming went quite smoothly, although there were some mishaps. In one scene I had to have a tumble in a haystack with Sandor Eles. His character had a moustache but, rather than grow one, Sandor let the make-up man do his magic. Sandor looked up at me from the hay to murmur his hot and sexy lines when I suddenly noticed that half his moustache was missing. I called out '*Cut*!' Sasdy was immediately on the case, telling me that if anyone called 'cut' it would be him. I pointed to Sandor's pruned moustache and explained I didn't want to waste my emotions on half a man. Make-up man Tom Smith hastily looked through his box of tricks and found that he was out of moustaches.

Everyone started shouting, running around, searching the haystack, but the missing item refused to show itself. I got bored and went into my winnie-bago. I shed my voluminous frock and tried to stretch out on the divan but my corset was killing me so I whipped that off as well. As I walked past a mirror I saw something black and ugly trying to claw its way out of my belly-button. Before I could faint or scream, I recognised the ugly beastie. It was Sandor's lost face fungus. Everybody was delighted with my find and we were able to get on with the shoot. How the nasty little thing managed to get through my outer clothes *and* my corset I'd prefer not to think about.

The film was finally wrapped and we all went home happy. At least, I thought we had all gone home happy. Evidently not Peter Sasdy. Throughout the film he had said I was wonderful and my old Countess the best thing he'd seen since Hydra. Then, as soon as I was off the set, he took my voice away. I found out by accident, when an actress, who'd previously only done commercials, sent me flowers and thanked me for the opportunity of getting such a grand job. Her voice was prissy and very 'English rose', and didn't fit a serial killer. Livid, I phoned Sasdy but he wouldn't speak to me. I got in touch with Jimmy and he seemed furious too. He said that one of the reasons he wanted me for the role was my accent. I suggested he got on to Sasdy and ordered him to restore my voice, but the next day he rang to say that Sasdy had already thrown away the voice tracks.

Much later I asked Sasdy why he had done it.

'It wasn't the Queen's English,' he replied.

'But she wasn't supposed to be English!' I said.

'If you play a Royal, you speak like a Royal.'

'So how about Sandor?' I demanded. 'He stands out like a sore thumb. He's the only one left with an accent.'

'Oh, it doesn't matter how he sounds. It's the Countess who matters.'

I was post-apocalyptic but could do nothing. Later he rang to ask me to talk to Jimmy Carreras about changing the title of the film. He thought *Countess Dracula* was too vulgar. Suddenly he seemed to see himself as Eisenstein and to be embarrassed to be a director of something he perceived as beneath him. I told Jimmy about Sasdy wanting to change the title and, as I'd guessed, he was enraged – a small but sweet victory.

I was beginning to like my work. It seemed that everything I sucked was sugar free and did me good. Work was being offered on a fairly constant basis so I was playing the star to the hilt and turning down anything I didn't fancy. I was starting to feel slightly secure about my future.

Domestically, however, there were a few problems. George was still around and getting heavy if he heard I had tea with anyone who wasn't female or under ninety-five, and was putting on the pressure about us living together. I spoke to Matka on a more or less daily basis and she always assured me that she was fine, but one day I received a call from a neighbour. She told me that my mother was far from well. She was finding it very hard to get around and had, on more than one occasion, fallen over and been unable to get up. I was shocked. Somehow, while I was feeling hard done by because I'd lost a couple of movies, my mama was doing what she always did: soldiering on without complaint. I rang the travel agent and booked a flight immediately. As I was packing I suddenly remembered I had promised George I would join him at a première in Leicester Square.

I rang him to tell him that I couldn't go. He was not happy; moreover, he had a producer coming with us who was interested in casting me in his film. I tried to hang on to my principles but he said that an extra day wouldn't make any difference, one way or the other.

I was glad I took time out to go to the première. It was another case of sitting in front of the right plate at the right table at the right time. The man beside me turned out to be Ronnie Lee from United Artists. He said they were about to start pre-production on a film of *The Merry Widow* and asked if I could sing.

'Sure,' I said, while mentally crossing my fingers. He told me to come and see him when I returned from Berlin.

Matka was worse than I expected. She'd always been thin but now she was skeletal. She had also developed a horrendous bronchial condition. It was so debilitating that she seemed to have been robbed of her spirit. She sat in the big old armchair that had been my father's favourite and appeared to fade into the upholstery. I sat and held her hand, and fought back the tears. Until then I'd taken it as my right that my mother should look after me. Sitting there in that gloomy room I prayed that she wouldn't die so I could prove to her and to myself that there was more to me than a fixation that I could entertain people. I told Mascha that I would tidy up the house, sell it and that she was coming with me to live in England. She started arguing that she was too old, that she couldn't leave the place she was used to, that old and young don't mix – all kinds of silly arguments which I didn't bother to answer. I just told her she was coming and that was final. I rang a number of estate agents and put the house on the market at once, then set about sorting which things we would ship to England and what we would leave behind. In a few days Matka was smiling once more, helping me decide and talking about how much my father had loved England.

We had goodbye dinners with Haneli and some of her friends, and in little over a week we were on our way. Steffka was happy as a sandboy to have her grandmother living with us. They played chess, went to the pictures and had a whale of a time together. Slowly Mother lost her cough and walked with a spring in her step once more. Only Maria seemed to feel that her domain had been infringed. I thought that eventually they would work it out.

I rang Ronnie Lee and reminded him that he was about

to launch the next diva in his *Merry Widow* film. He set up a meeting with the ranking members of his company and a singing coach, Gustl Sacher. Now we had got down to the hooks and eyes I wasn't sure I could do it, but Ronnie didn't want to hear my doubts. Before I knew what I was up to, Gustl was banging away on the piano and I was tralalaing fit to bust.

There was also the dancing lesson. As a dancer I was definitely designed to twist, maybe jive a little and probably do the locomotion, which was awkward because *The Merry Widow* is all about the waltz. I tried my best and, unbelievably, it seemed to be good enough to get me a screen test. It was the hardest thing I ever had to do in the film business. I was so worried that instead of not sleeping the night before the test, my usual lunacy, I didn't sleep for a week. Feeling like a gutted rabbit in a butcher's shop I turned up, and to the sound of my recorded trilling my partner, a well-known choreographer whose name I forget, strutted up decked out in full costume and looking like a seventeenth-century fag on New Orleans' Main Street. The next few minutes were a high-speed blur. Suffice it to say that my partner hardly limped at all as he led me off the floor.

Ronnie Lee was generous with his applause. I went to change and when I got back he told me that I had the job. I was astonished. The actual shoot was ages away but in the meantime I was to have singing and dancing lessons. I was delighted to be working – and earning – and to be able to say when asked that I was making *The Merry Widow*.

I found a house in Richmond, one of those three-bedroomed, bow-windowed jobs that uninspired architects scattered across the country in the Thirties. Steffka and Mascha liked it and we rented it. It wasn't exactly what I wanted but it had a pretty garden with a view over a mausoleum at the back and millions of trees. Just as we moved in I was invited to Romania for a horror documentary so Maria and my mother had to cope with the move as I toured the land of vampires surrounded by a vast media crowd. On returning to our hotel in Bucharest I was confronted by the man who owned the house we'd just rented in Richmond. Having discovered through the newspapers that I was in Bucharest, he'd tracked down my hotel and now begged me to buy his house. Apparently, he had fallen in love with a Romanian girl and wanted to stay. I wasn't terribly keen on the place but he was persistent and invited the entire crew to dinner for the duration of our stay, so I told him about the poor paintwork and leaking roof. In the end he lowered the price considerably and I negotiated some repair work. I did a 'subject to survey' deal with him and flew back to England feeling rather smug.

With the house organised, I could get back to my singing. Steffka was on holiday and I thought it would be nice for her to come along to the studio and see her old mother exercise the epiglottis. Gustl Sacher pounded away at the ancient upright piano, I cleared my throat and prepared to impress. I was well into my coloratura before going into one of the arias from Puccini's *La Bohème* when I noticed Steffka, her back to me, staring out of the window. I was a mite hurt. To appreciate my versatility properly she should have been facing me. Then I realised that her shoulders and pony-tail were shaking. I stopped in mid-flight and went across and turned her round to face me. Her face was scarlet with the effort she was making not to laugh. I knew then that Maria Callas had nothing to fear. Kids are the most honest critics and I think Steffanie got it about right. In the end it mattered not at all. The production was put on hold when the original investors withdrew their finance. I was told to hang loose and the producer would be in touch when the new financiers were lined up. I'm still waiting . . .

Twenty-Six

Matka loved England. She had been afraid that the renowned English fog and damp would play havoc with her rheumatism but within a month she was dashing about, aided by her A-framed walking stick, and soon became a well-known figure around Richmond. As she steadily grew stronger she virtually took over the running of the house. It made us both happy. She loved the idea that she had a purpose and was contributing, and for me it was a relief. Maria had gone back to Spain – to retire, as she had put it. I knew Steffka would be utterly safe with her grandmother.

I was still getting a reasonable amount of work but nothing really substantial, so it was back to the obituary of thespian dreams, *PCR*. Among the list of films completed was a notice saying that Robin Hardy was about to launch a venture called *The Wicker Man* in Scotland. The story was described loosely and the piece ended with the information that the part of the nymphomaniac librarian was still not cast. It was a Sunday but I wasn't going to wait until office hours before getting on the case. I rang George and obtained Robin Hardy's home telephone number. Apologising for phoning on a Sunday morning,

I said it was absolutely imperative that I spoke to him at once. He talked about the film for a while, then asked me to call round to discuss the part further.

'When?' I asked.

'Now.'

I drove in record time to his home in Chelsea. We talked for a couple of hours and got on so well that Robin decided to ring Peter Snell, the producer. I was beginning to like this company: they didn't hang about. Peter was on the point of leaving for Scotland but wanted to see me so I flagged down a taxi and sat impatiently while the cabby, enlightening me as to his philosophy on life in general and Sunday drivers in particular, picked his way across London to St John's Wood. Peter thought I would be perfect for the part and a week or so later I was on the sleeper to Dumfries.

The car that picked me up from the railway station sped along the hilltop overlooking the Irish Sea – not a reassuring sight. It was October, and mist and rain obscured everything but the waves gnawing up the rugged coastline. Even with the heaters going full blast I could feel the icy wind blowing into my pores. I wondered how we'd avoid the goosebumps showing in the first scene, as we pranced around naked celebrating the joys of spring.

The Kirroughtree Hotel, outside Newton Stewart, was the HQ for the production. After a snooze I went in search of a pot of tea. The decision whether or not to have a second was postponed when Peter Snell walked in. He was looking wind-swept and miserable. I waved the teapot at him and he joined me. Over tea we discussed our schedule and he let slip that his dishevelled appearance was due to being stuck on top of the cliffs of Burrowhead overseeing the construction of the Wicker Man. Of course, I had to squeak and demand that he took me to see it immediately. As we drove up, the mighty Wicker Man towered over us, the setting sun shining through its intermeshed branches creating a magical effect. Peter explained that the compartments which made up the body were for the sacrificial animals and that the larger one in the centre was for Edward Woodward.

We all had dinner that night in the main hall of the hotel with its oak-panelled walls, massive doors and large leaded windows overlooking the cliffs. Tony Shaffer, the writer, and I talked for hours. He was not happy with the ending of the film. In fact, all through the shooting he kept going to Dumfries library in search of a better ending. Every night he and I would sit on the floor between our rooms discussing this *ad infinitum* until I could no longer stand trying to convince him that he'd done it right the first time round. The producer also argued the point and at last, after considerable coaxing, Shaffer resolved that his first ending *was* the best.

The Wicker Man was beset by difficulties. British Lion, the production company, changed hands three times during filming. Peter Snell had to do some fast footwork to keep the film from collapsing. The cold got worse as we nudged into November. We all huddled under blankets, clutching rapidly cooling hot-water bottles until the shot was set, then we'd throw off our coverings and prance about pretending it was spring and the sun was warm. Poor Edward Woodward had to run around barefoot in a shroud. On 'cut' he would rush over to where I sat trying to convince my body that it was really spring, and stick his freezing feet under my hot frock. Britt Ekland had this fabulous sable coat which she'd throw into the bramble bushes on 'action'. She was pregnant with her son Nikolas at the time and I think she would have been happier anywhere else but on that windy Scottish coast. Diane Cilento, Britt and I shared a car every morning driving to the location. I like to talk but never got a word in. Their entire conversation revolved around what bad chaps Sean Connery and Peter Sellers had been and trying to outdo each other with the level of poverty they had been left in.

When shooting was finally over and everyone went back to London the battles over the film really began, which must have been hell for Peter Snell.

The nasty bottom line to *The Wicker Man* was that George refused even to look at the film, claiming it was not commercial. The Rank Cinema circuit therefore wouldn't show it. Later, in one of our frequent rows, he said that any other film I might manage to make would suffer the same fate. I thought how absurd he was, but I was naive. He subsequently showed that he was a man of bitter action.

Eventually, Bob Webster of EMI, the only other cinema circuit in Britain, took the film with the proviso that it went out on a double bill with *Don't Look Now.* The two producers, Peter Snell and Peter Katz, were rather annoyed. Nevertheless, they took the offer as no one else was beating a path to their doors. Neither film deserved the double-bill treatment – each stood up on its own. And both have become classics.

Twenty-Seven

I must have been the wimp of the decade for I continued to escort George wherever he wanted to go and I hated myself for it. I told myself repeatedly that everything would turn out for the best, while other wiser people just waited to see how best to avoid the fall-out. I had given up the idea that I'd ever meet a man I could fall in love with and had settled for my friendship with George. I thought that once he saw that I really wasn't interested in a physical relationship with him he would go back to being my friend. One day I believed it, the next I didn't. It was a routine. And, like all routines, it was hard to break. The real problem, which I wasn't willing to face, was that I still wanted him to find me work. He realised this and continued to dangle this carrot. His telephone calls always started with, 'I was talking to Lew Grade . . .' or Eric Pleskow or Joe Levine or Disney or anyone else who would impress me. He'd then go on to tell me about deals he was putting together on my behalf. I don't think I really believed it but I didn't admit it, just in case.

With our relationship not improving, it was a relief when I was offered a job in Switzerland. It was a children's television show called *Ski Boy*. I was over my

Hollywood film fixation and would accept anything where a camera might possibly be focused on me, followed by a pay-cheque. I told the producer I would love to do the job but unfortunately Steffanie was just getting over flu and needed me.

'Bring her with you,' he said.

It was what I wanted to hear.

There were four other actors, Steffka and I on the flight. I didn't know any of them so sat in the rear of the plane, with Steffanie beside me by the window and my belongings on the aisle seat. I settled down but suddenly became aware that a man stood over me, looking at the seat piled high with my cast-offs. *Sod him!* I thought. *There are plenty of other seats.* But he continued to stand there. I looked up and gave him my best drop-dead look but he merely smiled and asked if I would mind shifting my things. I couldn't believe it. I sat up and pantomimed looking around at the rows of empty seats. It didn't faze him. He still looked expectantly at my gear. Before I could get really crude a stewardess came into view. She wanted to know what the hold-up was. I explained. She regarded my oppressor. He looked at me and kept his smile firmly in place. His body language suggested he was prepared to remain there indefinitely. The stewardess backed down first. She told me that if I insisted on keeping my goods on the seat I would have to buy another ticket.

I switched my drop-dead look to her, thought through the situation and decided the hassle wasn't worth it. I slung the bags under my seat, the stewardess hung up my coat and the lout sat down. I hated him utterly. He pulled out an *Evening News*, turned to the crossword, searched unsuccessfully for a pen and then had the impudence to ask me if I had one he could borrow. I was more furious than ever but made a production of getting a pen out of my handbag. He sat there staring at the crossword for a while, then handed the pen back. 'Too hard,' was his explanation.

We sat in silence for a while. Steffka was staring out at the clouds and occasionally looking past me at our uninvited companion. He gave her a smile and she responded. *Traitor,* I thought. He refolded the paper and found the junior crossword. Again he had the temerity to ask for my pen. Seething, I slammed it on the table in front of him. As he picked it up I noticed he was wearing a bracelet with his name on it. *Cretin! Can't even remember his own name . . .* I thought.

The fool studied the simple puzzle with furrowed brow and sighed in resignation. 'That's too hard as well,' he said, returning my pen.

As we neared the Pyrenees the weather changed and the plane started jiving about. I love flying but am not at all keen on crashing. I gripped Steffka's hand and braced myself for the inevitable. Steffanie looked across me to my persecutor and explained my behaviour. He reassured her that everything was all right. We'd just hit some thermals approaching the mountains. Once we were over them everything would be calm again.

I was feeling seriously pissed off, not only because he seemed to be sympathetic to my malaise but because he was trying to reassure me. I hate being reassured. It's so condescending. 'You'd know about that, would you?' I asked cuttingly. After all, someone who couldn't do the children's crossword was hardly an Einstein. He confessed he was a pilot.

I looked at him with a smidgen of respect. 'So you say,' I said haughtily.

He shrugged and continued talking to Steffanie. As if I were invisible, he asked her what her mother did. She told him I was an actress.

'Not another one!' he said rudely.

Prat! I thought. I pointed towards his bracelet with his name on it. 'That's in case you forget your name, is it?' I asked smugly. He explained that he was a racing driver and for the purpose of identification the bracelet had his name and blood group on it.

Toughski shitski, I thought. *So you fly, you race cars and you've had enough of 'actresses' . . . What else can you do? It sure ain't crossword puzzles.*

Steffka carried on flirting with him, smiling and talking to him as though I wasn't there. The flight calmed down as we left the mountains behind and little by little I calmed down too.

I hate being ignored so gradually I let my guard slip. He told me he had just returned from the *temporada* – season – in Buenos Aires and was on his way to stay with a racing mate at his chalet in the mountains outside Geneva. I told him we were going on location for *Ski Boy* in St Luc and he apologised for his derogatory remark about actresses, explaining that every hot-panted dolly bird strutting the pit-lanes of the world classified herself as either a model or an actress. He seemed quite intrigued that I actually had a job to go to.

At Geneva airport he not only schlepped my bags off the aircraft but was happy to be left with Steffanie while I went off to change some currency. I smiled to see them in animated conversation, Steffka's pony-tail bobbing up and down as she chatted away a mile a minute. He was laughing at what she was saying and I had to admit he was growing on me.

Driving out to the location, I sat in the car and wondered if I would ever see him again. He'd asked for my telephone number before going off with a friend and to my surprise I'd actually given it to him. I thought about him for a while, then decided it was just one of those things . . . passengers that go bump as they pass in the air.

Ski Boy went like a dream, and Steffanie loved Switzerland and the snow. I played a journalist and had great fun both with the part and working with a pro like Michael Culver. Steffanie's birthday was on the penultimate night of the shoot. I arranged a party for her and the cast and crew. We had a great fondue and I suddenly thought of this funny guy I'd met on the plane. I wondered how his skiing was going and realised that I wouldn't mind hearing from him. I had to admit he was outrageously sexy and I don't feel that way often.

Filming over, Steffka and I jetted back to England. I was just wrestling my oversized suitcase into the bedroom when the telephone rang. It was my aeroplane tormentor. He had returned early from his skiing holiday and wanted to take me out. Not wishing him to think I was one of his pit-ponies, I tried to keep my voice cool and to act distant, but when I put down the phone I had somehow agreed to have dinner with him the next evening. I insisted on calling him Tonio instead of Tony and on choosing the restaurant. That night he had me in stitches all through dinner as he told me about his life in the RAF and motor racing. I'd never laughed so much on a date, nor got so hot and bothered either . . . Back at my place he insisted on a cup of tea before he got down to business and an apple afterwards. As I stood in the doorway, weak-kneed, and waved him goodbye I wondered what I was letting myself in for. Years later, Tone confessed that he'd watched Steffanie and me horsing around in the VIP lounge and thought it was Christmas when he saw we were on the same flight. He was having me and that was that.

By May, Tonio and I were an item. He knew about George and insisted I told him what was going on but I was fearful of the harm George could do me in the business. So far I had managed to keep the work coming in. I was a panellist on *New Faces* and doing a reasonable amount of television. That could all be jeopardised if I broke off with George. But I knew I should have to make a choice pretty soon. I was going to too many motor-racing parties and public events for our liaison to remain a secret for ever and I was telling George so many lies that when I told the truth I instantly felt a tremor of panic. Then one of my 'friends' phoned George, met him for dinner and filled him in on my passionate love affair. He had already sensed it. I had changed. I was quite relaxed about my life and career, and contented within myself. I didn't care that George knew. I was so incredibly happy to have discovered my knight in shining racing cars. Love had at last found me.

To distract me from my problems, Tonio began teaching me to fly. He kept a Cherokee Arrow down at Elstree and whenever we went anywhere he let me take the controls for most of the flight. No switching on the auto-pilot and getting your feet up for me, I sat there clutching the yoke and responding to every twitch or lurch. When George heard about this he went bananas, unable to stand the thought of me being independent. I couldn't ignore him or his urgent notes, telegrams and messages any longer. Our relationship had to be settled once and for all. I arranged a meeting with him at his flat in Dolphin Square. Although I had long lost any hope of George behaving like a gentleman and honouring his promise to release me from our marriage should I find true love, I now saw a side of him I hadn't known existed. He raged and screamed at me, demanding I leave Tonio at once to move into a family house with him. He threw insults at me about my family and Tone.

I was shaking with fury and felt sick. 'Why did you marry me? Why did you lie to me?' I cried. '*You* said we could be *friends*. *You* promised nothing would change . . .'

'Well,' he said and laughed. 'Things will change now. You'll see. Your future has always been behind you. I alone kept you going. You don't have a career now, that's for sure. Perhaps you've already noticed that nobody is falling over himself to hire you? Just wait until I really get to work. I guarantee you won't be able to get a walk-on part in a skin flick. So just stop seeing this dago' – which is what he called him, because I called Tone 'Tonio' – 'and we'll say no more about it.'

The argument was getting us nowhere. I turned to leave, only to find George had locked the door of the flat. As I scrabbled to escape he seized my shoulders and threw me on the floor. Demanding that we consummate our 'marriage' there and then, he tried to force himself on me and started violently pulling at my clothes. He was a big man and my karate lessons were of no use as he pushed his full weight on to me. Able only to move my neck, I head-butted him on the nose and the pain propelled him backwards. A well-directed kick to the groin sealed the matter. As he screamed with pain, I jumped up, unlocked the door and ran.

George now dedicated his life to turning mine into a morass of hatred and venom. He wrote to tell me that, had he only the courage, he would kill my child because it would hurt me most, but since he was a coward he would kill my career instead.

Tonio said, 'Forget it, he'll get over it.' But I knew he would make good his threat and was even frightened that he would hurt Steffanie. I went to the police and filed his letter, just in case. Tonio and I went to the town hall and filled in my divorce papers. We wanted George out of our lives.

Michael Cort had signed me up to do a sort of Bond film in Turkey, *Click*, with Tom Adams, and not long afterwards Howard Pays offered me a film in Malta with Rossano Brazzi. I loved both scripts. They were totally different stories and each of them fitted me perfectly. Suddenly, however, I received a phone call telling me the film in Malta was off. Then Michael Cort came to see me and told me that George had phoned and threatened him. He said that if he employed me George wouldn't play the picture in the Rank cinemas. I couldn't believe it. George had told me about some of the dirty tricks he had played on people who had got on the wrong side of him. I had always assumed he was just showing off. Now I was forced to realise just how powerful and malicious he was. When I confronted him, he just sneered. 'Prove it!' he said. 'You don't think any of those idiots out there are going to put their arse on the line for you, do you?' and he was right. No one in the industry spoke to me. Word had got out that I was *persona non grata.* When Tonio and I attended a première not a soul spoke to me, no one said hello. At lunch with Tone at the White Elephant, the 'in' place for the film industry at the time, people I'd thought were my friends gave a forced smile and turned away.

Tonio could see what it was doing to me and suggested we go to Argentina to shoot a film script I'd optioned. I thought of Perón, back in Argentina, President for the third time. Tonio had met him many times at the Automobile Club in Buenos Aires and at the Admirante Brown circuit. Perhaps he would help to get things going. Together we wrote Perón a letter.

Meanwhile the press learned about my problem with George. They asked me to tell all and help them do a hatchet job on the film exhibiting business, revealing how the circuit was booked and what backhanders were exchanged. I was sorely tempted, especially when they encouraged me to name my price. In the end I took Tonio's advice. 'Forget it!' he said. 'They'll tear you to pieces in the process. We'll go to Buenos Aires. If nothing happens at least you'll be out of the way for a while and who knows . . .?'

It was decided that Steffanie would finish her school year and then come out to Buenos Aires to join us, either with Matka or alone, depending on how things went. But a week later we read in the paper that President Perón had died. In Argentina, at that time, you had to be in with the powerful if you expected to get anything done. Isabel was Perón's deputy and had taken over the Presidency, but we didn't know how long that would last.

While we dithered I received a call from Bruce Gyngell at ITC, offering me a job. I asked Bruce whether he knew I was no longer with George. Had he seen the bad PR I was getting? He said he came from Australia and didn't give a shit about the bloody Rank Organisation and their personality problems. He wanted me for the female lead in an episode of a TV drama series called *Thriller*. I was delighted. I had one friend at least. And he was giving me a job.

'Where the Action Is' was filmed at Elstree with Eddie Burns from *77 Sunset Strip*. Tonio drove me to the studio every morning and came to fetch me home at the end of the day. We put our longer-term worries at the backs of our minds and enjoyed ourselves like a couple of kids.

I was offered another film but pessimistically waited for the call of doom. Sure enough, George did his stuff and a week later it came.

'Let's go to Buenos Aires,' I said. 'I can't bear all this hate.'

We left almost at once.

Twenty-Eight

The sweep of the wide Rio de la Plata was under our left wing as the plane lined up for landing. As we came on to finals Buenos Aires stretched to the horizon. From the air it was ugly but once on the ground I loved it.

We booked into the Sheraton opposite the Plaza de los Ingléses and were given a message that Juan Manuel Fangio, five times world motor racing champion and a friend of Tonio's, would take us out to dinner that evening with his 'natural son', Manuel Bordeu. I was touched. With everyone treating us like lepers in London it was nice to have someone like Fangio wanting to dine with us. His visit did a lot for our standing in the Sheraton: in Argentina Juan Manuel Fangio was next to God.

A couple of days later, as we were moving into a flat on Calle Posadas, Hector Olivera, a top Argentinian producer not entirely unknown in Europe, rang. He had heard that we were in town and wanted to invite us to dinner. There were about thirty guests at Olivera's house, which was big, even by the Republic's standards, and Hollywood-decorated. I was seated near Hector and opposite Juan Manuel. Naturally, the conversation turned to motor racing and, much to Tone's amusement, I insisted on putting the great Fangio right on the application of one of the rules. Luckily Juan Manuel was also amused.

After the meal, Olivera led us on to the terrace where a dozen gauchos were lined up. Eight of them banged massive drums, two played guitars and others the accordion, but the most impressive sight was the two gauchos standing surrounded by the drums. Slowly they started to tap with their heels on the stone floor. Gradually their feet moved faster, louder and they began to swing *boleadoras.* These are leather-bound bones or boulders about the size of a cricket ball, plaited on to thongs about two metres long, which on the pampas are used for bringing down cattle or game. As the rhythm picked up they began to twirl the *boleadoras* faster, closer, until the balls were brushing the hair of the dancers. A tiny error and the hard missiles would have smashed through their skulls. In a frenzy other dancers pulled from their belts huge silver-handled *facones* – razor-sharp small swords that all true gauchos carry – and threw them at the stomping feet of their partners. There was a stunning primitive beauty to this dance, the Malambo, which seemed to capture the gaucho heart of Argentina.

On our return the porter told us that Luis Sojit had been to see us and wanted us to telephone him as soon as we came in. Sojit, who I'd met at Perón's party in Spain, had now been taken back into government and was Minister for Communication. He had a big surprise for us: he had told President Isabel Perón that we were in town and now we were invited to lunch at her residence in Olivos. At this rate we reckoned we would be taking over the Argentine film industry before the week was out.

Lunch in Argentina invariably means *asado* in the garden cooked by a couple of cardboard gauchos. Isabel was friendly but distracted by political problems. She put on a brave face and chatted about my visits to Puerta de Hierro and Perón. She also asked after my work and, fascinated by horror, asked if she could see my movies. I offered to have them sent out for her.

Olivera invited us to visit him again, this time for lunch. His garden and pool were laid out like the Beverly Hills Hotel. The friends sitting around the pool were equally spectacular: long-legged women in micro-swim-suits and suntans that didn't stop, and balding, leather-tanned men, loaded down with gold fertility symbols and taking every opportunity to run experienced hands over obliging fillies. When we had devoured a small herd of cows and a flock or two of sheep, Hector took us to a table in a small arbour and got down to business. If we were serious about making films for consumption in Europe, he was our man, he said. Olivera owned some studios and a few days later he took us to visit Laboratories Alex, where the chairman, Alex Sessa, swore that his *raison d'être* was to process every bit of film we cared to expose – and all for love. This was getting heady.

The following weekend we were invited to the Hurlingham Country Club, a bastion of Englishness in the pampas. Our host was Gaston Perkins, one of Argentina's top racing drivers and one of Tonio's oldest friends. Gaston's brother-in-law, Herbie Henderson, was also in the party. He had made a killing selling farm equipment and fertiliser, and was interested in investing in something more exciting, such as movies. We laid out our wares and he rather liked the idea of *El Ultimo Enemigo*, the Spanish title of the script I had optioned.

By now, everybody seemed to know about us and why we were in Argentina. We were even invited to a poetry evening at the great Luis Borges's apartment. Borges was almost completely blind but seemed to love having people around him. Our names also reached the ears of the British Ambassador, who invited us to tea with his wife. I'd already fallen in love with Argentina and its people so when the Ambassador made derogatory remarks about the country I, as usual, spoke my mind. The atmosphere became decidedly frosty and we left, secure in the knowledge that we would not be invited back.

Meanwhile offers of partnerships continued to flow in and we began to look at the finer details of the deals. Gunter Jeanee, a macho Argy if ever there was one, was building a reputation as an action director of note. He was working for a company called Dinam, which wanted to make English-language films, and invited us to meet one of the partners, Orlando de Benedetti. Dinam's offices were decorated like Disney's idea of a fairy grotto. Orlando was tanned, Italian-looking, in his late thirties and had a penchant for wearing his jacket over his shoulders without his arms in the sleeves. But he was making all the right sounds. He wasn't talking just one film but six, and a television series based on a script that Tonio had written. He had a partner, Emilio Perina – who had connections in Montevideo, in particular with Uruguay's leading newspaper *El Pais* – whom he wanted us to meet. Meanwhile Hector was panting for an answer, although we were not enthusiastic about his insistence that he should be the director of any film we should choose to make, and Herbie was still wanting to find a home for his cash. We decided we'd keep these two waiting until we'd met de Benedetti's and Perina's Uruguayan friends.

The school term ended in England and Steffanie caught the first flight to Buenos Aires. I went to meet her at the airport with warnings from Tone ringing in my ears not to embarrass her by shouting 'Baby, Baby . . . !' as was my wont. So I played it fashionably cool and watched as Steffka, still in her British fur-lined anorak, long scarf and woolly hat, came out of the aeroplane, looked around, decided I wasn't there and went back in. I didn't know what to do, but a few moments later she emerged with a stewardess and they walked across the tarmac and into Immigration. I dashed downstairs, cursing myself for having heeded Tonio's advice, threw open the door of the Custom's shed and stormed in. Steffka was standing by one of the tables, the contents of her bag strewn around. I marched in, scooped everything into the case, picked it up with one hand and grabbed my child with the other. The Custom's officers looked on, stunned, but didn't make a move to stop me. Steffi told me later that it was like a scene from a James Bond movie. When I'd crashed through the door in my rather skimpy waistcoat and eye-wateringly tight jeans the sun had been behind me and even she had felt as if the SAS had arrived. We took her straight down to the Costa Nera, the embankment on the Rio de la Plata that boasted hundreds of tiny *asado* stalls. It was heaven to have her there with us. I felt whole and ready to take on whatever was thrown at me: Perina, Olivera, de Benedetti – they would all bend to my will and do exactly what I wanted.

When copies of my films arrived, Isabel Perón asked if we would come to the presidential residence for lunch and a viewing. With uninspiring guests we scoffed an uninteresting meal, then went to the projection room. I had brought *Countess Dracula, The House that Dripped Blood* and *The Vampire Lovers.* I had wanted to bring *The Wicker Man* but even then it wasn't easy to come by. We watched *Countess Dracula* and I felt everyone was bored sockless, so at the end of the film, before anyone had a chance to upstage me, I yawned and declared I had to be off. Isabel suggested one for the road and we drifted back to the drawing-room. When the drinks were served she drew me to one side and said she wanted to show me something before I left.

She led me down into the cellar, which was lit by a sort of ceramic chest of candles and an incongruously bare 40-watt bulb. The ceiling was high and plastered, and supported by half a dozen or so brick pillars with metal braces in between. The floor was stone-flagged and scrupulously clean. It was the centrepiece of the room, however, that held my gaze and sent a shiver down my spine. I realised that I was looking at the sarcophagus of the embalmed Eva Duarte de Perón.

Isabel led me closer. 'I'm looking after her while we sort out where her final resting place will be,' she said softly. 'She speaks to me.' When Isabel had run for the office of vice-president all her publicity had been along the lines that she was the reincarnation of Evita. She pointed to a plain plastic kitchen chair beside the coffin. 'I sit here for a while every day,' she explained. 'Why don't you sit there. I'm sure she'll talk to you.'

I was not at all keen but Isabel seemed so happy at the thought of my spending time with her soul mate that I let her talk me into it. After all, she was the President of the Republic.

'I'll just say goodbye to the others,' she said brightly. 'You come up whenever you like.'

I like now, I thought but, coward that I am, I sat and watched as Isabel disappeared up the stairs and all fell still.

I slowly went close to the sarcophagus and stared through the glass top at Evita's mummified face. It looked like wax at first and she seemed so small, like a child. How incredible it was that this was once the magical Eva Perón. I sat on the little chair in that cold room and looked at her, wishing I had known her. I imagined I could hear the adoring crowds shouting her name: 'Evita! Evita! Evita!' I thought of the day her body arrived in Madrid and Perón sat and sobbed whilst Isabel washed and repaired her torn, dusty white frock, gently cleaned her face and combed her hair. It was eerie sitting there and the longer I stared at Evita's face the more I thought she'd open her eyes. I was getting morbid.

Thoughts of death were depressing. I wanted to get away. I laid my hand on the glass top of the sarcophagos and said farewell to the embalmed Evita, then found my way up to where the stiffs were at least warm.

Tonio's racing friend Gaston Perkins invited us to stay at his *estancia* for a week. We took the lunch-time train from Buenos Aires and arrived at nightfall in a tiny station called Perkins in the middle of nowhere. A lone, massive gaucho, dressed in typical gaucho gear – *bombachas, rastra,* shirt and sombrero – waited for us with a clapped-out Dodge pick-up. He introduced himself as Ramirez, the foreman at the Perkins *estancia,* 'La Corona'. Steffanie and I stared at the sea of stars above, the Southern Cross that I'd dreamed of seeing since scrawny girlhood when I'd sat listening to my father describe the night skies. We seemed to drive for miles, until finally we reached the Victorian house, covered with vines, and seemingly straight from a horror film. As the car stopped, everyone came out of the house to welcome us.

A big *asado* had been arranged. We sat under the stars and ate massive chunks of beef and swilled back the magnificent Mendoza wine. Gaston told us that over the next two days wild horses were to be brought in for breaking and, relaxed by the wine and company, I began to wax lyrical about Tone's horseback skills with the result that he was invited to join the ritual. Tonio tried to chicken out, but he didn't have a chance.

The next morning when Tonio had to leave at daybreak I tried to feel sorry for him but I had such a headache from the wine that I couldn't quite manage it. The men drove the wild horses to a massive corral and evaluated them to see which were suitable for breaking. Tone was still trying to excuse himself from anything to do with the hard work that was to come the next day. When I eventually surfaced and asked him why he was so reluctant, he told me he had seen the way gauchos broke horses and it hurt the breaker more than the horse. I wasn't listening to any of that. I'd told everyone he was the greatest horseman since Genghis Khan and I wasn't backing down.

The next morning the locals started gathering early. Several people had flown in from other *estancias* and everyone was talking about El Inglés who was going to break some of the horses. I smiled brightly and acted as if it was something Tonio did every day. Tone, looking pale, was evidently still searching for a way out.

The day started with a bit of lassoing, which differed from the lassoing one sees in cowboy films. Instead of rushing around with a lariat and dropping it over the berserk beast's head, the gauchos sneakily throw it under the horse's feet, snap it tight and when the horse falls, leap on it and truss it up. Around midday they got around to the breaking. Tonio watched what was going on and it didn't make him any more relaxed. Each horse, frenzied, bucking, kicking and rearing, was led to a post in the middle of a large paddock. A bridle was put on its head and it was forced to lie down on its side with its nose clamped against the pole. A sack was put over its head and the rider carefully got into place. As soon as he felt ready for the fray he nodded, one of the gauchos pulled off the hood and let the frightened animal loose. It immediately went bananas. The gaucho hung on grimly until he was dumped or managed to get to safety on one of the other horses.

At last it came to Tonio's turn. He was looking decidedly peaky but I was still as brave as ever and jollied him along. Once he was in the paddock he perked up. He'd clearly decided that if he was going to die he might as well look as if he were enjoying it. Everybody was interested. After all, it's not every day you get the chance to see a foreigner break a bone or two.

Tone eased himself on to the horse and sat there, still trying to think of a good excuse to be somewhere else. Then he made the mistake of looking at the gaucho holding the horse's head. He took it as a signal and let go. The beast's first movement was vertical, its second horizontal. Tonio stayed with the vertical; he stayed with the horizontal. I was proud. Then the horse took off, humping and twisting. A couple of times it looked as if Tonio was off but an injudicious lurch of his mount kept him on board. A couple of riders moved in to help him off but at the last moment the animal did a horizontal and a vertical move together, Tonio went up and when he came down his ride had departed. He lay on the ground for a few seconds. I thought he was hurt but he was just offering up thanks for his survival. Everyone was very complimentary and old Ramirez made a big thing of presenting Tonio with the black, red-tasselled beret of the *dorminadores* – the horse breakers. Tonio said they were teasing but I prefer to think he earned it.

It was a sad day when we had to leave Perkins but we returned again and again and it became like a second home to us.

We decided to sign with de Benedetti and Perina. Perina convinced us that *El Ultimo Enemigo* should be shot in Uruguay and wanted us to go there to meet the financiers and do a recce. The financiers of *El Pais* newspaper confirmed de Benedetti's six films and a TV series but the recce wasn't too successful. Though Perina insisted that the sort of mountains we wanted for our major locations existed, we were a bit put off by the opening line in the official guide book which stated categorically that 'there are no mountains in Uruguay'.

Back in Buenos Aires, a news conference was called at the splendidly baroque Circulo Italiano. De Benedetti laid on a feast and then we all gave our two pennyworth to the press, posed for photographs and went home. To my relief, Olivera didn't seem at all put out. It looked as if at last I had hit that movie Klondike that producers dream about but which is always just out of reach.

We had hardly drawn breath after the press conference when news came in that President Isabel Perón had been arrested. No sooner had our good luck kicked in, it seemed, than it was to run dry again. Luis Sojit advised us to get out of the country: Argentina was heading for a revolution. Tonio rang Juan Manuel Fangio and asked what we should do. He didn't think we were in too much trouble but he advised us to take a vacation. We should either go back to London or skip across the Rio de la Plata into Uruguay with everyone else and see what happened. Tonio agreed that it made sense and Fangio sent a car to take us to the airport. The trip was uneventful but occasionally frightening. Everywhere there were road blocks and lorry-loads of soldiers, who pointed their rifles at us and made firing motions, which they clearly thought hilarious.

At the airport there was a concentration of heavily armed troops, but they didn't seem interested in what was going on. People were packed into the departure lounge like penguins on the last available iceberg. A state of emergency had been declared and for the foreseeable future no international flights were being allowed in or out. Tonio dumped Steffanie and me in a corner and went off to see what the chances were of hiring a private plane. He had his pilot's licence with him and reasoned that there might be someone needing a pilot to get his plane out. We were too late for that, but he tried the General Aviation Flight Movements office and struck lucky. There was a Fokker just in from Brazilia and about to leave for Montevideo with a load of freight. Tonio tackled the pilot, flashed his pilot's licence and appealed to the bloke's sense of aviational fraternity. At last the man agreed. Tonio said he would pick up his baggage and meet him on the tarmac. He carefully avoided saying that Steffanie and I were part of it. The pilot was sitting at the controls, ready to leap across the water to the safety of Uruguay when Tonio wrenched open the door, threw in our cases, then pushed us in after them. For a moment it looked as if we were going to have an argument but I think the pilot remembered the armed men, idle and looking for something to do, and decided he was going to get away more quickly by biting the bullet. I was never happier to leave the ground.

Twenty-Nine

We stayed in Uruguay, eating into our reserves, for about two months. With us sitting on their doorstep, virtual refugees, our backers seemed less keen to commit themselves. Orlando de Benedetti, a staunch Perónista, had had his wings clipped by the new military government and was lying low in Venezuela. The financiers claimed that it was de Benedetti's judgement they were backing and without him the deal was off.

We decided that Tonio should return to London and see if he could raise some finance there, perhaps by mortgaging the house. We also decided that Steffka had to go back. She had already missed a term of school and it was unfair to keep her hanging around while we sorted ourselves out. I wept for days after they had gone and during the three desperately lonely weeks of Tone's absence.

Tonio ran around Britain trying to raise money and interest in our projects. There was lots of interest but no money or commitment. He put in motion the paperwork for getting a mortgage on the house but even that was going to take weeks. Things were not looking good. To take his mind off the bad news and in the hope that someone might want a representative in Uruguay he decided to go to a motor race at Brands Hatch. He was walking through the paddock when he heard his name called. It was a friend from the flying club, Robin Ellis, and they went off to the bar for a drink.

At that time Robin was a rich young man with all a rich young man's toys: a Ferrari Boxer, a Kawasaki motor bike and an international hobby racing model cars that cost him a packet. Tonio told him what we were doing in South America and Robin thought for a bit, then asked how much we needed. He thought some more and made a counter offer to pick up our living expenses while he sussed out whether he wanted to commit himself further. Tonio almost snatched his hand off accepting. Robin also warned him that he was negotiating a deal with a huge construction firm that might take up a lot of his time. The deal was with Bairstow Eves. That sounded good. John Bairstow had served with Tonio in the Navy as snotties and they had been friends for years. Tone had joined the Merchant Service to avoid conscription, a common ploy in those days. However, his idea of sailing the oceans of the world was strictly limited to Amyas Leigh and *Westward Ho!*, and he hated it. So he left the Navy and joined the RAF.

A week later Tonio turned up with Robin in Montevideo. While he had been away I had talked on the telephone with Hector Olivera. Somehow Hector had bridged the political chasm and come out ahead. He said he was ready to start shooting a film with us. I asked him about our chances of survival and he assured me that the new government was focused on weeding out local dissidents, not international investors. So we decided to go back to BA.

Our move back was well timed. Business, especially the entertainment industry, was beginning to pick up. The only drawback was that the military now occupied all significant positions. The film industry was given an admiral to whom scripts had to be submitted for approval. While Hector was doing that de Benedetti and Perina came back on the scene. Both companies wanted to make *El Ultimo Enemigo*. We massaged them along, hoping one of them would come up with the goods. With Perina, we decided to recommence the recce while waiting for our projects to be approved. Perina's military buddies, through the governor of San Juan province, lent us a helicopter and we spent days zooming around the Andes looking for suitable locations. We saw mountain villages and incredible waterfalls, landscapes that were Martian and pockets of unbelievable fertility, but what we were looking for was a bridge like the one over the River Kwai. The governor said he knew just such a one. On the morrow he would send his car to take us there. Our party consisted of the producer, Emilio Perina, Juan Sires, the production manager, Gunter Jeanee, the director, Tonio, me and the driver. Robin had been scheduled to come with us but he had been recalled to Buenos Aires. There was some problem with his property deal and he had to see his lawyers urgently. It was a good thing, as it worked out, for Robin is six foot two and bony, and the car we were assigned was a small Renault. The driver assured us that we could all fit in and that anyway, we didn't have far to go. Piled on top of each other we headed towards the Andes.

The 'not far' turned out to be very far indeed. The desert road we bumped along ran out. Every few hundred yards we had to jump out of the vehicle and heave it out of a patch of soft sand. Tempers were getting frayed. All we could see was miles of featureless desert shimmering in the heat haze. None of us had thought to bring any water and our bodies jammed into the car were creating a temperature that would have coddled a coconut.

Again we hit a sandpit. I sat on the ground and gazed around, trying to imagine how I would look when some seasoned traveller stumbled across my whitening bones. The radiator was close to melting and it was clear we could not continue. Despite the fact that it was hardly likely that anyone would come along and steal the tyres, the idiotic driver insisted on staying with his machine. We decided to walk towards the mountains, where there was a railway line, in the hope that we might catch a train. Almost straight away one came along. We waved and the passengers waved back – and the train shimmered off into the heat haze.

We stopped and looked around us. In one direction there was endless track. In the other, the same. It was a toss-up. Reasoning that the train had to have come from somewhere we decided to go north. I wanted to point out that it was also *going* somewhere but didn't wish to seem unconstructive. We walked for hours. I couldn't get the picture of my bleached bones out of my head. So far everyone had been philosophical and amazingly hopeful but the midday sun began to take its toll. Sires, a sprightly seventy-year-old, was – incredibly, in this land of leather – wearing plastic sandals and they were melting. Tonio offered to carry him on his back and Sires showed how far gone he was by letting him. After a while, however, Tonio had to put him down. He suggested Gunter took a turn but Gunter declined the invitation, arguing that we had no idea how far we had to go but however far it was we weren't going to make it if we had to carry Sires. Tone ploughed on for another three or four hundred yards but by this time he was on the verge of collapse. With Sires's permission, we found a cutting under the line, in the shade, and stowed him away so that we could find him later. The men suggested I stayed with him but Tonio wouldn't allow it and I was relieved.

We walked and walked along the endless track. After about four hours we saw a *boliche*, a decrepit-looking hut, in the far distance by the side of the track. It was the station of a tiny village. When we eventually arrived, no one seemed to be around. At the back was a little patio covered with vines. A water bottle was suspended from a beam. I grabbed it and got stuck in but Tonio took it way from me at once and poured the water over my head. It seems you don't drink water when you're dehydrated.

We wandered around to the front where, in a lean-to, stretched out on a leather sofa, was an Indio-looking fat man dressed only in pants and singlet. When he saw me, he did one of those cartoon take-offs and disappeared into another part of the *boliche.* We stood around wondering if we should follow but soon the door opened and the man reappeared dressed regally in his station-master finery. We tried to explain our plight to him, about Sires slowly dying in the desert, but he insisted that we left matters of business until he had finished welcoming us. He made tea for everyone, reminded us that it was the Queen's birthday and pointed to a brass plaque, shining brilliantly on the wall, which claimed that the station had been built in Birmingham. Finally we were allowed to share our problems with him and he conjured up a boy who was detailed to take Gunter to some unspecified place to fetch a lorry. About half an hour later Gunter turned up on the back of a load of wreckage which I was assured by our station-master was a truck. Gunter wasn't too keen on ploughing off into the desert again as it was getting dark now, but nobody else volunteered so, with bad grace, he finally agreed to navigate if Tone would drive. When they eventually got back with Sires we were all tucking into a huge feast of steak. Sires wasn't much disturbed by his adventure. He just asked what had happened to our car and driver. We all looked at each other and dissolved in laughter. Hours later a Land Rover arrived from the governor and we piled in. We were told that the driver had walked back along the tyre tracks of his car and had been home for hours.

Back at the governor's *estancia* we were in bad odour. He had, unknown to us, laid on an *asado* at which we were meant to have been the guests of honour. We decided that we had 'done' San Juan and slipped away gracefully the following morning.

Gunter decided that we needed a break, as much to avoid any of the fall-out of our souring the relationship between the San Juan governor and de Benedetti as to rest after our adventure. Gunter's *finca*, or small farm, in San Marcus Paz outside Buenos Aires was all ponchos and leather. We sat under the Southern Cross and talked of gauchos and horses. London and Steffanie seemed a galaxy away and I missed her.

The next day Gunter was keen that we should watch him play a game of 'pato', which turned out to be rather like rugby on horseback. The game is called pato, which means duck in Spanish, because in the old days the ball had been a live duck. Two teams would fight to grab the unfortunate fowl by the neck and ride with it to the far end of the field without being flattened by the opposition. Nowadays the duck has been replaced by a leather ball with a number of loops jutting from it.

As Tonio and Gunter brought the horses into the paddock, I had a brilliant idea, but before I could voice it Tonio caught my eye and said, 'Forget it!' It would have been fun to watch him join in.

After the match, which Gunter claimed his team had won, although he could have told me anything, everyone was invited back to the *finca* for *asado*. Gunter was really laying on a feast. He had an accordionist, four *guitaristas* and some *bombos* (drummers). The entertainment went on well into the night. Someone sang Tango. The *guitaristas* did a *duello*, where two or three gauchos sit and challenge each other with their guitar playing. Then the story-tellers got into their act.

I was exhausted and went to bed, dreaming about stars and horses and Steffi – so far away . . .

Thirty

I had not spent much time in BA since our return from 'exile' in Uruguay and had been unaware of the changes that had taken place. Returning from a horror conference in New York, I was struck by the large number of road blocks. Soldiers swaggered around with lethal-looking weapons in their hands and a glint in their eyes which said they would just love an excuse to use them.

In Buenos Aires we discovered that Robin had found out from his solicitors that all was not well with his property deal. Although he had already signed over the cash and received shares, Bairstow Eves had decided that the deal was dodgy and had withdrawn, a fact that the property developer had neglected to pass on to Robin. Without the underpinning of the wealthy Bairstow Eves group the whole deal was coming unstuck. Reluctantly Robin decided he had to get back to London.

One morning as I sat outside the Piccolo, the little cafeteria beside the hotel in which we were staying, reading the English-language *Buenos Aires Herald*, the headlines on the entertainment page jumped out and grabbed me by the windpipe: 'Pinches kills industry inches by inches'.

George had been given a golden handshake from the Rank Organisation. When Tonio joined me I said we could go home now. He thought about it but said it wasn't the right time. Olivera was ready to start shooting and, anyway, he'd already sent a ticket to Steffanie and she was due out the following week. It was the greatest surprise I could have imagined.

Tone explained that while we'd been away the *Ultimo Enemigo* project had been shelved. The admiral in charge of the Film Institute had not been keen on a story featuring a woman taking on the military, overthrowing them and taking over the government with the help of US mercenaries. Olivera now planned to shoot *Gaucho Girl,* a sanitary tale about a young orphan girl who inherits a rich *estancia* in Argentina. It was doubly exciting for me because Steffanie was to be the eponymous heroine while I played the Cruella de Ville-type, trying to get my hands on her loot.

Every seventeen days it rains in Buenos Aires, and, when it does, the streets all look like Venice. It was on one of those days that Steffanie arrived. This time I didn't hold back. She knew I was there the minute she stepped out of the Jumbo. Tonio and I stood at the bottom of the gangway, right on the tarmac. She sorted out the blokes at Customs all by herself and had no problem with them wanting to unravel her Christmas presents. She just wouldn't allow it. It was wonderful to be together again and we were both excited at the prospect of working together.

Steffka had not really slept for a couple of days so instead of going out to celebrate our reunion we sat outside the Piccolo with our favourite *boccadillo de Roquefort* and *cappuccino.* We were just about to go in to bed when a couple of Ford Falcons slewed up on to the grass and half a dozen men, waving guns, leaped out.

Everybody froze, knowing from bitter experience to sit tight and keep their hands on display. The likelihood was that the men were the police, but this was not reassuring. If they shot you, you would be found with a gun in your hand and nobody would investigate the matter further. The young men didn't bother to identify themselves. They made us line up against the wall and went along the line. Steffanie thought it all very exciting. I was petrified. When they found out we were British they were quite civil and waved us back to our seats. I wanted to go inside and jump into the safety of my bed but Tonio told us to sit down and see what happened. After they had searched everybody and found nothing of interest to them they went inside the hotel. We sat and waited. No one left. Everyone felt that they had passed some sort of test and might not be so lucky if they moved off and were put to the question again. In the hotel, the police rounded up four men and a woman. They put a man in the boot of each car and the woman and the other two men in the back seats. Without looking at us again they jumped back into the Falcons and powered away.

Instantly everybody began to talk. I gripped Steffanie's hand and made for the door of the hotel. Although I had seen similar instances on the streets I had never before been directly involved. When we had first arrived in Buenos Aires, in spite of the bad publicity surrounding the Peróns and the crippling inflation, there had been a sense of freedom. People sat around in cafés and said what a fool Perón was, how stupid Isabel was. Now, no one dared say a word. I wanted to get out and prayed that we would soon be able to afford to leave.

Olivera had brought together a group of fantastic character actors and a boy called Cacho to play opposite Steffi. Cacho was a budding Adonis and could ride like a Tartar. It was decided that he would give my daughter some extra riding lessons. Steffka and I did make-up tests, had our wardrobes made and learned our lines. Tucked away in the security of the studio for two weeks, everything was calm and orderly. We then went to an *estancia* near Santa Fe where the outdoor locations were to be shot and had started shooting the interiors when Olivera called Tonio into his office and asked him where his half of the production budget was. This was the first mention of our buying in. Steffanie and I were not being paid and Tonio had written the script for nothing. Now Olivera wanted cash. When Tonio pointed out our contribution, Olivera became irritable and said we would be paid when we'd put up our share of the budget. He didn't seem happy to be making the demand and we suspected he was under pressure from the military, now running the industry. Olivera's request brought us up short but we didn't panic. Herbie Henderson had said he was keen to invest so we visited him. He seemed delighted with our proposal and we had the impression that things would now move very quickly.

We worked until the end of the week, daily expecting to receive funds from Herbie. When nothing happened I contacted him. He seemed overwrought and said he had personal problems. 'It's nothing to do with our deal. Why don't you come round on Monday and we'll sort it out on the spot?' I didn't like the further postponement. Alarm bells began to make a deafening sound. At the studio, Tonio was doing some fast talking. He had coaxed Olivera into giving us another week so I didn't tell him about my reservations.

On Monday Steffka and I went to the studio and Tone went to Herbie's office. When he asked for Herbie the receptionist gave him a letter. Herbie was sorry he was unavailable. The previous week he'd had a big bust-up with his wife and over the weekend there had been a reconciliation and they had jetted off to Paris to replight their troth. He would attend to our business when he returned – whenever that might be. We knew it was the end.

We confessed our problem to Olivera. He was sympathetic but couldn't be persuaded to continue without money up front or a distribution contract for the UK in his pocket. It was time to go. We'd spent over two years in Buenos Aires and had sunk practically every penny into it. Maybe George's successor, Stan Fishman, wouldn't carry on the vendetta and I could get work back in England.

It was January, the jacaranda trees down the Avenida del Libertador were in blossom and it was time for the Grand Prix. We decided to stay for it, then go with the teams to Brazil and afterwards back to London. It was a great finale to our South American adventure.

Thirty-One

It was great to be back in England. Now that George had left Rank we hoped it might make a difference to my re-emergence. Unfortunately it didn't. The ban on me had run for so long that I was virtually a non-person. To fill the empty hours I began to write a thriller, *Cuckoo Run*, based on one of the scripts I had touted around Argentina. I had almost completed it when I received a call from Bill Kenwright. Bill managed a touring theatre company, which kept a lot of actors in work. He ran things on a tight budget but was also firm and faithful. He asked if I'd do *Dial M for Murder* for him on a theatre tour and I quickly accepted.

We opened at the Opera House in Glasgow. Tonio came up for opening night and then went back to London. He was playing with the idea of forming a touring theatre company himself and was working on finding a backer. He drove back up on Saturday, had a kip in my dressing-room, then took me to our house in Richmond.

In the morning he suggested we ate breakfast in the garden. It was perfectly situated, faced south, had huge horse-chestnuts to provide shade and was surrounded by an ancient brick wall. The only thing that spoiled it was the Anderson shelter, a relic from World War Two. When my eyes adjusted to the light I couldn't believe what I saw. The Anderson shelter was gone and in its place was a bed full of beautiful flowers. I looked around the rest of the garden. In the short time I had been away he had planted flowers everywhere. It was so wonderful that I dissolved into tears.

I'd been crying a lot recently and had also been feeling sick and getting terrible stomach cramps. I knew that I was ill but couldn't admit it. After all I had gone through, I needed to feel strong. To be ill was to be weak and inferior. So I hadn't said anything to anyone, not even to Tonio or Steffka. Tone had sensed that I wasn't well but as I only saw him at weekends while I was touring I'd managed to hide my pain from him.

We were on our way down to Brighton, where I was to open at the Theatre Royal. I'd been feeling unwell all weekend but had covered it by saying I was merely tired and needed to rest. Half-way to Brighton, I had to get Tonio to stop the car so I could be sick. When I finally got back in I was exhausted. Tonio wanted to turn back immediately but I told him not to be silly, that I'd eaten something which didn't agree with me. He wasn't convinced. He made me promise that I would go to the doctor the following morning. I said yes but had no intention of going. I was more frightened of finding out something vile than continuing to suffer. But Tonio read my mind and insisted on staying over and taking me to the surgery.

The next morning the doctor made an appointment for me to go immediately to the hospital for tests and within a week ovarian cancer was diagnosed. My initial reaction was anger with myself and with the world, and disbelief. 'I couldn't possibly have an operation now,' I told the surgeon. 'I'm in the middle of a tour.'

'Fine,' he replied. 'But you'll be dead before you finish the tour.' That set me back.

For a while I continued to come up with terrified excuses. I was booked up for only another seven weeks, surely nothing could happen before then . . . But Tonio held the doctor's line and, moreover, accused me of being selfish: who was going to cook his eggs and bacon on Sunday morning? What about Steffanie . . .?

I dreaded having to tell Bill Kenwright but he was brilliant. When he heard my tale of woe he insisted that I went into hospital at once. Having thought myself indispensable, I was a bit taken aback. Bill told me he would find a stand-in for however long I was away and that as soon as I was better I could take over again, which was the kindest thing he could have done, for it gave me a reason to get on with my recovery.

I didn't tell my mother about the operation as I didn't want to upset her, or for her to think I was a weakling, so I pretended I was away in some theatre where it wasn't possible to get home for the weekend. When I later told her about it she said she had known all along. I've no idea how because no one told her.

They wheeled me into theatre and got ready to put me under. I hate that final period before you pass out, when you think you're never coming back. Steffka and Tonio had been with me all morning until it was time to go. I was morose. I said goodbye and thought I would die. And if I didn't die, I wouldn't be quite a woman any more. When I suggested to the doctors that they shouldn't take everything out – the ovaries, the womb, the lot – a kind nurse leaned over me. 'Listen, darling,' she said, 'I've had all that stuff out and it's bliss not having the . . . well, you know . . . those days once a month.' I'd been bleeding all over the place, even on stage, and her words were a great consolation.

When I came to, I was in a foul mood. Steffi did her best to cheer me up and while she was there I was fine, but as soon as she left this great big black dog leaped out of the closet and gnawed at my entrails. I felt empty – as though I wasn't a woman any more. I thought stupid thoughts like perhaps my Tone would go off me. He had a horror of hospitals, and when he came to see me he was tongue-tied and couldn't wait to get out of the place. I would have to do some serious 'pumping myself up' if I wanted to get my equilibrium back. After all, what they'd taken out wasn't anything I still had any use for . . .

Renee Wilson of Worldwide Films came to see me. She had always been a firm friend and proved it by ordering me to go and live in her house in Bexhill until I had fully recuperated. It was right by the sea, had a live-in maid and was ideal for convalescing. I didn't need much persuading.

After a week at Bexhill I was determined to get back to the theatre. I thought it would prove a point, although I'm not sure I ever knew what that point was. Tonio tried to talk me out of it but realised at last that there would be no living with me unless I had my way. I phoned Bill at his office and told him I was ready to come back. I quite expected him to say that there was no point as there were only three and a half weeks of the tour remaining but he simply asked when I wanted to start. I told him I was ready to leap out of the wings immediately. He suggested I saw a performance to get back into the play and then took over on a Friday. With the weekend coming up it would give me a chance to rest. Steffanie was on holiday and came with me to look after me. She became my dresser, gofer, comforter, food provider and general 'feel-good' factor.

Going back to work was both a good idea and a bad one. Good because it stopped me worrying about myself: I was too exhausted most of the time. And bad because I was so weak and in pain. Between my entrances I lay down on a sleeping bag that Steffka put on the floor in the wings for me. At times I had to sit or lean on the furniture while I was on stage because I was so weak I couldn't stand up unsupported for any length of time.

At last the tour finished and I was able to go to bed. I was in pain and popping pain-killers like Smarties. Every time I moved it felt as if the huge scar transversing my belly was about to rip open. The hospital told me the cause was the lesions, the aftermath of the operation, and advised me to exercise. Tone suggested I try golf. It would take me out into the fresh air, was difficult enough to make me forget my other problems – and would give him an instant partner when he felt like playing a round. He found me a wonderful golf pro, an ex-Ryder Cup player called Jimmy Adams and before long I was clouting the ball with maximum enthusiasm and minimum result, but the exercise was working. Each time I swung the club the lesions stretched a little more until the pain lessened. Jimmy suggested I play in some charity matches and introduced me to Garfield Morgan who played Chief Inspector Hoskins in *The Sweeney*. He was, and is, big stuff on the charity circuit and before long I was a regular as well.

My health was not our only worry. Matka had always run the house for us. It was her territory and we intruded on her routine at our peril. However, she was finding it increasingly painful to maintain her high standards. Her legs – the legs that had kept her mobile and on her feet during all the horrors of the camp and had carried us around Europe for nearly two years – were failing. She didn't complain but I knew how much she resented the toll they were taking on her general health. She had once said that when she couldn't walk any more it would be the end of her and now she was having trouble, especially with the stairs.

One night we came home from the cinema to find her lying at the bottom of the stairs. She had fallen down and hadn't been able to get up. She needed her granny flat now.

There was a small plot of land at the side of the house, so Tonio put in building plans to the council and dug the foundations. By the time planning permission was through the oversite was laid. It was only a matter of time before the walls were up, the roof on and the granny flat, with bathroom *en suite,* was ready for occupation. Mama loved it and it gave her a new lease of life.

While Tonio was building the flat, he enlarged the kitchen to make the huge farmhouse kitchen we'd always wanted. He also extended the terrace in the garden and built an Argentinian-style barbecue. *Asados* became our thing and at the drop of a sombrero we had a party and invited everyone we knew. Weather didn't come into it. If it rained, we just handed out golf brollies and everyone got on with it and loved it.

While I had been sampling the high life of a provincial tour, Tonio had been setting up a touring company of our own: TRIP, which stood for Tonio, Robin and Ingrid Pitt. I wasn't too sure that it was a prudent thing to do but Robin Ellis was back on the scene and liked the idea. We were to put on a new play by the *Emmerdale Farm* writer Neville Siggs. Called *Duty Free,* it was a country cottage farce. I played the much put-upon wife and Nick Tate from *Space 1999* played the two-timing husband. Eunice Gayson of Bond fame and Tim Barratt, a veteran comedy actor, played the nosy neighbours. We opened in Bristol, went on to Brighton and a couple of other theatres before we took a week off, during which Tonio and I went to the Cairo Film Festival.

It was all a film festival should be: bags of dinner parties, flash cars and a need to impress the guests. The main British film entry was Euan Lloyd's *Wild Geese*, starring Richard Burton, Roger Moore, Richard Harris, Stewart Granger and Hardy Kruger. To promote it the Film Producers' Association invited Susannah York, Judy Geeson, Georgina Hale and several others, including me, who had nothing to do with the film. On the opening night we were all supposed to be introduced on stage but the public address system was on the blink. The cinema was packed to the rafters with enthusiastic and very vocal Egyptians, who were making the most of the non-functioning mikes. One by one we girls tripped on to the platform, nodded timidly at the raging audience and hurriedly left the stage. Tonio had been roped in to do a public bow, although he hates that sort of thing. He was wearing a white dinner jacket à la Perón and entered holding his arms aloft in imitation of the South-American President. The audience went wild. We never found out who they thought Tonio was but when we left he had to have a police escort while we bimbos walked freely to the waiting cars without any interference.

The festival was due to go on for another week but I had to bow out. I was due back in England to tackle a new venue. When I told the press that I was leaving Cairo to open in a play in Cleethorpes the journalists wouldn't believe me. I'm not sure I did either. It was a bit of a change: one day enjoying the exotica of the pharaohs – the next holed up in digs with the smell of boiling cabbage, Dettol and damp.

It was in Cleethorpes that I learned that I was about to become a published author. After Tonio had cut down my novel, *Cuckoo Run*, from 250,000 words to a more manageable 120,000, I had stuffed it under the bed. I had written the book merely to prove I could and didn't feel like holding myself up to ridicule by trying to get it published. However, Tonio decided to get cleaners in to do the carpets, my manuscript resurfaced and he took it along to Futura without telling me. Just before curtain up he rang to tell me that Futura's commissioning editor, Marjory Chapman, had phoned to say she wanted to publish *Cuckoo Run.* Amazed and thrilled, I slammed down the telephone, ran in the pouring rain along the pier to the dressing-rooms and told everybody that I was about to be a published author.

Thirty-Two

Duty Free did great business in the provinces and we had theatres vying for dates and offering wonderful guarantees. Even the mighty Moss Empires wanted us. Louis Benjamin, their boss, badgered Tone to bring the play to London but Tonio didn't think he had enough experience to take on the West End. When Moss Empires were persistent, however, he began to waver. He discussed the idea over lunch with John Pact, his business manager. John was a theatre junkie and the thought of coming into London excited him. They left the restaurant, walked immediately to Coutts Bank in Cavendish Square, and successfully buttonholed the manager.

We had to pay penalties to provincial theatres for abandoning the rest of our tour, remodelled our wonderful sets to West End standards, changed the name from *Duty Free* to *Don't Bother to Dress*, papered the house . . . and got lousy reviews.

On the opening night I had planned a small party at the Embassy Club after the show. In my excitement I ended up inviting over fifty people. Bill Kenwright took me aside and told me that he gave the play three weeks. He was wrong. It lasted five weeks and was a constant haemorrhage on the bank account. At last we were forced to face the fact that the coach parties Moss Empires had predicted weren't going to materialise. There was no miracle in the offing. Traditionally and legally, you have to put up notice to quit two weeks in advance. We intended to put it up on Saturday but Tonio talked to the managing director of Durex, the condom manufacturers, and persuaded him that it would be a capital idea to underwrite a play in the West End: 'Durex presents: *Don't Bother to Dress.*' The publicity would be breath-taking.

Tonio put the plan to Moss Empires, who did not seem to have a problem with it so he rushed around, had a fresh sign made for the marquee, set a printer to designing a new programme and the PR agent to writing a press release. He estimated the change-over would take a couple of weeks.

On Monday we were told that Louis Benjamin wanted a word. It sounded ominous. Benjamin announced that he didn't like his theatre being used to advertise French letters. Tonio told him that it was our only chance of survival but Benjamin was adamant. Durex were disappointed but there was nothing they could do.

The play was losing us an estimated £3000 a week. I spoke to the cast and asked them to consider accepting a back-dated notice to the previous Saturday and luckily they agreed.

We were still in a terrible fix for money. Tone rang his best friend and fellow pilot, Joe Khan, and told him his problem. Joe wasn't interested in investing in the play but he proved what a good friend he was by instantly offering to lend us money to get out of the West End. Tonio gratefully accepted. We got the play off two weeks later. It had eaten up the reserve we had built up on tour, the loan we had from Coutts and another chunk of the house.

It was time to go back to the mortgage company to ask for more money.

We decided to take another play on tour. *Woman of Straw*, a wonderful story about greed, had been a movie with Gina Lollobrigida and Sean Connery. Tonio again sought commercial sponsorship and went to British Caledonian who, to my surprise, agreed. We got the sets built, the tour signed up and Harry Hitchcock, boss of British Caledonian, came to the première. It went well, we made a small profit and I loved the play.

Meanwhile, my book was being prepared for publication. My editor's husband, Ian Chapman, published Alistair MacLean and asked him to read the manuscript of *Cuckoo Run*. Perhaps he would be prepared to write a line or two which they could use to push the book? Alistair, one of the kindest men I've ever met, rang Ian Chapman and said, 'I love it! Tell Ingrid, bloody well done.' Sadly, he died soon afterwards so didn't get to write anything on the cover of *Cuckoo Run* but what he said to Ian meant a lot to me. The book was such a success that it sold out its entire print run in eight weeks.

One day Tonio and I were watching John Wayne in *True Grit* on TV when the broadcast was interrupted to bring live action from the SAS assault on the Iranian Embassy. It was nail-biting stuff that had us on the edge of our seats. Euan Lloyd, a first-class producer who has a string of action hits to his credit, lived right around the corner from the Iranian Embassy and watched the entire nightmare. Never one to hang around, he was the first producer to register the film of the siege with the title *Who Dares Wins*, the motto of the SAS. I heard about it, rang him immediately and asked him round for lunch. It was a marvellous summer day, the garden a kaleidoscope of colour and I had bought some great T-bone steaks. In spite of all that, I couldn't get Tonio away from the television. When Euan arrived I tried to take him through to the garden but he wasn't interested.

'You have got television?' Euan asked, seriously concerned. I nodded and pointed to where Tonio was crouching on the sofa in semi-darkness. It was the day that Botham did the impossible and dragged England to victory over Australia by 129 runs. I accepted defeat. There was going to be no glorious *asado* on the sun-drenched terrace. No artful to-ing and fro-ing while I angled for a chance to suggest his film could not but be enhanced by my presence on the screen.

When the game was finally won, Euan suddenly remembered he had work to do, jumped up, practically kissed Tonio for sharing such a wonderful experience with him, and made for the door. I was seething but managed to paint a suggestion of a smile on my face. Euan kissed me, stepped out of the door, turned and said shortly, 'If you want the part of Helga, it's yours. Second lead, great part. I'll send you a script.' And he was gone.

A couple of days later the script arrived and Euan phoned to ask me what I thought. This was the first film script I had been offered since George went on the rampage and the thought of it was enough to bring tears to my eyes.

My friend Tom Pendry MP invited Euan and Ian Sharp, the director, to come to the House of Commons to watch a debate so that the scenes in the House would look authentic.

The film – and making it – was great. The SAS guys impressed me to the bone. It was Lewis Collins's best film. I thought he was totally brilliant as Captain Peter Skellen of the SAS. The only sad bit was that Euan was determined to use Judy Davis when he could have had

Jane Fonda for the main lead. The Americans didn't like an Australian imitating a Yankee terrorist and the film didn't do all that well in America, where it was called *The Final Option*.

After *Who Dares Wins* I worked on *Smiley's People* for the BBC. I had a fun cameo part. Alec Guinness would bring Fortnum & Mason biscuits to lighten up rehearsals. He was the most caring and generous actor I have ever worked with and would give close-ups to me that he could have had for himself. Curt Jurgens played my lover. I'd known Curt since *Eagles* and we'd chat about old times with Alec.

Through Chris Chrisafis – Euan Lloyd's co-producer – I landed a part in *Wild Geese 2,* a feature film about breaking Hess out of Spandau where he had been imprisoned since the war. Laurence Olivier was to play Hess and Richard Burton the mercenary sent in to spirit him away and deliver him to the West, where he could impart some great secrets.

I flew to Berlin, where the film was to be shot, the day before filming started. I was very excited at the prospect of working with Richard again so when some American friends asked me out to a polo match I judged it a distraction. Later that evening I was in my room when one of the Yanks phoned to ask me if I had heard the news: Richard Burton had just died. I was shocked and wandered downstairs where I ran into Euan and babbled out the bad news. Euan turned ashen and hurried to his room. Later that night he flew back to London to sign another actor and make sure the funding was still forthcoming from EMI.

Edward Fox took over Richard's part and shooting continued on *Wild Geese 2*. To be in Berlin was horrific for me. We were filming near the border and I was paranoid. I felt binoculars were trained on me, rifles aimed at me, I even imagined I could hear gunfire. I was jumpy and nervous and tried to stay in my hotel room as much as possible. I wondered if the tormenting images imprinted on my brain in my youth would ever fade and leave me in peace. I longed to return home.

I sat in luxury on the aeroplane flying back to beautiful England, looking forward to my two treasures fetching me home from the airport.

At London Airport Tone and Steffanie picked me up and took me to the VIP lounge since the news they had to tell me couldn't wait until we got home. It was fantastic: Thames TV were going to make *The Peróns* into a series. Tonio and I had written the book some time before and it had been published by Methuen in 1982. John Frankau wanted Hugh Whitemore to write the scripts. The news of getting a TV series off the ground and some dosh at last was so great that after considerable celebrations Tonio and I agreed to let Steffanie go to boarding-school. My father had always said that the one thing parents owe their children for bringing them into the world is to give them a proper education. What you have between your ears will give you a chance for a better life. Tonio insisted that she would have the best, whether or not we could afford it, and we chose Hampden House in Amersham. She went at once and I missed her so much that while our agent and John Frankau sorted out the contract for *The Peróns*, we motored down to Steffi's school and took her out to lunch, dinner or even brought her home for the weekends. Tone threw in driving lessons on the school estate since Steffanie was car-mad.

At last we got our contract backed up by some much needed cash. Then the TV technicians went on strike. What did we care? We were actually paid more money because Thames was closed down while they were out. We were going to work on the project with Hugh

Whitemore, who was not an expert on the subject matter. He seemed to love the whole idea. But he had to finish the script of *Return of a Soldier*, a film for Alan Bates and Glenda Jackson. Then something else delayed him. I offered to write the scripts with Tone but John Frankau was determined to have Whitemore. Without warning we learned that Frankau had been replaced by Verity Lambert. By this time we were under the impression that Hugh's work was coming along like a house on fire. Production, scheduled originally for November, was put forward to the spring of the following year. Verity asked to see the scripts and Hugh had to admit that he hadn't even started. She cancelled the project. We were paid off and that was the end of yet another dream. Disappointment wasn't the word for it.

I called Lew Grade. He was receptive and asked to read the book. We had a number of meetings. Then I was invited to breakfast. His breakfast meetings were legendary. I sauntered into his sumptuous office suite, we discussed the series over croissants and coffee, and he was excited. It was all going my way when he got a telephone call. It was unbelievable. I was about to agree my contract with the customary handshake but I knew from the way Lew reacted on the phone that I was in trouble. His face just folded over. When he hung up he shook his head and stood up. I was stunned. He told me that Faye Dunaway was playing Evita and Robert Mitchum Perón – in Hollywood. I thought I would throw up all over the table. In the end, Mitchum backed out and the whole thing was a disaster. But not as great a disaster as it was for us.

Still, one good thing came out of it all: my kid got a good education.

Thirty-Three

On 15 January 1986 my mother died. She was nearly eighty-four. She had spent fifteen years with us and I'm sure both coming to England and having the granny flat had lengthened her life. Looking after us had made her happy and given her a purpose in her final years but as she'd lost strength and felt herself to be a burden she'd turned despondent. She became increasingly frail and disorientated. Twice the police had to bring her home because she'd lost her way. She started focusing on the past, talking about the war, my father and the camp; about when the Nazis had lined up prisoners and shot them; when they hanged Annie Jadkowska. She repeatedly reminded me of the hanging and about a red cabbage she had stolen, which had nearly cost her her life. It was disturbing to hear my mother, who had not talked of the camps for forty years, reviving these memories. Steffanie, who was at drama school, stayed at home. I didn't leave the house either. We both wished to be with Mama. I couldn't bear the idea of her being alone when the time came.

A few days before her death Mama looked at her door and shook her head. She seemed to see someone there but she wasn't ready to go. 'No, no, no,' she said gently. On the day she died, she looked at the door and smiled. She waved her hand at somebody she saw standing there and nodded. 'Yes,' she said firmly. I like to think it was my father. It is said a loved one comes for you when your time is up.

At the very end, Steffanie was with her and she called me. I was sitting on Tonio's lap, crying. I ran to my mother's room and Steffanie and I held her in our arms as she died. She seemed to be very peaceful and was not in any pain.

Matka was gone. She was the strongest person I've ever met. She taught me so much: particularly about love being the only thing worth living for. She always supported me and understood completely that I gave my life and future to my child and to Tonio. She never cared about my career or our lack of money and material goods. She just wanted us to love one another and to see the three of us happy. And at the end of her life she made me promise that Tonio and I would be together always.

Things got really hard after Mama died. Not only did we suffer the grief of bereavement, we were virtually on the breadline. I was delighted when work came along as it not only provided much needed funds but distracted me from our problems.

Hanna's War, Menahem Golan's film about Hanna Szenesch, a Hungarian freedom fighter who was arrested on her first assignment, was a gruelling story but I was glad to be part of it. Peter Weir was going to direct it but in the end he couldn't stand Menahem's insistence on changes to the script and he told him to direct it himself.

It was an interesting experience going to Hungary. Luckily I had no scenes to do which would give me nightmares. The problems with the production were incredible. I don't know whether it was because of the language difficulty or plain inefficiency. Two thousand extras were waiting at the railway station to be loaded on Eichmann's train for deportation. They waited and waited. The train arrived at nine in the morning instead of two o'clock at night. The next day the extras waited again. This time the train was spot on time but didn't stop. It went on and on like this. I had to admire Otto Plaschkes, the line producer, for keeping his cool. Menahem totally lost his. He kept yelling at me. I too lost my cool: 'What are you, a bloody Nazi? Only Nazis ever shouted at me like that.'

He was fantastic after that – he never shouted again.

Whenever I wasn't working on a film or on stage, I was bashing out treatments and synopses by the trunk-loads – and that's where most of them stayed. At one time Tone and I had fifty-four projects on the go at the same time. One was the script based on my mother's life and experiences that I had written fifteen years earlier at the Hilton when I did *Eagles*. Johnny Hough loved the story but said that to get it financed he needed a book. We set up a meeting with Methuen, a deal was struck, and I started writing.

When *Katarina* was published, it too sold out its first print run. I worked day after day with John Hough, sending books to producers and directors, and received some wonderful replies, especially from Alan Parker. It looked good for a while but then he decided to do *The Commitments*. Then *Sophie's Choice* came out and that was the end for *Katarina* for the time being.

Although jobs came in for me we still suffered dire financial problems. We seemed to be paying for everything – recces, budgets, costume design, travelling expenses – and the only money dribbling in was from half a dozen books we had written. When we found another potential investor we did a business plan, budgets, had several meetings with lawyers and accountants, and at last it looked as if things were going our way. With the mortgage company breathing down our necks because we had missed payments, arrangements were made to pick up the first cheque.

I was due at our investor's apartment at three o'clock. I turned up on time and was asked by his secretary to wait. When she returned, she told me that her boss couldn't see me.

'But this has all been arranged,' I insisted.

The woman looked unhappy. Reluctantly she took out a letter and gave it to me. It said that our potential investor had, after due consideration, decided not to go ahead with our deal. After all the meetings we had had to thrash out an equitable arrangement I could not believe he would renege at this late date. I demanded to see him. His secretary confessed that it was impossible: he was drunk and insensible. I sat down and fought against the feeling that I should lie on the floor and scream and cry.

Yet even as I issued the threats to sue our 'investor' I knew it was pointless. I had no idea what I would tell the mortgage company. I thanked the secretary, who called a taxi to take me home. All the way I thought how incredibly happy we had been, Tone, Steffanie, Matka and me: a family. Our problems were just part of life. You know you're alive when you have challenges to contend with.

Tonio opened the front door. He knew instantly what had happened. He took me in his arms and said it didn't matter.

It was time for a reassessment. We had to do something positive. I rang the lawyer acting for the mortgage company and told him they could come and take my house. This was Tuesday and I set Friday as the date when we would leave.

We started packing at once. Now it was decided that we would go, I wanted to get it over with. Our departure turned into a three-day party. All my friends came, loaded down with cartons, bubble-wrap and champagne to help me sort out and pack our belongings. One of them, Dinah Earle, offered her barn to house my accumulated junk and others offered lodgings. Nasrine Grayson, my beautiful Iranian friend, a civil engineer by profession, roamed the house making sure we left nothing of value behind. Susie Weaver, an old motor-racing friend, organised boxes and made meticulous lists of what was in them. Pat Lasky miraculously cooked with next to nothing, conjuring up meals, feeding more than a dozen, and we all sat at the long kitchen table Tonio had made out of the back door in our big farmhouse kitchen, munching and laughing and remembering glorious dinner parties we'd had.

As I looked into the garden for the last time, at the trees I had planted with my mother, I suddenly remembered the urn with her ashes buried under the big willow at the end of the plot. Now we were going, I couldn't leave her behind. I dug up the little box and took her ashes to scatter on the River Thames. She loved that river and she would have liked being one with it.

We lived at Dinah's farmhouse in West Sussex for a month and then another friend, John Woods, invited us to stay with him in Hurley, on the Thames. All the time Tone and I worked hard writing.

One night we were invited to dinner at Nasrine Grayson's in Sheen. We passed the most delightful little cottage in her road which had a 'For Rent' sign out front. It had everything: wisteria growing up the front, a tiny Romeo and Juliet balcony, big bay window, conservatory and a little garden. Again Tom Pendry, my MP friend, came into bat and furnished a guarantee so that we could move in at once. I worked like a berserker to make the place perfect. I loved it to death. It was the prettiest home I'd ever had.

One evening in the bath in our new cottage, I felt a round hard lump in my breast. I ran to Tonio screaming, shedding water everywhere, and he felt it too. We rushed to the doctor the next morning. The GP was on holiday and her stand-in suggested I should wait for two weeks until she got back. I thought he was mad. We tore off to the hospital but they wouldn't look at me without a referral from my GP so we had to wait two weeks for her to return and send us to Queen Mary's Hospital in Roehampton. I saw five doctors who looked like brand-new housemen but not one surgeon. All of them said I shouldn't worry, it was just a pimple. I tried to convince myself that they must be right.

The 'pimple' did not disappear and for three months I continued to go back until I finally saw the man who, I reckon, saved my life, Doctor Stephen Andrews. After examining my 'pimple' he insisted I see the surgeon at once. I told him I'd been trying for months to see a surgeon but no one would let me. Doctor Andrews rushed out and came back in no time with a surgeon, who examined my breast and whipped me into theatre. They did a biopsy at once, which showed that the 'pimple' was malignant.

When I heard the verdict I threw myself screaming and sobbing into Tonio's arms. He held me, quietly caressed my hair, my head, my face, just as my father had always done.

Hot fury rose through my whole being and engulfed my mind. I started swearing like the worst fishwife on earth, shouting at Tonio, screaming that the Nazis didn't get me and a bunch of fucking cancer cells wouldn't either. I hadn't died in Stutthof and I wasn't going to die now. I would fight – like I'd seen my Matka fight. In my mind the cancer was a living thing, like the Nazis, and I would face it as I had faced my childhood enemy and survive. *I was not going to bloody die*. I went into hospital and they cut out the cancer: two and half centimetres of it.

I think it was worse for me to have my breast under the knife than my womb. After all – you can't see the womb. I'm mad about breasts, especially mine. Then I thought of the day we were to breathe the gas at Stutthof. Fear would never be like that again . . .

After the operation I was referred to Charing Cross Hospital and was assigned to Professor Coombs, the resident oncologist, who explained that becoming a gym junkie and doing my regular weights exercises every day since my first cancer operation had helped me survive the months of misdiagnosis. Hard exercise apparently lowers the oestrogen level in the body which cancer cells feed on. Nevertheless, if it hadn't been for Doctor Andrews's rapid and decisive action it would have been too late to operate and the cancer would have spread into the lymph nodes and the bone. Doctor Andrews is now a Fellow of the Royal College of Surgeons, specialising in cancers. I don't know how I can ever thank him for what he did for me.

Each day I had to undergo radiotherapy. My therapist was an angel. Joana Lukawska, from Poland, in the end took away my fear of the massive radium machine. I was terrified of it. Every time I was put into it, I would shake all over and couldn't control it. I'd have a massive attack and be unable to breathe. Joana kept telling me to love the machine because it would make me well. She would say that she was watching me all the time, nothing would go wrong, she would be right there. Without her, and her incredible patience, I might not have been able to complete my course of daily sessions for eight weeks. She told me how few people actually do. That is stupid but then they don't all have Joana to look after them. She is now in her final year of qualifying as a doctor.

I had to go back into Charing Cross Hospital for corrective surgery. By the third time I was thoroughly sick of it. To keep my mind off the knife, I concentrated on a convention being held in Nottingham which I intended to go to no matter what. The advertising had been big on my being there. The medical staff told me I would be out in plenty of time but a week before the event I was still in hospital. Tonio wanted to cancel but I told him I would be out by the weekend. On Tuesday I informed him I would definitely be home on Wednesday. On Wednesday I promised I would be ready on Thursday. On Thursday I swore that the doctor said I could go but I had to wait for something or other. We planned that Tone would pick me up on the Friday and we would leave immediately for Nottingham. Unfortunately the doctor still didn't want to release me as I had a catheter discharging into a bottle.

When Tonio arrived I grabbed the overnight bag I had packed and hustled him out of the hospital before a nurse might apprise him of the situation. I wasn't being butch, I just wanted to prove to myself that I wasn't condemned to be sick for the rest of my life. I tied the bottle to a belt I had put round my waist and it dangled against my shins, hidden under a kaftan I had kept at the back of my wardrobe since my trip to Cairo.

Half-way up the M1 I began to worry if my bolshie act wasn't going to turn out badly. The bottle wasn't getting any fuller. I checked the needle but it seemed all right. As soon as we booked into our hotel I had to tell Tone that I had a problem. He looked as if he had been whacked with a mallet.

At the local hospital I explained my predicament. They

checked the catheter and changed the almost full plastic bottle for an empty, heavy glass one, but it remained dry. We were scheduled to dine that evening with our hosts, David and Pat Cutts. I didn't want to think about my catheter so ignored Tonio's pleas to spend a quiet night in our room. It was less easy to ignore the glass bottle. Every time I moved it clinked against the chair or the table. I managed to get through the meal with a lot of hilarity to cover up my clanking bottle and had a great night worrying whether or not my catheter was sucking.

The next morning the bottle was still empty and I was beginning to feel scared about what I had done. Nevertheless I had a great day, hugging and embracing friends and fans, my bottle banging into their shins. What must they have thought I was hitting them with? We left about six o'clock. When I confessed to Tonio that I was worried about the catheter he wanted to take me straight to Nottingham hospital but I chose to return to Charing Cross to confess my sins.

It was nearly midnight when we got there. Typically nobody wanted to see me, but I tracked down a Sister to her lair and persuaded her to look at my catheter. I didn't have a problem. The reason my bottle had remained dry was that the incision had stopped leaking. I was allowed home to my own bed.

While all this running to the hospital was going on, the owner of my dream cottage decided to return from South Africa and to sell it. Moving again was the last thing I needed in the middle of this medical trauma but it worked out well because I found, through a local property paper, an apartment overlooking Richmond Park. When I came out of hospital that's were I recuperated. From every window there is a wonderful view of all the trees. It's high up and airy with picture windows and gardens all around. I lay in my sumptuous bed, looked out at the trees and the sky, watching the herons race past my window like the old Spitfires, and I thought how lucky I was. I love it here. Tonio likes it wherever I am; as long as we are together he doesn't mind where he is. I had to go back into hospital for more operations but I was no longer frightened. I saw it as part of getting well. I would pump myself up every day into a positive frame of mind. I'm in the clear now. I love every day. But then I always have done. The sun or the rain, cold or stifling heat. I love the moon and the stars, the dark nights with the wind blowing around the house, telling tales of goblins and gnomes and demons and elves rushing through the park – just like that Polish forest, lifetimes ago.

Through the good times and the bad times in my life I have learned that however much hatred and however many obstacles one meets, with iron in the spine one can make it.

I'm lucky. I have a daughter and a man who both love me to distraction. All is well with love like that pouring into your soul . . .

Epilogue

Without doubt my entire life was overshadowed by my childhood and the tormenting acts of violence and hate I had to witness. Although I was a child and got the impression that what was happening around me and to me was normal, to be surrounded by barbed wire and watch towers, men pointing guns at you all the time, to live with constant fear, cruelty, beatings, screaming, shooting, endless mental and physical torture and death, and to be called a non-person during your formative years, leaves a scar. And throughout my life I have been aware of that scar, sometimes minimally, sometimes powerfully.

People ask me if I blame my father for the suffering we had to endure. He could have put aside his beliefs in right and wrong, and become a hero of fascism, been part of the killing machine. I'm proud of him for not taking the easy way out, for understanding the consequences of his actions, for not becoming part of the national hate, a quiescent part of the assassination machine. His courage was limitless. If it had killed us all, he still could not have chosen any other way. For my father there was never a possibility of compromise. And he willingly paid the price for his convictions.

My mother's obsession with saving my life at any cost gave her a superhuman strength, which I have tried to live up to all my life. Eventually I did not believe any longer that I was part of the *Untermenschen*, the non-persons, who don't deserve to live. I survived the hell, but hardly anyone else did: ninety-eight per cent of all deportees died. Surviving doesn't make one special – but it does make one extraordinarily lucky.

Although I have appeared on the stage, on television and in films, and have had several books published, I believe that my most important achievement was to bring into this world an extraordinary human being who will carry on what my mother taught us about love and inner strength – about the destruction hate breeds; about happiness; contentment and not blaming others when things don't work out. She taught us not to lead a useless life, to strive to become a better person, to live with love in one's heart . . . to be happy.

Index